Bureaucrats as Law-makers

The Council of Ministers is one of the most powerful institutions of the European Union (EU) and plays a major role in the European policy-making process. Drawing on formal theory and combining quantitative and qualitative methods in an innovative fashion, this book provides novel insights into the role of national bureaucrats in legislative decision-making of the Council of the EU.

The book examines and describes the Council of Ministers' committee system and its internal decision-making process. Relying on a wide quantitative dataset as well as six detailed case studies in the policy areas of Agriculture, Environment and Taxation, it provides a comprehensive and systematic assessment of the extent to which national bureaucrats act as law-makers in the Council. It also examines the degree to which theories on collective decision-making, delegation and international socialisation can account for variation in the involvement of bureaucrats. Investigating how often and why national officials in working parties and committees, rather than ministers, make legislative decisions in the EU, this book addresses the implications of bureaucratic influence for the democratic legitimacy of Council decision-making. The author finds that ministers play a generally more important role in legislative decision-making than often assumed, alleviating, to some extent, concerns about the democratic legitimacy of Council decisions.

Bureaucrats as Law-makers will be of interest to students, scholars and practitioners in the field of European Union politics and policy-making, legislative decision-making, intergovernmental negotiations and international socialisation.

Frank M. Häge is a Lecturer in Politics at the University of Limerick, Ireland.

Routledge/UACES Contemporary European Studies

Edited by Federica Bicchi, *London School of Economics and Political Science, Tanja Börzel, Free University of Berlin,* and Mark Pollack, *Temple University, on behalf of the University Association for Contemporary European Studies*

Editorial Board: Grainne De Búrca, European University Institute and Columbia University; Andreas Føllesdal, Norwegian Centre for Human Rights, University of Oslo; Peter Holmes, University of Sussex; Liesbet Hooghe, University of North Carolina at Chapel Hill, and Vrije Universiteit Amsterdam; David Phinnemore, Queen's University Belfast; Ben Rosamond, University of Warwick; Vivien Ann Schmidt, University of Boston; Jo Shaw, University of Edinburgh; Mike Smith, University of Loughborough and Loukas Tsoukalis, ELIAMEP, University of Athens and European University Institute.

The primary objective of the new Contemporary European Studies series is to provide a research outlet for scholars of European Studies from all disciplines. The series publishes important scholarly works and aims to forge for itself an international reputation.

1 **The EU and Conflict Resolution**
Promoting peace in the backyard
Nathalie Tocci

2 **Central Banking Governance in the European Union**
A comparative analysis
Lucia Quaglia

3 **New Security Issues in Northern Europe**
The Nordic and Baltic states and the ESDP
Edited by Clive Archer

4 **The European Union and International Development**
The politics of foreign aid
Maurizio Carbone

5 **The End of European Integration**
Anti-Europeanism examined
Paul Taylor

6 **The European Union and the Asia-Pacific**
Media, public and elite perceptions of the EU
Edited by Natalia Chaban and Martin Holland

7 **The History of the European Union**
Origins of a trans- and supranational
polity 1950–72
*Edited by Wolfram Kaiser, Brigitte
Leucht and Morten Rasmussen*

8 **International Actors,
Democratization and the
Rule of Law**
Anchoring democracy?
*Edited by Amichai Magen and
Leonardo Morlino*

9 **Minority Nationalist Parties and
European Integration**
A comparative study
Anwen Elias

10 **European Union
Intergovernmental Conferences**
Domestic preference formation,
transgovernmental networks and the
dynamics of compromise
*Paul W. Thurner and Franz Urban
Pappi*

11 **The Political Economy of State–
Business Relations in Europe**
Interest mediation, capitalism and
EU policy making
Rainer Eising

12 **Governing Financial Services in the
European Union**
Banking, securities and post-trading
Lucia Quaglia

13 **European Union Governance**
Efficiency and legitimacy in
European commission committees
Karen Heard-Lauréote

14 **European Governmentality**
The liberal drift of multilevel
governance
Richard Münch

15 **The European Union as a Leader
in International Climate Change
Politics**
*Edited by Rüdiger K. W. Wurzel and
James Connelly*

16 **Diversity in Europe**
Dilemmas of differential treatment in
theory and practice
*Edited by Gideon Calder and
Emanuela Ceva*

17 **EU Conflict Prevention and
Crisis Management**
Roles, institutions and policies
*Edited by Eva Gross and Ana E.
Juncos*

18 **The European Parliament's
Committees**
National party influence and
legislative empowerment
Richard Whitaker

19 **The European Union, Civil Society
and Conflict**
Nathalie Tocci

20 **European Foreign Policy and
the Challenges of Balk an
Accession Sovereignty
Contested**
Gergana Noutcheva

21 **The European Union and
South East Europe**
The dynamics of Europeanization and
multilevel governance
*Andrew Taylor, Andrew Geddes and
Charles Lees*

21 **Bureaucrats as Law-makers**
Committee decision-making in the
EU Council of Ministers
Frank M. Häge

Bureaucrats as Law-makers
Committee decision-making in the
EU Council of Ministers

Frank M. Häge

LONDON AND NEW YORK

First published 2013
by Routledge
2 Park Square, Milton Park, Abingdon, Oxfordshire OX14 4RN

Simultaneously published in the USA and Canada
by Routledge
711 Third Avenue, New York, NY 10017

First issued in paperback 2014

Routledge is an imprint of the Taylor & Francis Group, an informa business

© 2013 Frank M. Häge

The right of Frank M. Häge to be identified as author of this work has been
asserted in accordance with sections 77 and 78 of the Copyright, Designs
and Patents Act 1988.

All rights reserved. No part of this book may be reprinted or reproduced or
utilised in any form or by any electronic, mechanical, or other means, now
known or hereafter invented, including photocopying and recording, or in
any information storage or retrieval system, without permission in writing
from the publishers.

Trademark notice: Product or corporate names may be trademarks or
registered trademarks, and are used only for identification and
explanation without intent to infringe.

British Library Cataloguing in Publication Data
A catalogue record for this book is available from the British Library

Library of Congress Cataloging-in-Publication Data
Häge, Frank M.
Bureaucrats as law-makers: committee decision-making in the EU Council
of Ministers / Frank M. Häge.
p. cm.—(Routledge / UACES contemporary European studies ; 21)
Includes bibliographical references and index.
1. Council of the European Union. 2. Council of the European
Union—Committees. 3. Decision making—European Union countries.
4. Legislation—European Union countries. I. Title.
JN34.H34 2012
341.242'222—dc23
2012004350

ISBN 13: 978-0-415-68967-0 (hbk)
ISBN 13: 978-1-138-82224-5 (pbk)

Typeset in Times New Roman
by Book Now Ltd, London

Für meine Eltern

Contents

List of illustrations	xii
Acknowledgements	xiv
List of abbreviations	xv

PART I

Introduction and background   **1**

1   Bureaucratic decision-making in the Council   **3**

Contributions of the study 4
Research approach and methods 6
Plan of the book 10

2   The Council's committee system   **12**

Council committees in EU legislative decision-making 13
The organisational structure 18
Long-term trends in Council committee activity 24
The role, organisation and activities of Council committees 29

3   Existing research on Council decision-making   **31**

The extent of committee decision-making 32
Committee communication and co-operation patterns 35
Committee member socialisation 36
Committee interaction styles 38
Policy outcomes of Council decision-making 39
Process characteristics of Council decision-making 40
Summary of the literature review 41

x   Contents

4   Theoretical perspectives on committee decision-making   43

Preferences, institutions and policy stability 44
Committee socialisation 49
Policy uncertainty, salience and delegation 54
The theoretical arguments in brief 59

PART II
Quantitative analysis   63

5   Sample selection   65

Selection criteria 65
Selection procedure 67

6   Describing the extent of committee decision-making   70

Measuring committee decision-making 70
Results of the descriptive analysis 72

7   Explaining the variation in committee decision-making   75

Operationalisation of variables 75
Results of the statistical analysis 80
Summary and discussion 86

PART III
Qualitative analysis   89

8   Methodological issues   91

The complementarity of quantitative and qualitative research 91
Advantages and disadvantages of a nested design 92
Case selection criteria 94
Data sources and collection 98

9   Agriculture   103

Geographical Indications Regulation 104
Leaf Tobacco Regulation 113
Comparative analysis 121
Appendix: development of individual negotiation issues 127

Contents xi

10 Environment 130

Ambient Air Directive 131
Batteries Directive 138
Comparative analysis 150
Appendix: development of individual negotiation issues 157

11 Economic and Financial Affairs 162

Parent-Subsidiary Directive 164
Mergers Directive 172
Comparative analysis 180
Appendix: development of individual negotiation issues 187

12 Summary and between-sector comparison 189

Summary of the within-sector comparisons 189
Between-sector comparison 192

PART IV
Synthesis and conclusion 197

13 Discussion of research results and theory building 199

Synthesis of the quantitative and qualitative research findings 200
Towards a procedural theory of Council decision-making 206

14 Conclusion 208

The legitimacy of Council decision-making 208
Challenges for future research 209

References	213
Index	220

Illustrations

Tables

2.1	Working parties and sub-areas by Council formation	22
3.1	The extent of committee decision-making: previous research	33
6.1	Decision-making level by Council formation	73
7.1	Description of variables and data sources	77
7.2	The linkage of Council formations with party policy positions	78
7.3	Determinants of committee decision-making	81
7.4	Effects of changes in the explanatory variables	85
8.1	Characteristics of selected cases	96
8.2	List of case study interviews	101
9.1	Geographical Indications Regulation: main decision-making events	107
9.2	Leaf Tobacco Regulation: main decision-making events	115
9.3	Agriculture: types of negotiation outcomes by Council level	124
10.1	Ambient Air Directive: main decision-making events	133
10.2	Batteries Directive: main decision-making events	141
10.3	Environment: types of negotiation outcomes by Council levels	153
11.1	Parent-Subsidiary Directive: main decision-making events	166
11.2	Mergers Directive: main decision-making events	174
11.3	Taxation: types of negotiation outcomes by Council levels	184
12.1	Summary of the within-sector and between-sector comparison	194

Figures

2.1	The internal decision-making process of the Council	14
2.2	Organisational structure of the Council	21
2.3	Yearly meeting days of ministers, 1958–2004	25
2.4	Yearly meeting days of Coreper, 1958–2004	26
2.5	Yearly meeting days of working parties, 1958–2004	27
2.6	Distribution of meeting days across Council levels, 1958–2004	28
4.1	Unanimity and qualified majority core	46
4.2	Small and large preference divergence unanimity cores	47

4.3	Qualified majority committee core and co-decision core	48
4.4	Performance norms winset of socialised committee members	52
4.5	The delegation set of the minister in a one-dimensional policy space	56
9.1	Geographical Indications Regulation: negotiation process	107
9.2	Leaf Tobacco Regulation: negotiation process	115
9.3	Agriculture: comparison of negotiation processes	122
9.4	Geographical Indications Regulation: negotiation issues	127
9.5	Leaf Tobacco Regulation: negotiation issues	129
10.1	Ambient Air Directive: negotiation process	134
10.2	Batteries Directive: negotiation process	142
10.3	Environment: comparison of negotiation processes	152
10.4	Ambient Air Directive: negotiation issues	157
10.5	Batteries Directive: negotiation issues	159
11.1	Parent-Subsidiary Directive: negotiation process	167
11.2	Mergers Directive: negotiation process	175
11.3	Taxation: comparison of negotiation processes	182
11.4	Parent-Subsidiary Directive: negotiation issues	187
11.5	Mergers Directive: negotiation issues	188

Acknowledgements

This research project benefited from many comments and discussions on various occasions. Earlier versions of parts of the study were presented at the Annual Work Conference of the Netherlands Institute of Government (NIG, 2004 and 2006), at the Third Pan-European Conference on EU Politics of the ECPR Standing Group on the European Union (2006), and at the 36th Annual Conference of UACES (2006). Furthermore, elements of the study were discussed several times in the AiO Seminar at Leiden University and in the European PhD Research Colloquium on 'Democracy and the European Union'. I would like to thank the participants of these conferences and seminars for their valuable comments and constructive criticisms. Special thanks go to Michael Kaeding and Dimiter Toshkov, who provided continuous feedback and valuable advice throughout the entire life of the project. Of course, I am also grateful to my PhD supervisor Bernard Steunenberg for his invaluable guidance and support. Needless to say, any remaining errors are mine.

From a more practical point of view, I would like to thank the investigators of the Chapel Hill expert survey for providing their data on party positioning on European integration and the officials of the Council Secretariat for their patient and comprehensive responses to my rather extensive requests for access to Council documents. Finally, I am most grateful to the European and national officials I interviewed for sharing their precious time with me and for answering all my questions about the intricacies of Council decision-making.

Abbreviations

AT	Austria
BE	Belgium
CAP	Common Agricultural Policy
CFSP	Common Foreign and Security Policy
CoR	Committee of the Regions
Coreper	Committee of Permanent Representatives
CY	Cyprus
CZ	Czech Republic
DE	Germany
DG	Directorate general
DK	Denmark
TEC	Treaty establishing the European Community
ECJ	European Court of Justice
EE	Estonia
EL	Greece
EP	European Parliament
ES	Spain
ESC	Economic and Social Committee
EU	European Union
FL	Finland
FR	France
HU	Hungry
IE	Ireland
IT	Italy
LT	Lithuania
LU	Luxembourg
LV	Latvia
MT	Malta
NiCad	Nickel-cadmium
NL	Netherlands
PAH	Polycyclic aromatic hydrocarbons
PL	Poland
PSC	Political and Security Committee

xvi *Abbreviations*

PT	Portugal
SCA	Special Committee on Agriculture
SE	Sweden
SCIFA	Strategic Committee on Immigration, Frontiers and Asylum
SK	Slovakia
SL	Slovenia
TRIPS	Trade-Related International Property Rights
UK	United Kingdom
WP	Working party
WTO	World Trade Organisation

Part I

Introduction and background

1 Bureaucratic decision-making in the Council

The Council of Ministers is the main legislative institution in the European Union (EU). Although the European Parliament (EP) has been granted more and more legislative rights over the last two-and-a-half decades, the Parliament has still no say in a number of policy areas. In contrast, no legislative decision is made in the EU without the explicit agreement of the Council. Corresponding to this important role as a legislator, decision-making in the Council has received considerable attention from a theoretical point of view. A number of scholars offer sophisticated theories modelling Council decision-making (Steunenberg 1994; Tsebelis 1994; Crombez 1996, 1997; König and Proksch 2006a); and the predictive power of some of those models has been tested and compared relying on painstakingly collected positional and salience data (Thomson *et al.* 2006; Thomson 2011). Yet, systematic empirical analyses that open up the black box of the Council's internal decision-making process are largely missing. In recent years, a number of studies have examined the voting behaviour (Mattila and Lane 2001; Mattila 2004; Heisenberg 2005; Hayes-Renshaw *et al.* 2006; Hagemann 2007; Mattila 2009; Plechanovová 2011) and co-operation patterns (Beyers and Dierickx 1997, 1998; Naurin 2007) of Member States in the Council. While these studies might tell us something about the conflict dimensions underlying Council negotiations, they are silent on the internal decision-making process that leads to Council decisions. There are a growing number of works that investigate the internal working and organisation of the Parliament (Kaeding 2004, 2005; Hoyland 2006; McElroy and Benoit 2007; Rasmussen 2008; McElroy and Benoit 2010; Yordanova 2010), in particular the composition, functioning and effects of its system of standing committees (Bowler and Farrell 1995; Whitaker 2005; McElroy 2006; Settembri and Neuhold 2009; Yordanova 2009). Similar systematic quantitative or comparative research on the Council's internal workings is virtually non-existent.

The absence of research on the internal decision-making process of the Council is not due to a lack of importance, relevance or interest. On the contrary, Council committees play a major role in Council decision-making. The work of ministers is supported by more than 250 Council working parties and committees consisting of diplomats and national officials. The Council's organisational structure is not only horizontally divided, with different sectoral ministers making decisions for their respective policy areas, but also vertically between different layers of

4   *Part I: Introduction and background*

committees. At the bottom of the hierarchy, ordinary working parties begin the negotiations on a dossier. These working parties report to more senior committees on the middle layer, and these senior committees in turn answer to ministers. According to the EU treaties, only ministers have the right to make Council decisions related to legislative acts. However, in practice, a considerable proportion of Council decisions are de facto made by committees. Decisions agreed at lower levels of the hierarchy are formally adopted by ministers without discussion. According to a prominent estimate, the Council committees are responsible for 85-90 per cent of all Council decisions (Hayes-Renshaw and Wallace 1997).

Much of what we know about the work of committees in the Council decision-making process is based on anecdotal evidence. Given the lack of public information on the proceedings within the Council, previous work had to rely on the subjective opinions and judgements of insiders. The current study takes advantage of newly available information to investigate the role of committees in legislative decision-making of the Council. More precisely, the study answers two research questions. The first research question is of a descriptive nature. The question asks what proportion of legislative Council decisions is made by committees. This descriptive question logically precedes the second research question, which is concerned with explaining the variation in the extent of committee decision-making. The second question asks why some legislative decisions are made by committees and others by ministers. In general, the scope of the study is restricted to decision-making on legislative Commission proposals concerned with the substance of internal EU policies. Thus, I do not examine administrative, institutional, budgetary or foreign policy decision-making. The study focuses on legislation adopted through the classic Community method: the Commission proposes legislation, and the Council and the Parliament decide about adopting the act. Methodologically, I employ both quantitative large-N as well as qualitative comparative case study methods. The quantitative analysis is based on 439 legislative Council decisions and the qualitative analysis consists of a comparison of six decision-making processes in three policy fields.

Contributions of the study

The results of the study inform both the normative debate about the legitimacy of Council decision-making and several strands of scholarly literature concerned with positive explanations of aspects of EU decision-making. The answer to the question of what proportion of legislative Council decisions is made by committees is of particular normative relevance. A domination of legislative decision-making in the Council by committees would increase doubts about the democratic legitimacy of Council decisions. A main source of legitimacy for Council decision-making derives from the accountability of governments to their directly elected national parliaments (see, e.g. Moravcsik 2002). This chain of accountability from citizens of Member States to Council decision-makers is at least further stretched when national officials rather than government ministers decide about legislation in the Council. One could even argue that this chain is broken, as national officials do not answer directly to Parliament at all. Of course, the answer to the question about what factors explain whether or not ministers become involved in Council decision-making also affects any normative evaluation. Even if the general rate of committee decisions was high, this finding would be less disturbing if committees focused only on routine decisions and technical proposals and left the important 'political' decisions to ministers. Conversely, a rather low overall rate of committee decision-making would still be considered problematic if there was no discernible difference in terms of importance and technicality between decisions made at the committee level and decisions made by ministers.

The study also promises insights for the scientific study of Council and EU decision-making in general. The results of the study are relevant to a number of fields of research in EU politics. Firstly, the study examines the consequences of formal and informal rules. Much disagreement exists in the current literature about the precise effects of the voting rule and the legislative procedure on Council decision-making. Some scholars (Steunenberg 1994; Tsebelis 1994; Crombez 1996, 1997) argue that the voting rule has a decisive influence on decision-making outcomes in the Council, while others (Heisenberg 2005) argue that a 'culture of consensus' operates against such an effect. Existing studies present empirical evidence for both perspectives. Studies of EU decision-making efficiency generally find that the possibility of qualified majority voting increases decision-making speed (Golub 1999; Schulz and König 2000; Golub 2007; Golub and Steunenberg 2007; König 2007; Hertz and Leuffen 2011), whereas studies of voting behaviour conclude that actual voting is the exception rather than the rule (Mattila and Lane 2001; Heisenberg 2005; Hayes-Renshaw *et al.* 2006; Mattila 2009; Plechanovová 2011). Whether and how the possibility of adopting proposals by a qualified majority of Member States affects committee decision-making is an interesting question. The answer to this question should also inform the more general debate about the effects of the voting rule on Council decision-making.

Besides the voting rule, the legislative procedure is a major factor structuring EU decision-making. After early contributions (Steunenberg 1994; Tsebelis 1994; Crombez 1996, 1997) focused on theoretically modelling the consequences of formal aspects of different legislative procedures, recent years have seen a number of more empirically driven studies that focus on the effects of the actual practices that have developed alongside the formal legislative procedures and complement them now (Farrell and Héritier 2003, 2004, 2007; Häge and Kaeding 2007; Judge and Earnshaw 2010). Several reasons exist to assume that the involvement of the EP as a co-legislator under the co-decision procedure might affect the dynamics of internal Council negotiations.[1] Attempts to reach early

---

1 The time period studied precedes the entering into force of the Treaty of Lisbon in 2009, which introduced amongst other things a number of terminological changes, including new names for legislative procedures. Thus, I use the pre-Lisbon Treaty terminology throughout the book.

6   *Part I: Introduction and background*

agreements in the first stage of the co-decision procedure are increasingly common. If the EP and the Council make such an attempt, intra- and inter-institutional negotiations often overlap. But even if the institutions do not attempt to reach a first-reading agreement, the anticipation of the EP position in future rounds of negotiations might affect Member States' negotiation behaviour in committees. The effects of EP involvement on the internal decision-making process of the Council have received little systematic attention to date. Thus, the results of the current study should inform the literature on the consequences of formal and informal aspects of the co-decision procedure.

The study presents novel insights in other respects as well. A burgeoning literature on the international socialisation of officials working in EU institutions has developed (Beyers 1998; Egeberg 1999; Trondal 2001, 2002; Beyers and Trondal 2003; Beyers 2005; for a review, see Quaglia *et al.* 2007). The quantitative empirical research in this field focuses mainly on supranational role perceptions. However, a crucial element of international socialisation theory is its claim that socialisation does not only affect role perceptions but also the behaviour of officials. In the case of the Council, socialised national representatives are supposed to take on a more co-operative negotiation style. Case studies support this suggestion (Lewis 1998, 2003b, 2005), but the claim has not been examined through either statistical or comparative methods. The current study improves on this situation by investigating the hypothesis through both a quantitative large-N analysis as well as qualitative comparative case studies.

The results of the study also speak to the literature on delegation and discretion. Existing EU research finds that uncertainty about the consequences of a dossier is a major factor determining the extent of delegation from principals to agents (Franchino 2000, 2004, 2007). The current study investigates whether this pattern also holds for the division of labour between bureaucrats and ministers in the context of the Council. Finally, the study investigates the effects of issue salience on Council decision-making. Existing empirical research on EU decision-making either focuses exclusively on highly important legislation (e.g. Thomson *et al.* 2006) or disregards the possible effects of salience (e.g. Golub 2007; König 2007). The likely consequence of either treatment is biased research results. The current study sheds some light on the question of whether and why the salience of a dossier matters for Council decision-making

Research approach and methods

Research strategies can be distinguished along numerous dimensions. As in many other studies, the approach taken here does not fit neatly into any single textbook category. Thus, a few words about the main characteristics of the research strategy are in order. Two general distinctions are useful in this respect (Gerring 2001): the differentiation between X- and Y-centred studies on the one hand, and the distinction between confirmatory and exploratory research on the other. The distinction between X- and Y-centred studies points to the focus and the goals of the study. The letters X and Y are normally used to denote the independent and dependent variable in theoretical or statistical models. Accordingly, X-centred research focuses on the causal effect or effects of a specific explanatory variable stipulated by theory. In other words, X-centred research aims to answer the question 'What are the various effects of X?'(Gerring 2001: 137). The work by Tsebelis (2002) is a prime example in this respect: after outlining his veto-player theory, Tsebelis examines the effects of veto players in different areas of policy-making and on several characteristics of political systems.

In contrast, Y-centred research focuses on the cause or causes of a specific empirical phenomenon of interest to the researcher. A Y-centred study attempts to answer the question 'What causes Y?' (Gerring 2001: 137). Both X- and Y-centred studies have their merits and the goals of the researcher usually lead to the selection of one or the other approach. The main goal of the current study is to find out why some decisions are made by committees while others are not. The aim is to identify the causes of committee decision-making in the Council, not to make a case for the importance of any specific theory. Thus, the study is clearly Y-centred. Note that the distinction between Y- and X-centred studies does not necessarily imply differences in the logic of inquiry. Given their focus on investigating the consequences of a well-specified theory, X-centred studies do not usually follow an inductive logic. The goal of these types of studies is to test one or several hypotheses logically deduced from the underlying theory. But the Y-centred approach is consistent with both the deductive and the inductive logic of inquiry. The distinction between different logics of inquiry seems similar to the second differentiation of research strategies into exploratory and confirmatory approaches, but there exists only a partial relationship between the two distinctions.

The distinction between exploratory and confirmatory research refers to the status and relative importance of existing theory and empirical data in the research process. In confirmatory research, the researcher approaches the subject under study with one or several clearly delineated theories in mind that purport to explain the phenomenon. The empirical data is then solely used to test the validity of the pre-established theories. Thus, the confirmatory approach relies exclusively on the deductive logic of inquiry. In contrast, exploratory research contains both deductive and inductive elements. The researcher first approaches the subject under study with some more or less elaborated theories, ideas or simple hunches about possible causes in mind. Like in confirmatory research, the researcher examines the validity of these candidate explanations deductively by confronting them with the empirical data. But exploratory research does not stop here. If a theory has been found inadequate in the light of the empirical evidence, the researcher modifies it to improve its fit with the data. Also, the researcher examines whether patterns in the data suggest possible explanations not considered at the start of the research process. As the research project evolves, these new or modified explanations are then compared with new evidence and again adjusted if necessary. In this respect, exploratory research is best described as 'a process of mutual adjustment such that ... concepts, theories, and evidence are

8 *Part I: Introduction and background*

properly aligned' (Gerring 2001: 231). Both induction and deduction are essential parts of this mutual adjustment process.

Whether a confirmatory or exploratory approach is more useful for a study depends crucially on the degree of empirical knowledge and theory development present in a certain research field. If a phenomenon has been extensively described and its causes theorised in great detail, a purely confirmatory approach might be warranted. However, if we do not know much about the phenomenon in question and theorising is still rather rudimentary, examining solely the validity of existing insights might lead us astray from discovering other or even more important causes of the phenomenon.

The study of Council committees lacks mature theories and the amount of reliable empirical information is limited. At this early stage of research on committee decision-making in the Council, an exclusive focus on testing hypotheses derived from other fields could result in the neglect of important explanatory factors. In such a situation, an exploratory approach is more fruitful than a strictly confirmatory one. As the following chapters will show, taking such a perspective does not imply approaching the object of the study without reliance on prior theoretical ideas. However, these ideas have usually been developed in different contexts or with other purposes in mind. Like in a purely confirmatory approach, one goal of the study is to evaluate the validity of these theories. Indeed, this evaluation is an important starting point of the research strategy. But confirming or rejecting pre-existing theoretical ideas is neither the final nor the exclusive goal of this study. Identifying additional factors that influence committee decision-making and refining and further developing theory in the light of new empirical evidence are goals that are just as important.

In summary, the research project is Y-centred and, while it includes an important confirmatory component, rather exploratory in spirit. The aim is to find out how much Council committees decide and, more importantly, why they decide what they decide. To investigate these questions, I employ a mixed-method design. In the first step, I investigate committee decision-making through a quantitative analysis of 439 Council decision-making processes. The quantitative analysis serves three purposes: first, it sheds some light on the descriptive question about the proportion of Council decisions made by committees. Second, it forms an important initial step in the evaluation of existing theoretical ideas. In fact, the explanatory statistical analysis constitutes the major confirmatory component of the study. Finally, the results of the descriptive and explanatory quantitative analyses allow for an informed selection of cases for the qualitative analysis.

With respect to the explanatory goals of this study, the strength of the quantitative analysis lies in its transparent inference procedure and the more generalisable results it generates. Given the data and a certain model specification, statistical techniques and the associated conventions about significance levels lead to relatively unambiguous conclusions about the relevance of a certain explanatory factor. Even if the claim to generalisability in a strict statistical sense, that is generalisability to an underlying population, can be disputed, the quantitative analysis assures at least that findings are not the result of potentially peculiar characteristics of a limited number of cases. The quantitative analysis is very useful for yielding insights about the validity of potential explanations of committee decision-making drawn from the existing literature. However, this purely deductive approach is also one of the quantitative analysis' limitations. As discussed above, important additional explanatory factors might be overlooked by such a procedure.[2] A second limitation of the statistical analysis is its exclusive reliance on examining the co-variation among variables to investigate causal relationships. Even if sound theoretical reasons exist to expect that two variables are causally related, an empirical finding that they co-vary could still be a coincidence or caused by a neglected third variable influencing both of them in a similar way.

In order to improve on these two problems, I also conduct intra- and intersectoral comparisons of Council decision-making through qualitative case studies. The case studies form the second step in the empirical analysis. Given the preliminary nature of the results of the quantitative analysis, I only use the most robust findings from the quantitative analysis as case selection criteria for the qualitative studies. In contrast to the quantitative analysis, the case study analyses combine both deductive and inductive elements. The potential explanatory factors identified from the existing literature and examined in the quantitative analysis are further scrutinised in the qualitative analysis. In particular, the case studies are used to examine the plausibility of the posited causal mechanisms and to improve the precision of theoretical concepts. However, the case studies are not only valuable for verifying the correlational results of the quantitative study. They are also helpful for identifying additional explanatory factors not suggested in earlier work. Finally, case studies have advantages for determining whether and how different explanatory factors interact to produce a certain outcome. In this sense, comparative case studies are an invaluable tool for further theory development.[3] The combination of insights from both quantitative and qualitative analyses promises to result in more valid conclusions than a reliance on either type of analysis on its own. The two types of analysis are complimentary in so far as one type of analysis omits some of the shortcomings of the other.

---

2 Not all statistical techniques employ a deductive approach. Many statistical procedures follow an inductive logic, especially procedures designed to aid the description and exploratory analysis of data. Still, the researcher has to make a decision on what type of data to collect before she or he can apply such a procedure. In order to guide the data collection, any quantitative study requires that the researcher knows a priori what variables might be of relevance. In contrast, data collection and analysis are almost seamlessly interwoven in exploratory qualitative research. In this type of research, data collection consists of assembling documentary evidence to describe a certain case rather than collecting specific information in order to code a set of pre-specified variables.

3 Interactions can also be incorporated into statistical models, but their inclusion is usually not suggested by the data themselves. In contrast, comparing evidence within and across cases often points to the conditionality of causal relationships. The comparative approach regularly demands the consideration of interactive relationships among the explanatory variables in order to yield a logically consistent explanation.

Plan of the book

In the following chapter, I give a stylised account of the role of Council committees both within the internal decision-making process of the Council and the EU legislative process more generally. The goal of this description is to locate Council committees and their work in their institutional environment. The chapter also presents an empirical picture of the Council's committee system in different policy sectors and describes changes over time. The empirical record illustrates the large size of the Council's committee system but also gives background information on the structural variation of the committee system across policy fields. Finally, I discuss the absolute number and relative distribution of meetings of different Council bodies over time. This discussion shows that reasons exist to expect that working parties and senior committees play a vital role in the functioning of the Council.

Chapter 3 reviews the existing literature on Council decision-making. First, the existing empirical results on the extent of committee decision-making are discussed. I argue that crucial methodological problems prevent us from having confidence in the rather divergent findings of earlier work and outline how the current study improves on these problems. Then I discuss different areas of research on the Council and its committees in order to summarise the existing knowledge in this field and to explicate the added value of the current study. Through the discussion of previous research, several theoretical factors that could be of relevance for explaining committee decision-making are identified. In Chapter 4, I rely on formal tools from social choice and game theory to discuss the theoretical rationales underlying these factors in more detail. I also draw on general theories of delegation to distinguish further potential explanations for committee decision-making.

Part II of the book presents the quantitative large-N analysis. Chapter 5 outlines the sample selection. First, the selection criteria are described and justified. The descriptive as well as the explanatory research question relate only to certain types of Council decisions. I outline the population of decisions considered to be of relevance for the study. Furthermore, I describe the practical process through which the sample of decision-making cases was identified and through which the data was collected.

Chapter 6 gives the main answer to the question about the proportion of Council decisions made by committees. First, I discuss advantages and disadvantages of the approach used to measure the extent of committee decisions. I argue that the measurement approach used in this study yields more reliable results than other approaches used in previous work. The second part of the chapter presents the descriptive results of the analysis. The findings indicate that ministers are much more involved in Council decision-making than often assumed. In this respect, they clearly challenge the conventional wisdom. However, the results also show enormous variation between different Council formations in the proportion of decisions made at the committee level.

Chapter 7 further examines this variation. In this chapter, I discuss the main quantitative results with regard to explaining why certain decisions are made by committees and others are not. I begin the chapter with a description of the operationalisation of the variables for the statistical analysis. Subsequently, the results of the regression analysis are presented. The chapter ends with a summary of the results and preliminary conclusions.

Part III of the book presents the comparative case study analysis. Among other things, the qualitative case studies serve to further investigate the validity of the quantitative findings. Before describing the cases, I begin this part of the book with a discussion of some methodological issues in Chapter 8. In particular, possible ways of fruitfully combining quantitative and qualitative methods are discussed. I also defend the decision to rely only on the most robust findings of the quantitative analysis to guide the case selection for the qualitative analysis. Then the selection of the six cases is described. Finally, I give details on the different data sources used to reconstruct the decision-making processes.

In the following three chapters, I present qualitative descriptions and analyses of decision-making cases in different Council formations. Each chapter is devoted to a specific policy area. Chapter 9 compares two decision-making cases in the field of Agriculture. Chapter 10 compares two instances of decision-making in the field of Environment and Chapter 11 compares two instances of decision-making in the field of Economic and Financial Affairs. In every chapter, I first give a brief outline of the history of the policy area and the organisational structure of the Council formation. Then I describe the decision-making process for each of the two selected proposals. Finally, I conclude with a within-sector comparison of the two cases with respect to the negotiation process and the involvement of different Council levels in decision-making.

In Chapter 12, I summarise the findings from the intra-sector comparisons. In this chapter, I also discuss which explanations hold up in a cross-sectoral perspective. The descriptive findings of the qualitative analysis qualify the results of the quantitative study to some extent. Although ministers are actively involved in negotiations on a relatively large number of dossiers, the ministers discuss only a very limited number of issues during these occasions. Still, the issues discussed by ministers belong to the most salient ones. The results of the qualitative analysis also point to the need to revise and supplement some of the explanatory findings from the quantitative study.

In Part IV of the book, I present a synthesis of the quantitative and qualitative findings. In Chapter 13, I summarise the research results and discuss in how far the different results can be reconciled. To a large extent, the findings yield a coherent account of committee decision-making in the Council. In Chapter 14, I build on these insights and elaborate on them to make a first step towards a procedural theory of Council decision-making. In this chapter, I outline an explanation for the level at which a legislative decision is taken in the Council. Finally, I conclude the study in Chapter 15 with a discussion of the normative and scientific implications of the findings as well as an outline of promising avenues for future research.

2 The Council's committee system

In this chapter, I present background information on the organisation of the Council's committee system and its role in EU legislative decision-making. Besides presenting context information necessary for evaluating some of the choices made in the descriptive and explanatory analyses that follow, the descriptions in this chapter also serve to illustrate the size, complexity and potential importance of the Council's committee system. Thus, this chapter presents additional justification for researching the role and functioning of Council committees in EU decision-making. An equally important purpose of the chapter is to provide the procedural and organisational context in which the studied cases were embedded. Therefore, the descriptions portray the procedures, rules and organisational structures in operation during the study period from 2000 to 2005.[1]

I first give a stylised account of the involvement of working parties and senior Council committees in the legislative decision-making process. In line with the overall focus of the thesis, I concentrate on a description of a typical legislative decision-making process under the consultation and co-decision procedure, respectively. In the second section of the chapter, I consider the hierarchical structure of the Council organisation in more detail. I also describe differences in the Council's committee system across policy sectors and discuss changes over time. Finally, I depict the growth in the overall number of working party and Coreper meetings per year since the foundation of the European Communities and compare this development to the changes in the number of ministerial meetings during the same period of time. This description indicates that the practical relevance of Council committees is substantial and that it has been steadily increasing over the last 50 years both in relative and absolute terms. While practical or functional relevance should not be equated with political influence and power, these stylised descriptions and aggregate statistics about the number of committees and their meetings suggest that committees are potentially important political decision-making bodies that deserve more systematic empirical study.

---

1 Note that the description does not take into account the subsequent changes introduced as part of the Lisbon Treaty amendments. Wherever relevant, these changes are mentioned in footnotes.

Council committees in EU legislative decision-making

The EU institutions adopt legislation through a number of formal procedures, varying mainly in the degree of powers granted to the European Parliament and in the degree of inclusiveness of the Council's voting-rule (i.e. qualified majority or unanimity). The EU treaties specify the decision-rules applicable in a certain issue area.[2] To keep things simple, I describe only the two main procedures for adopting legislation on internal EU policies: the consultation and the co-decision procedure.[3] The main difference between the two procedures regards the decision-making rights of the Parliament. Under the consultation procedure, the EP can only give a non-binding opinion. In effect, the Council is the sole legislator under this procedure. In contrast, the co-decision procedure grants equal rights to the Parliament. In both procedures, the Commission has the exclusive right of initiative and can withdraw and amend its proposal during the procedure.[4]

The Commission initiates both procedures by transmitting a proposal for legislation to the Council, the Parliament and, if required by the relevant treaty article, to the Committee of the Regions (CoR) and the Economic and Social Committee (ESC), respectively. The latter three institutions are all asked for their opinions and can suggest amendments to the draft legislation. The EP adopts its opinion by a simple majority of votes. The Commission is not obliged to incorporate any of these amendments into its text. In the case of the consultation procedure, the EP has the 'power of delay' (Hix 2005: 78; Kardasheva 2009). The European Court of Justice made clear in its 1980 'isoglucose' ruling that no legislation can be passed until Parliament has given its opinion.[5] Thus, the EP can pressure the Commission to amend its proposal according to the EP's wishes by delaying the formal adoption of the EP opinion. In contrast, the Council or the Commission can impose a tight time schedule on the delivery of the opinions of the CoR and the ESC. Thus, the non-delivery of an opinion within the set time period by these institutions does not constitute an obstacle for the legislative process to proceed (Nugent 2006: 405–406).

At the same time as the EP, the CoR and the ESC prepare their opinions, the Council starts negotiations on the dossier. As noted, the Council can only take a formal decision after the Parliament has delivered its opinion. In reality, Council decisions are de facto often taken before the EP adopts its amendments, but with

---

2 The following versions of the treaties were applicable during the study period: Consolidated Version of the Treaty Establishing the European Community. 24 December 2002, OJ C325, pp. 33–159; and Consolidated Version of Treaty on European Union. 24 December 2002, OJ C325, pp. 5–32.

3 For an overview of legislative procedures and decision rules in different policy areas, see (Hix 2005: 99–102, 415–421). The Lisbon Treaty amendments extended the range of policy areas in which the co-decision procedure applies considerably and renamed the procedure to ordinary legislative procedure.

4 Exceptions exist in some areas of Justice and Home Affairs, where the Commission shares its right of initiative with Member States.

5 ECJ judgement on SA Roquette Frères v. Council of the European Communities. Isoglucose production quotas. Case 138/79, 29 October 1980.

14 *Part I: Introduction and background*

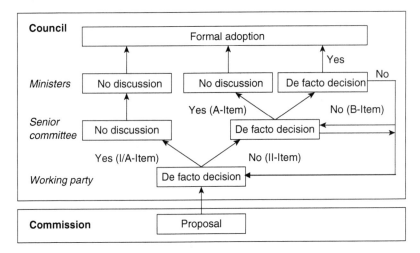

Figure 2.1 The internal decision-making process of the Council.

Source: Figure 1 in Häge (2008).

Note: The term 'Council' refers to the Council as an organisation, not to the Council as a legal entity as described in the Treaties. The Council as a legal entity refers only to meetings of ministers. The possibility that a proposal fails completely is not considered in the figure. In general, a proposal can fail at all levels of the Council hierarchy.

the restriction that they are 'subject to Parliament's opinion' (Nugent 2006: 504). Before ministers discuss a proposal, a number of subordinate committees of national officials first deal with it. I distinguish three main Council levels: working parties at the bottom of the hierarchy, senior committees in the middle, and ministerial meetings at the top. Figure 2.1 illustrates the internal decision-making process in the Council.

The dossier first enters the internal decision-making process of the Council at the level of working parties. The Committee of Permanent Representatives (Coreper) is usually responsible for establishing and dissolving working parties.[6] The Council Presidency, assisted by the Secretariat, decides when and which working party discusses a certain dossier. Working parties consist of policy experts, which are either based in national ministries or temporarily seconded to the Member States' permanent representations in Brussels. As in other Council bodies, the Commission is also represented in working parties. A delegate from the country holding the Presidency chairs the meetings and the working party members can draw on the support of the Council's secretariat and the Council's legal service.[7] The working party members aim at reaching agreement on as many

---

6 Art. 19(3) of the Council Decision 2002/682/EC, EURATOM of 22 July 2002 adopting the Council's rules of procedure. 28 August 2002, OJ L230, pp. 7–26.

7 Since the establishment of the External Action Service by the Lisbon Treaty, several External Relations working parties have been chaired by officials of that service.

issues as possible in order to relieve higher decision-making levels of workload. The responsible working party often discusses the proposal during several meetings. Meetings usually last either half a working day or a full working day.

After deliberations in the working party, the working party chair hands the dossier up to the senior committees at the second Council level. The two formations of Coreper and the Special Committee on Agriculture (SCA) form this level of the hierarchy.[8] Coreper II consists of the permanent representatives of the Member States and prepares the meetings of the General Affairs and External Relations, Economic and Financial Affairs, and Justice and Home Affairs Council formations. The members of Coreper I are the deputy permanent representatives. They prepare the meetings of Council formations in the areas of Employment, Social Policy, Health and Consumer Affairs, Competitiveness, Transport, Telecommunications and Energy, Environment, Education, Youth and Culture. Coreper I shares the responsibility for preparing ministerial meetings in 'Agriculture and Fisheries' with the SCA. The SCA consists of senior officials from national agriculture ministries. The SCA is responsible for issues related to the common agricultural policy, whereas Coreper I is responsible for food safety issues.[9] After the initial discussions in the working party, the dossier forms either a I-item or a II-item on the senior committee's agenda. If the working party reached complete agreement, the Presidency includes the dossier as a I-point on the senior committee's agenda. In this case, the senior committee approves the agreement of the working party without further discussion and decides to forward the proposal to ministers for a formal adoption. If the working party was not able to resolve all issues, the dossier forms a II-point on the committee's agenda. Only II-items are subject to further deliberation by the senior committee.[10]

After the senior committee discussed the dossier, the Presidency transmits the proposal to one of the ministerial meetings. Ministers from the Member States meet in nine different formations.[11] These formations are distinguished according to policy areas. Together, the different ministerial formations represent the apex of the Council hierarchy. If either the working party or the senior committee

---

8 The role and functions of Coreper are laid down in Art. 207 of the Consolidated Version of the Treaty Establishing the European Community. 24 December 2002, OJ C325, pp. 118–119; and Art. 19 of the Council Decision 2002/682/EC, EURATOM of 22 July 2002 adopting the Council's rules of procedure. 28 August 2002, OJ L230, pp. 15–17. The SCA was set up by an intergovernmental decision of representatives of the governments of Member States on 12 May 1960.

9 As described further below, a number of committees composed of more senior officials exist in the Council structure. The SCA stands out among those committees because it reports directly to ministers (Hayes-Renshaw & Wallace 2006: 95). In contrast to other more senior committees, the SCA does not have to seek the approval of one of the Coreper formations to put an item on the ministers' agenda.

10 The SCA is an exception in this respect; during the study period, it did not divide its agenda into I- and II-points.

11 The official list of Council formations during the study period is laid down in Annex I to the Council Decision 2002/682/EC, EURATOM of 22 March 2004 adopting the Council's rules of procedure. 15 April 2004, OJ L106, p. 37. The Lisbon Treaty changes includes a split of the General Affairs and External Relations formation into a General Affairs and a Foreign Affairs formation.

16   *Part I: Introduction and background*

have reached a settlement, the proposal forms an A-point on the agenda of a forthcoming ministerial meeting. A-points are adopted without discussion at the beginning of ministerial meetings.[12] In many instances, the ministers adopting a dossier as an A-point are not even responsible for the policy area in question (Gomez and Peterson 2001: 62–63). Of course, the adoption of acts by ministers holding a different portfolio is of no concern in legal terms, as the EU treaties do not distinguish between different Council formations. If neither the working party nor the senior committee reached a complete agreement, the proposal forms a B-point on the agenda of a meeting of the relevant ministerial formation. Ministers discuss the dossier only in this case to resolve the remaining outstanding issues. Formally, only ministers may adopt legislative decisions of the Council. But as this description of the internal Council decision-making process shows, many decisions are de facto made at lower levels of the Council hierarchy. Of course, the description is somewhat simplistic. In reality, proposals can move up and down across the different levels of the Council hierarchy several times before ministers can finally adopt them. In these cases, the higher-ranking Council bodies discuss the dossier but refer it back to lower levels with new instructions. In Figure 2.1, I indicate this possibility through feedback arrows from higher to lower Council levels.

The consultation procedure ends at this stage with a decision on the legal act by ministers. Depending on the voting rule referred to in the relevant treaty article, the adoption of an act requires either a qualified majority of votes or a unanimous decision. If ministers reach no decision, the legislation fails.[13] In contrast, the complete co-decision procedure formally consists of three readings by both the Parliament and the Council. In the case of the co-decision procedure, the Council can adopt the law at this stage only if either the EP has not made any amendments or if the Council approves all the amendments made by the EP. Without any co-ordinated efforts on the part of the EU institutions, the Council is unlikely to approve all EP amendments in its first reading. However, the EU institutions increased their attempts in recent years to reach more first- and second-reading agreements under the co-decision procedure. These efforts are part of a more general programme to increase the efficiency of EU legislative decision-making. In order to reach a first-reading agreement, delegations from the Commission, the Parliament and the Council meet to negotiate a compromise solution. The EP subsequently adopts this compromise solution in the form of amendments to the Commission proposal. The Council is then in a position to accept all EP amendments in its first reading. First-reading agreements are usually

---

12 However, any Member State or the Commission can demand that an A-point is withdrawn from the agenda. The withdrawal can only be prevented through a negative decision by the Council as a whole. See Art. 3(8) of the Council Decision 2002/682/EC, EURATOM of 22 March 2004 adopting the Council's rules of procedure. 15 April 2004, OJ L106, p. 25.

13 Of course, the procedure can also end through the failure of the proposal at lower levels of the Council hierarchy. The Presidency stops discussions on a dossier when it becomes apparent that the necessary majority will not be reached.

The Council's committee system   17

negotiated at the level of working parties and Coreper. The Presidency represents the Council in the negotiations with the other institutions. The Presidency often does not have a clear mandate during first-reading negotiations, because the Member States have not yet agreed on a common Council position.

If the institutions do not reach a first-reading agreement, the Council adopts a common position. The Council's common position either confirms or, more commonly, amends the Commission proposal. In either way, the adoption of the common position requires a qualified majority of votes. The Council then communicates the common position to the EP for a second reading. The EP has three months to act. If the Parliament does not act, the common position automatically becomes law. The common position also becomes law when the Parliament approves it by an absolute majority of its members. As in first-reading agreements, the direct adoption of the common position by the EP is usually a result of conscious attempts by all three institutions to conclude the procedure early. In this case, the Council's common position contains in fact an inter-institutional compromise agreement and is therefore directly acceptable to the EP.

If the Council's common position does not constitute a compromise or is otherwise acceptable to the EP, the EP rejects or amends the common position. Again, the EP has to decide by an absolute majority of its members. If the EP rejects the common position, the proposal fails. If the EP makes amendments, it returns the amended common position to the Council and the Commission. The Commission then gives an opinion on the amendments. If the opinion by the Commission is favourable, the Council can adopt the amended common position in its second reading by a qualified majority of votes. However, if the Commission issues a negative opinion on an EP amendment, the Council has to decide about this amendment by unanimity. The second reading in the Council constitutes the third opportunity to end the co-decision procedure early. The process is analogous to first-reading agreements. If the institutions can agree on a compromise before the EP adopts its second-reading amendments, the EP amendments to the Council's common position can be formulated accordingly. The Council can then directly adopt the common position as modified by the EP's compromise amendments.

If the institutions do not reach a second-reading agreement, the Presidents of the Council and the EP have to convene the conciliation committee within six weeks to negotiate a joint text. The conciliation committee consists of an equal number of representatives of the Council and the European Parliament. The conciliation committee delegation of the Council makes decisions by a qualified majority of votes and the EP delegation by a simple majority of its members. The committee has six weeks to agree on a joint text. If the committee does not reach an agreement, the proposal fails. If the committee manages to formulate a joint text, the text still has to be accepted by both the EP and the Council in their third readings. The ratification of the joint text has to occur within six weeks to enter into law. The adoption of the joint text requires the agreement of a qualified majority of votes in the Council but only a simple majority of votes in Parliament. If either institution does not accept the joint text, the act fails.

18   *Part I: Introduction and background*

In the consultation procedure, the Parliament can only make non-binding suggestions to the Council. In contrast, the Parliament is a real co-legislator under the co-decision procedure. The necessity for the Council to engage in negotiations with the EP under the co-decision procedure also affects the influence of Council committees in EU legislative decision-making. According to Bostock (2002), the co-decision procedure has further elevated the already central role of Coreper in the legislative process and the role of working groups supporting Coreper. After the Council has adopted its common position in the first reading, 'action on the Council side to complete the procedure has devolved almost entirely on Coreper (assisted as always by Council working groups)' (Bostock 2002: 219). A main indication of the increased importance of Council committees is that second-reading agreements are almost invariably reached below the ministerial level. Ministers only formally confirm these inter-institutional agreements through the A-point procedure. In addition, the Council side of the conciliation committee consists almost always of members of Coreper.[14] Only the head of the Council delegation is often a minister or a junior minister from the country holding the Presidency. To sum up, Council committees play a crucial role in ensuring the functioning of the Council machinery and the efficiency of the EU legislative process as a whole. Council committees were already very involved under the consultation procedure, but the co-decision procedure has further increased the reliance on committee work in the Council.

The organisational structure

In the preceding description of the role of Council committees in the legislative process, the actual organisational structure of the Council's committee system was strongly simplified. I referred only to the horizontal distinction along sectoral lines between different Council formations and the vertical division between ministerial meetings, senior committees, and working parties. In this section, I describe the organisation of the Council's committee system in more detail. A closer inspection reveals further vertical divisions in the Council hierarchy, in particular within the level of working parties.

Besides the senior committees mentioned above, that is the SCA and the two formations of Coreper, a number of specialised bodies exist whose members are similarly high-ranking officials: the Economic and Financial Committee deals mostly with matters related to monetary union, the Employment Committee is consulted by ministers on measures for the co-ordination of employment and labour market policy, the Social Protection Committee advises ministers on co-operation in social protection policies, and the Article 133 Committee assists the Commission in international trade negotiations and advises it in matters related

---

14 The co-decision procedure applies mainly to policy areas under the responsibility of Coreper I. Thus, the members of the Council delegation to the conciliation committee are mainly deputy permanent representatives (Bostock 2002: 219).

to the Common Commercial Policy.[15] All these committees deal with matters that are part of the classic Community policy areas. In addition, the Political and Security Committee (PSC) gives advice in the area of Common Foreign and Security Policy and exercises 'political control and strategic direction of crisis management operations', and the Article 36 Committee advises ministers and co-ordinates policy in the field of Justice and Home Affairs.[16] The Member States established all these committees through treaty articles. Larsson (2003: 41) suggests that Coreper usually does not further discuss the issues handled by these committees. In this case, the approval of Coreper to put an item on a ministerial agenda would be a pure formality. While this suggestion seems plausible, no reliable empirical data exists on the extent to which Coreper interferes with the work of other relatively senior committees. In the absence of such data, the formal right of committees to prepare the agenda of ministerial meetings is the most straightforward criteria for the terminological distinction between senior committees and working parties. For the purposes of this study, I subsume all committees without the right to report directly to ministers under the heading of working parties. In cases where a distinction from ordinary working parties is necessary, I refer to higher-ranking groups as senior working parties.

The senior working parties are supported by several even more specialised committees set up by formal Council decisions: the PSC is supported by the Military Committee and the Committee for Civilian Aspects of Crisis Management. The Military Committee gives military advice and directs all military activity in the Union framework; the Committee for Civilian Aspects of Crisis Management reports officially to Coreper II but has also the task of advising the PSC.[17] The Economic Policy Committee and the Financial Services Committee assist the Economic and Financial Committee. The Economic Policy Committee is responsible for economic advice and the preparation of the Council's work on co-operation in economic policies of Member States; the Financial Services

---

15 The Economic and Financial Committee was formally established by Art. 114(2) of the Treaty Establishing the European Community. 24 December 2002, OJ C325, p. 80. The Employment Committee was formally established by Art. 130 of the Treaty Establishing the European Community. 24 December 2002, OJ C325, p. 89–90. The Social Protection Committee was formally established by Art. 144 of the Treaty Establishing the European Community. 24 December 2002, OJ C325, p. 96–97. The Article 133 Committee was formally established by Art. 133(3) of the Treaty Establishing the European Community. 24 December 2002, OJ C325, p. 90–91. The Lisbon Treaty amendments renamed it to 'Trade Policy Committee'.

16 The Political and Security Committee was formally established by Art. 25 of the Treaty on European Union. 24 December 2002, OJ C325, p. 19. The Article 36 Committee was formally established by Art. 36 of the Treaty on European Union. 24 December 2002, OJ C325, p. 25–26. The Lisbon Treaty amendments replaced it by a new Standing Committee on Operational Cooperation on Internal Security.

17 The Military Committee was formally established by the Council Decision 2001/79/CFSP of 22 January 2001 setting up the Military Committee of the European Union. 30 January 2001, OJ L27, pp. 4–6. The Committee for Civilian Aspects of Crisis Management was formally established by the Council Decision 2000/354/CFSP of 22 May 2000 setting up the Committee for Civilian Aspects of Crisis Management. 27 May 2000, OJ L127, p. 1.

20   Part I: Introduction and background

Committee provides advice on financial market issues.[18] The Security Committee is somewhat different to other committees in that its tasks do not concern public policy, but rather the administration of the Council itself. The Security Committee is concerned with all issues of security related to the Council's proceedings and advises the General Secretariat on those matters.[19] Besides the committees set up by a formal Council decision, a number of other higher-ranking working parties exist that were not established through a direct decision of ministers. These working parties stand out because they direct and co-ordinate the work of lower-ranking working parties in their field of responsibility. For example, in the field of Justice and Home Affairs, the Strategic Committee on Immigration, Frontiers and Asylum (SCIFA) oversees the work of the working parties on Asylum, Frontiers, Migration, and Visa; and in the field of Agriculture, the Working Party of Chief Veterinary Officers supervises the work of the different specialised working parties of Veterinary Experts.

Three other groups of national officials also occupy a special position in the Council structure. The Mertens, Antici and Friends of the Presidency Groups are referred to as groups 'closely associated with Coreper'.[20] The Mertens Group prepares the meetings of Coreper I and the Antici Group the meetings of Coreper II. These groups consist of close aids of the deputy permanent representatives and the permanent representatives, respectively. The Friends of the Presidency Group can be activated by the Presidency to solve a specific problem or conflict (Larsson 2003: 41). Finally, at the bottom of the hierarchy are the ordinary working parties, which form 'the Council's lifeblood' (Westlake and Galloway 2004: 200). Figure 2.2 summarises the hierarchical structure of the Council organisation.

The Council's committee system does not only show a wide variation in terms of the seniority level of different groups, but also in terms of the sheer number of groups in different policy areas. In Table 2.1, I present the number of working parties in different Council formations between July 2000 and December 2005. The numbers are derived from the Council's list of preparatory bodies. Senior working parties established by treaty articles or by Council decisions are not included in the counts. The General Secretariat continually updates the list of preparatory bodies to reflect new developments. The list indicates working parties as well as sub-areas within the remit of a working party. In practice, sub-areas usually constitute separate groups themselves. Therefore, I present both the number of working parties proper as well as the number of sub-areas in the table.

---

18 The Economic Policy Committee was formally established by the Council Decision 2000/604/EC of 29 September 2000 on the composition and the statutes of the Economic Policy Committee. 11 October 2000, OJ L257, p. 28. The Financial Services Committee was formally established by the Council Decision 2003/165/EC of 18 February 2003 concerning the establishment of the Financial Services Committee. 12 March 2003, OJ L67, p. 17.

19 The Security Committee was formally established by the Council Decision 2001/264/EC of 19 March 2001 adopting the Council's security regulations. 11 April 2001, OJ L101, p. 10.

20 For example, see Council (2000): List of committees and working parties involved in the Council's preparatory work. 5 July 2000, 9872/00, p. 3.

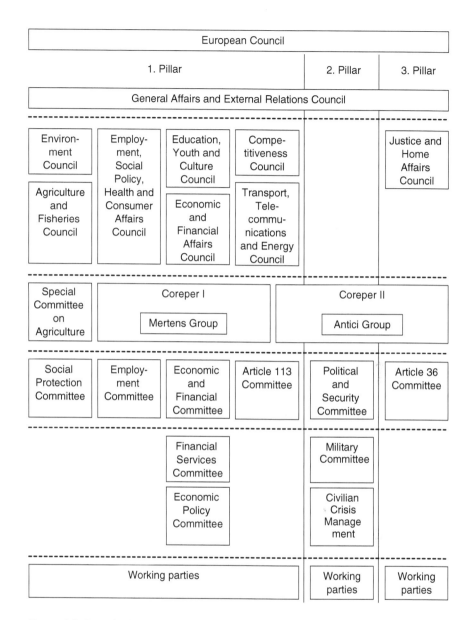

Figure 2.2 Organisational structure of the Council.

Note: The figure presents the organisational structure of the Council at the end of the study period in 2005. The size of boxes does not correspond to the importance of bodies, the graphical structure corresponds to the actual hierarchy only for classes of bodies (demarcated by dashed lines) within each pillar, e.g. the Military Committee is at the same hierarchical level as the Civilian Crisis Management Committee and both directly advise the Political and Security Committee at the next higher level. Similarly, that the Social Protection Committee is presented below the Special Committee on Agriculture does not imply that it reports to the SCA, but only to one of the committees at the next higher level, in this case to Coreper I. See the text for a more detailed description.

Table 2.1 Working parties and sub-areas by Council formation

Council formation (pre-Seville reform)	July 2000			October 2001			July 2002			March 2003			February 2004			December 2005			Formation (post-Seville reform)
	WP	SA	Tot	WP	SA	Tot	WP	SA	Tot	WP	SA	Tot	WP	SA	Tot	WP	SA	Tot	
General Affairs	16	0	16	16	1	17	17	1	18	18	1	19	16	1	17	17	2	19	General Affairs
External Relations	41	0	41	37	0	37	37	1	38	35	1	36	37	1	38	36	2	38	External Relations,
Development	3	0	3	3	0	3	3	0	3	–	–	–	–	–	–	–	–	–	Development
Budget	3	0	3	3	0	3	3	0	3	9	9	18	8	8	16	8	8	16	Economic and Financial
Economic and Finance	8	9	17	8	12	20	9	12	21	–	–	–	–	–	–	–	–	–	Affairs
Justice and Home Affairs	26	7	33	26	7	33	21	7	28	21	7	28	21	7	28	22	0	22	Justice and Home Affairs
Agriculture	37	67	104	29	73	102	29	73	102	25	78	103	26	78	104	26	80	106	Agriculture and Fisheries
Fisheries	3	0	3	3	0	3	3	0	3	–	–	–	–	–	–	–	–	–	
Industry	4	3	7	4	3	7	4	3	7	16	19	35	17	17	34	14	14	28	Competitiveness (Internal Market, Industry, Research)
Internal Market	13	28	41	14	20	34	14	20	34	–	–	–	–	–	–	–	–	–	
Research	3	0	3	3	0	3	3	0	3	–	–	–	–	–	–	–	–	–	
Telecommunications	2	0	2	2	0	2	2	0	2	7	0	7	7	0	7	7	0	7	Transport,
Transport	4	0	4	4	0	4	4	0	4	–	–	–	–	–	–	–	–	–	Telecommunications,
Energy	2	0	2	2	0	2	2	0	2	–	–	–	–	–	–	–	–	–	Energy
Information Society	1	0	1	1	0	1	1	0	1	–	–	–	–	–	–	–	–	–	
Labour and Social Affairs	2	0	2	1	0	1	1	0	1	4	0	4	4	0	4	4	0	4	Employment, Social Policy, Health and Consumer Affairs
Health and Consumer Affairs	2	0	2	2	0	2	2	0	2	–	–	–	–	–	–	–	–	–	
Environment	5	3	8	2	2	4	2	3	5	2	3	5	2	3	5	2	3	5	Environment
Education, Culture, Youth	4	2	6	4	0	4	4	0	4	4	0	4	4	0	4	4	0	4	Education, Youth and Culture
Total	179	119	298	164	118	282	160	120	280	141	118	259	142	115	257	142	112	254	Total

Sources: Own calculations based on the following Council documents: Council (2000): List of committees and working parties involved in the Council's preparatory work. 5 July 2000, 9872/00; Council (2001): Council preparatory bodies. 30 October 2001, 13204/01; Council (2002): Council preparatory bodies. 15 July 2002, 10183/02; Council (2003): List of Council preparatory bodies. 4 March 2003, 7003/03; Council (2004): List of Council preparatory bodies. 23 February 2004, 6124/04; Council (2005): List of Council preparatory bodies. 5 December 2005, 15180/05 + Corr. 1.

Note: WP = working party, SA = sub-area, Tot = Total.

In addition, I indicate the combined total number of working parties and sub-areas in a certain Council formation. In the following discussion, I assume that sub-areas can be treated as separate groups, and focus on the combined total number of working parties and sub-areas.

Regarding temporal changes, a considerable decrease in the overall number of working parties from 298 in the year 2000 to 254 in 2005 is apparent. This decline is mainly due to efforts to rationalise the working party system. Besides changes in mandates of individual groups, these rationalisation efforts led to abolitions and to mergers of groups. For example, the working party system in the Environment formation was reformed in spring 2001. Coreper decided to incorporate the Working Parties on Biodiversity, Biosafety, and Persistent Organic Pollutants into the Working Party on International Environment Issues and to dissolve the High-Level Working Party on Environment and Development.[21] Later in the same year, the Council rationalised the working party structure in the Agriculture formation. Although Coreper formally agreed to abolish eight working parties, six of them were just relegated to sub-areas of other working parties.[22] In 2002, Coreper decided to merge two working parties and to discontinue four more working parties as part of the restructuring of the Justice and Home Affairs formation.[23]

Another reform step took place in spring 2003. Among other things, this reform sought to bring the working party system in line with the reduced number of Council formations agreed to by Member States at the Seville European Council in June 2002. The reform affected working parties in the fields of General Affairs, External Relations and Development, Economic and Financial Affairs, Agriculture and Fisheries, Competitiveness, and Transport, Telecommunications and Energy. The reform reduced the overall number of working parties by 21 groups. Coreper decided to abolish 12 groups, to newly establish six groups, to subsume six groups into other groups, and to merge 16 groups into seven new groups.[24] Overall, the rationalisation efforts to prepare the Council structure for the accession of ten new Member States in 2004 explain most of the variation in the number of working parties over time. However, the changes in the Council's list of preparatory bodies also indicate that Coreper establishes and dissolves individual working parties and sub-areas in response to short- and medium-term needs to deal with specific policy issues.

Regarding cross-sectoral differences, the Agriculture and Fisheries formation stands out for having by far the highest number of working parties. At the end of 2005, 106 working parties prepared the work of Agriculture and Fisheries ministers. Most of the remaining working parties are concentrated in only four other

---

21 Council (2001): List of committees and working parties involved in the Council's preparatory work. 22 June 2001, 10279/01, p. 12, fn. 8.

22 Council (2001): Council preparatory bodies. 30 October 2001, 13204/01.

23 Council (2002): Council preparatory bodies. 15 July 2002, 10183/02; and Council (2002): Structure and number of Justice and Home Affairs working parties and activities other than legislative work (reports, evaluations, etc.). 1 March 2002, 6582/02.

24 Council (2003): List of Council preparatory bodies. 4 March 2003, 7003/03, pp. 1–3.

24   Part I: Introduction and background

formations. The meetings of foreign ministers are prepared by 19 working parties dealing with General Affairs and 38 working parties dealing with External Relations. Decisions in the field of Economic and Financial Affairs are prepared by 16 working parties and 22 working parties support Justice and Home Affairs ministers. Finally, 28 working parties deal with dossiers in the Competitiveness formation. In contrast, the number of working parties in the remaining four Council formations ranges only between four and seven groups. A clear explanation for these cross-sectoral differences in the number of working parties is not apparent. However, both the breadth and the complexity of the policy issues dealt with in different Council formations vary considerably. Divergent functional requirements of the policy area are likely to be at least in part responsible for differences in the number of working parties across Council formations. However, the Council formations also exhibit quite different histories in terms of their institutional development. Thus, path-dependencies are also likely to play a role in explaining the continued differences in the organisation of the working party system in different Council formations.

Long-term trends in Council committee activity

Up to this point, I have discussed the organisational structure of the Council's committee system as well as its more recent historical development. Detailed information on the long-term development of the committee system is generally lacking. However, the Council secretariat keeps track of the number of days different types of Council bodies met per year since 1958, the year of the establishment of the European Communities.[25] These statistics trace the involvement of different Council levels over time and allow for a comparison of their relative importance in managing the Council's workload. The figures show strong increases in the number of meeting days of all Council bodies. However, the pattern and the extent of growth in the activity of working parties, Coreper and ministers still exhibit significant differences. Figure 2.3 illustrates the development of the number of ministerial meeting days per year. The plot indicates two periods of strong growth. The first period of growth occurred soon after the foundation of the European Communities: between 1959 and 1962, the number of ministerial meeting days increased almost four-fold from 21 to 80 per year. The second major increase occurred in the period between 1982 and 1984. In just two years, the number of ministerial meeting days jumped from 86 to 133 per year.[26] Although the number of meeting days varied considerably between and after these two growth periods, a clear positive or negative trend is not identifiable.

Compared with the step-wise growth of ministerial meeting days, the number of Coreper meeting days plotted in Figure 2.4 shows quite a different development

---

25 General Secretariat of the Council of the European Union (1996): Review of the Council's work. Luxembourg: Office for Official Publications of the European Communities.

26 As far as possible, I checked the most extreme changes in this time series with information on the number of meetings from other sources. I could not find any indications that the numbers are affected by measurement problems.

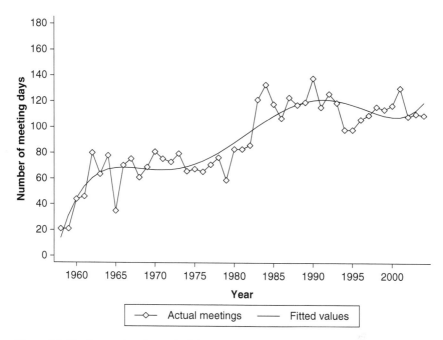

Figure 2.3 Yearly meeting days of ministers, 1958–2004.

Sources: Table 0.2 in Kassim (2003: 20) for the years 1958–1996 (several corrections were made on the basis of the original tables in various issues of the 'Review of the Council's Work', which was published yearly by the Council secretariat until 1996); Table 3.2 in Hayes-Renshaw and Wallace (2006: 98) for the years 1997–2004.

Note: The fitted values are based on a fifth-order polynomial regression of the number of meeting days (Y) against time (X): $Y = b_1 X + b_2 X^2 + b_3 X^3 + b_4 X^4 + b_5 X^5$.

over time. The number of meeting days of the permanent representatives and their deputies increased very strongly in the early years of the European Communities. Within six years after the establishment of the European Communities, the number of Coreper meeting days grew from 39 in 1958 to an all-time high of 177.5 in 1964. During the remainder of the time period, the number of Coreper meeting days fluctuated considerably but stayed mostly within a band of 100–140 meeting days per year. The figure does not show a clear upward or downward tendency after the extreme growth in the early days of the European Communities. This horizontal trend is similar to the pattern of stagnation observed in the number of ministerial meeting days since the early 1980s.

As illustrated in Figure 2.5, the growth in the number of working party meeting days indicates a step-wise growth over time. In this respect, the pattern is somewhat similar to the growth in the ministerial meeting days. However, the steps in the working party time series are much less abrupt than in the ministerial meeting days data. The steps in the number of meeting days of ministers and of the working parties also do not correspond in time. The number of working party meeting days first increased steadily from 302 in 1958 to 1439 in 1971; then a

26 Part I: Introduction and background

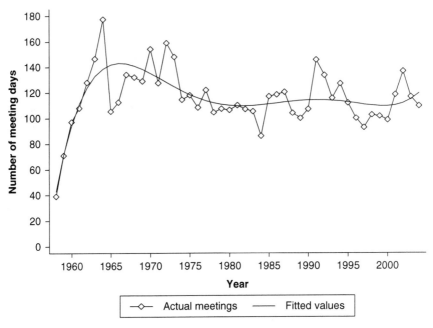

Figure 2.4 Yearly meeting days of Coreper, 1958–2004.

Sources: As Figure 2.3.

Note: As Figure 2.3.

relatively large jump to 2135 meeting days occurred in 1972, after which the number of meeting days remained relatively constant over the subsequent 20 years. However, the number of meeting days resumed its growth in the early 1990s and continues to do so until the end of the observed time period in 2004. Apart from the stagnation in the 1970s and 1980s, the number of working party meeting days shows a relatively clear increasing trend over the last half a century. Whether the slight decreases in 2003 and 2004 are signs of a renewed consolidation remains to be seen.

The comparison of the development of the number of meeting days of the different Council bodies suggests at least two conclusions. First, the Council committees play important roles in keeping the Council machinery running. In the case of working parties, this conclusion can be directly drawn from a comparison of the total number of meeting days of different Council levels. From the establishment of the European Communities, the number of working party meeting days was always more than ten times larger than the number of ministerial meeting days. In 2004, the last year of the time series, national officials spent 3037.5 days in working party meetings, while the number of Coreper and ministerial meeting days amounted only to 109.5 each. Thus, working parties were and are responsible for dealing with a vast part of the Council's work.

But beside the working parties, Coreper also plays an important role in coping with the Council's workload. In absolute terms, the number of Coreper meeting

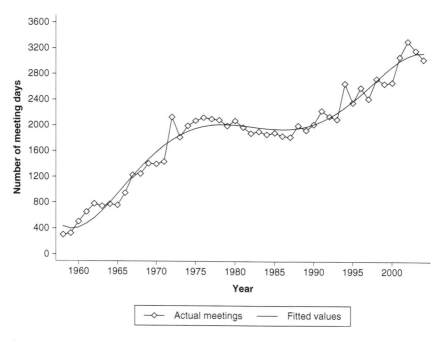

Figure 2.5 Yearly meeting days of working parties, 1958–2004.
Sources: As Figure 2.3.
Note: As Figure 2.3.

days is considerably smaller than the number of working party meeting days and is often not much larger than the number of ministerial meeting days. However, in relative terms, the two Coreper formations are the most involved decision-making bodies in the Council. The numbers of ministerial and working party meeting days both aggregate the meeting days of several groups, while the total number of Coreper meetings is only the sum of the meetings of its two formations. For example, the 109.5 meeting days of ministers in 2004 were accumulated by nine different ministerial formations, while the same number of meeting days of Coreper was accumulated only by the two groups of permanent representatives and their deputies. Due to their involvement in virtually all Council business, the two formations of Coreper are likely to play a central co-ordination function in the Council structure. In contrast, the ministers concern themselves only with the peak of the iceberg that constitutes the Council's work.

Another conclusion that can be drawn from these statistics is that the reliance on working parties in the Council has not only continually increased in absolute terms, but also in comparison to the reliance on other Council bodies. The number of Coreper meetings seemed to have already reached a natural upper limit early in the integration process. The permanent representatives and their deputies can spend only a finite amount of time in Council meetings. In contrast, the number of ministerial meetings was only partially affected by these natural boundaries. With the coverage of new policy areas in European legislation, the Council established

28 Part I: Introduction and background

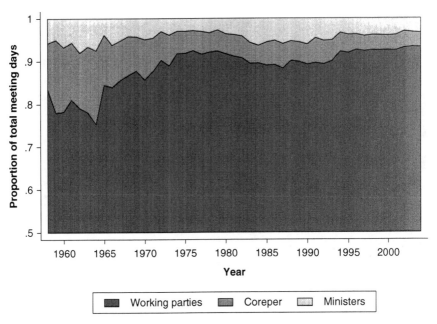

Figure 2.6 Distribution of meeting days across Council levels, 1958–2004.

Sources: As Figure 2.3.

Note: The *y*-axis does not start at zero but at 0.5. Focusing the plot on the region above 0.5 on the *y*-axis allows for a closer inspection of the changes in the proportions of Coreper and ministerial meeting days, but the resulting figure strongly understates the proportion of working party meeting days.

additional formations involving different groups of ministers (Steunenberg 2004).[27] However, to the extent that European legislative activity became more about consolidating and intensifying regulation in existing policy areas rather than about establishing European regulation in new policy areas, coping with increased ministerial workload by involving additional ministers also ceased to be an option. Thus, the number of ministerial meeting days reached a plateau in the early 1990s, while the number of working party meeting days continued its growth path at that time. Overall, the numbers presented in the figures above lend themselves to the interpretation that ministers and Coreper members have responded to the increased workload over time by relegating more and more of the Council's work to working parties, the lowest level in the Council hierarchy.

This trend is more clearly illustrated in Figure 2.6, which shows the number of meeting days of different hierarchical levels as a proportion of the total number of meeting days in the Council. With the exception of the period between the early 1980s and the early 1990s, in which the number of ministerial meeting days increased while the number of working party meeting days remained relatively

---

27 The number of active Council formations increased from 8 to 20 between 1971 and 1988 (Steunenberg 2004: 142).

stable, the proportion of Council meeting days grew continuously over time at the expense of the proportion of ministerial and Coreper meeting days.

The role, organisation and activities of Council committees

In this chapter, I first discussed the role of committees in Council decision-making within the wider context of the EU legislative process. According to textbook accounts, Council committees take care of the details of legislative proposals presented to the Council by the Commission. The collective aim of committee members is to reach agreement on as many issues as possible, supposedly to minimise the need to personally involve the ministers. First, the members of the relevant working party exchange their views on the Commission proposal. The relevant Coreper formation or the SCA only becomes involved if the members of the working party cannot reach a complete agreement. Similarly, the senior committee members refer the proposal to ministers for deliberation only if they cannot resolve all of the outstanding issues themselves. Thus, committees seem to play an important function in ensuring the efficiency and the technical quality of the output of Council decision-making.

Although these stylised textbook accounts of the role of committees in the Council give us an idea about their functions and importance, the extent to which these accounts represent the reality of committee decision-making in the Council is uncertain. These accounts are usually not based on systematic empirical studies but on common wisdom and the subjective perceptions of a few informed insiders. More importantly, they do not tell us much about the causal mechanisms underlying committee decision-making. What makes some proposals 'technical' enough to make an agreement at the committee level possible and others so 'political' that the involvement of ministers is required for their adoption? A major goal of this study is to shed more light on the question of why committees are able to reach an agreement in some instances but not in others.

In the second section, I described the organisation of the Council's committee system in more detail. The description showed significant differences in the organisational structure of different Council formations. Notably, the number of working parties varies considerably across policy sectors. For example, only a handful of working parties deal with Environmental policy, while the number of working parties concerned with Agricultural policy reaches more than a hundred. Beside the overall number of working parties, the hierarchical structure among different types of committees varies across Council formations. In most cases, the Council structure is characterised by three layers, the ministers at the top, Coreper in the middle, and the working parties at the bottom. However, significant exceptions exist to this pattern. First, much of the Council business in the field of Agriculture is not managed by one of the Coreper formations, but by the SCA. Thus, the SCA replaces Coreper to a large extent in preparing the meetings of ministers in this policy field. Second, a number of committees exist in certain formations that take a hierarchical position between normal working parties and senior committees that directly prepare the ministerial meetings. For example, the Justice and Home Affairs area is almost entirely characterised by a four-layered hierarchy: the SCIFA co-ordinates the work of the specialised working parties

30   Part I: Introduction and background

concerned with migration, asylum and external borders, while the Article 36 Committee co-ordinates the work of the working parties concerned with judicial co-operation in criminal matters and with policy co-operation. Both the SCIFA and the Article 36 Committee in turn report to Coreper II, which prepares the meetings of the Justice and Home Affairs ministers. This discussion indicates that treating the Council as a monolithic actor might not be warranted. Decision-making dynamics in the Council might not only differ across different hierarchical levels but could also be influenced by differences in the organisational structure of Council formations.

Finally, I compared the absolute and relative involvement of different hierarchical levels in the Council's work through a discussion of time-series data on the number of yearly meeting days of different Council bodies. The comparison clearly illustrated the vast reliance on working parties to manage the Council's workload. The development over time also showed that this reliance increased continuously not only in absolute but also in relative terms. The latter finding is of special significance, since it indicates that the higher Council levels cope with an increased workload by relegating more and more work to the working parties. Taken together, the discussion in this chapter suggests that Council committees play a vital role in sustaining the Council as a decision-making institution and that this role, at least with respect to working parties, is becoming more rather than less important over time.

Note, however, that the functional importance of Council committees cannot necessarily be equated with political importance. While large numbers of committees and committee meetings might be necessary to guarantee the efficient operation of the Council, these large numbers do not automatically imply that committees also have the power and influence to significantly determine the outcome of Council decision-making. Received wisdom and aggregate statistics suggest that committee members are potentially influential decision-makers, but such indirect indications cannot substitute for systematic empirical evidence. Like the stylised accounts of committee decision-making discussed earlier, aggregate statistics about the number of committees and their meetings also do not inform us about the extent or the conditions under which committees rather than ministers make decisions in the Council.

Knowledge about the factors influencing committee decision-making is not only important for a better understanding of how the Council works, but also for the normative evaluation of its decisions. The reliance on committees of diplomats and national experts might indeed have advantages by ensuring the efficiency and technical quality of Council decision-making, but do these advantages come without costs? To what extent does committee decision-making undermine the democratic legitimacy of Council acts? Do the advantages outweigh the losses in terms of direct accountability of ministers to their national parliaments? Do organisational differences exist across Council formations that move this trade-off in one or the other direction? The answers to these questions depend strongly on what types of issues committees decide, how they decide them, and which factors influence the decision-making behaviour of their members. In the next chapter, I discuss the extent to which the existing research has examined these questions.

3 Existing research on Council decision-making

Textbook accounts of the Council are not shy in using colourful metaphors to describe the overarching importance of committees for the functioning of the Council. For example, Hix (2005: 83) describes Coreper as 'the real engine for much of the work of the Council'. Similarly, Westlake and Galloway (2004: 200) refer to Coreper as 'the Council's backbone and engine room of Council business'. With respect to working parties, Westlake and Galloway (2004: 200) assert that 'of all the Council's component parts, the working parties ... are perhaps the least well-known yet among the most vital' and that they constitute 'the Council's lifeblood'. In the same vein, Hayes-Renshaw and Wallace (2006: 96) state that 'the working parties form the backbone of the entire process of European integration'. Despite the acknowledgements of the relevance of committees for the functioning of the Council, very little research has focused specifically on decision-making in Council committees and on the role and function of committees in the larger hierarchical structure of the Council.

A few existing studies elaborate on the descriptive question about the extent of committee decision-making in the Council. In this chapter, I first describe these findings, discuss methodological problems of these studies, and outline how the methodology employed in the current study should result in a more valid description of the division of labour between committees and ministers.[1] Next, I focus on literature that offers ideas about factors explaining why certain decisions are made by committees and others by ministers. The subject matters of the first three groups of studies that I discuss are most closely related to the current research topic. The first group of studies examines communication and co-operation networks in Council committees, the second group the socialising effects of participating in Council committees, and the third group the interaction styles prevalent in Council committees. While these three areas of research concentrate their empirical analyses directly on Council committees, we can also gain some relevant insights from the more general literature on Council and EU decision-making. I first review research on the outcome and process of Council decision-making. Regarding studies on the outcome of EU decision-making,

---

1 This part of the chapter relies on material previously published in Häge (2008).

32 *Part I: Introduction and background*

I discuss attempts to formally model Council interactions. With respect to the process of EU decision-making, I consider the results of more empirically focused studies investigating the factors influencing the speed of legislative decision-making as well as empirical studies of the voting behaviour of Member States. As a conclusion, I discuss the extent to which existing studies can inform the current research on Council committees.

The extent of committee decision-making

Quantitative studies of the extent of committee decision-making in the Council are rare. In fact, the most cited estimate of the proportion of Council decisions made by committees is based on an informed guess. In the first edition of their seminal textbook on the Council, Hayes-Renshaw and Wallace (1997: 40, 78) mention that committees are responsible for 85–90 per cent of all Council decisions.[2] Although Hayes-Renshaw and Wallace (1997: 40) are explicit in pointing out that the numbers are based on 'hearsay evidence', they are widely cited in subsequent research. Researchers of Council working groups and committees refer to the estimates to illustrate the relevance of their research topic (Beyers and Dierickx 1998: 291; Lewis 1998: 483, 2003a: 1009; Beyers 2005: 905), others rely on them in evaluations of the democratic legitimacy of the EU (Meyer 1999: 630) or use them to describe the division of labour in the Council in textbooks of EU politics (Nugent 2003: 165; Hix 2005: 83) and in other EU-related work (Egeberg 1999: 461; Niemann 2004: 403; Zimmer *et al.* 2005: 408).

Of course, the Council was a rather secretive organisation until recently, and relying on the judgements of informed insiders was the only feasible option to gain some insights into the phenomenon of interest. But some less well-known studies also exist that provide figures based on more systematically collected evidence, although only for certain policy sectors or other more restricted samples. The studies by van Schendelen (1996) and Gomez and Peterson (2001) rely on the agendas of ministerial meetings. Andersen and Rasmussen (1998) and van den Bos (1991) also provide important insights through data based on Council documents and expert interviews, respectively. Recently, Hayes-Renshaw and Wallace (2006) provide new figures in the second edition of their book, which are also based on an analysis of the agendas of ministerial meetings.

Table 3.1 shows the estimates for the extent of committee decision-making provided by these studies. For comparative reasons, the table also gives the original figures advanced in Hayes-Renshaw and Wallace (1997). The table shows wide variation in the size of the estimates. Again, Hayes-Renshaw and Wallace (1997) ascribe 85–90 per cent of decisions to committees. All other estimates of the extent of committee decision-making are considerably lower. Examining the agendas of all meetings of Agriculture ministers in 1992 and 1993, van Schendelen (1996) reports that 65 per cent of the items had already been decided by committee members. Using the same methodology, the new study by

---

2 According to Bostock (2002: 226), the original source for this estimate was a member of Coreper.

Existing research on Council decision-making 33

Table 3.1 The extent of committee decision-making: previous research

Author (year)	Data source	Policy/period	Committee	Ministers
Hayes-Renshaw and Wallace (1997: 40, 78)	Practitioner estimate	General unspecified	85–90	10–15
Hayes-Renshaw and Wallace (2006: 53)[a]	Ministerial agendas	General 2004	66	34
Andersen and Rasmussen (1998: 589)[b]	Council documents	Environment 1993/1994	26	74
Gomez and Peterson (2001: 540)	Ministerial agendas	GAER 1995–2000	48	52
van den Bos (1991: 232)[c]	Expert interviews	General 1987	53	47
van Schendelen (1996: 538)	Ministerial agendas	Agriculture 1992/1993	65	35

Sources: See the first column of the table.

Notes: All numerical cell entries are percentages. GAER stands for General Affairs and External Relations.

a The total number of B points and the total number of agenda points in GAER seem to be incorrect in the original Table 2.2. As a result, the percentage figures given in the original table are also incorrect. The percentages given here result from recalculations made based on the raw numbers given in the original table.
b Proportions refer to acts discussed at different levels and were calculated from raw figures as presented on p. 589.
c Proportions were calculated from raw figures as presented on p. 232, see also pp. 149–165. Decisions by the Article 133 Committee were counted as working party decisions.

Hayes-Renshaw and Wallace (2006) indicates a very similar proportion, with 66 per cent of the decisions being made at the committee level. Although the time period of their study is restricted to meetings that took place during the last quarter of 2004, the scope of their study is larger than van Schendelen's in that they considered agendas of ministerial meetings in all Council formations.

However, Gomez and Peterson (2001) report less committee involvement in a similar study focused on the GAER Council formation. Examining the agendas of foreign ministers over the period from 1995 to 2000, Gomez and Peterson found that only about half of all agenda items had already been decided at the committee level. This estimate is quite close to the estimate advanced by van den Bos (1991). Based on a sample of 74 legislative 'decisions which are important for the Netherlands' (van den Bos 1991: 62), van den Bos' expert interviews also indicated that committees took the most important decision in about half of the cases. Finally, tracing the history of the decision-making process on 43 environmental policy acts adopted during 1993 and 1994, Andersen and Rasmussen (1998) found that committees decided only about a quarter of all acts.

The disparate results point to some limitations of previous studies. First, the reliability of expert estimates as presented in Hayes-Renshaw and Wallace (1997) is questionable. Expert estimates are likely to be biased by selective perceptions. In this case, a comparison with the other estimates in Table 3.1 indicates that the expert estimates are likely to overstate the involvement of committees.

34   Part I: Introduction and background

Second, the studies based on a content analysis of ministerial agendas are also likely to overstate the involvement of committees. These studies do not trace policy proposals over time. Thus, the researcher does not know whether a dossier that ministers adopt without discussion has actually been decided by ministers during an earlier meeting. This issue has long been identified as the problem of 'pseudo' or 'false' A-points (de Zwaan 1995: 136; van Schendelen 1996: 540). A 'false' A-point is an item that is listed as an A-point on the ministerial agenda for adoption without discussion although it has in fact been decided by ministers in an earlier meeting in which it constituted a B-point. The occurrence of 'false' A-points is not exceptional but rather the rule (Häge 2008: 548): when ministers reach a decision on the substance of a dossier, the text is not directly adopted during the same meeting but first referred to the Council's legal-linguistic experts. After the text has been checked and translated by these experts, the dossier is adopted without discussion as an A-point during one of the following ministerial meetings. By neglecting the history of individual dossiers, the dossiers decided by ministers are counted at least twice. The correct count as a ministerial decision in the earlier meeting, in which the item was listed as a B-point, is offset by the incorrect count as a committee decision in the later meeting, in which the same item formed an A-point. In the aggregate, the neglect of the temporal dimension of Council decision-making therefore results in a systematic overstatement of committee decision-making. Finally, the remaining studies base their findings on very limited samples. Although the studies by Andersen and Rasmussen (1998) and van den Bos (1991) consider the whole history of proposals and report lower levels of committee decision-making than the studies of ministerial agendas, we cannot be sure about the extent to which the different estimates are a consequence of using a superior measurement approach or a result of relying on relatively idiosyncratic samples. The study of Andersen and Rasmussen focuses exclusively on decisions in the field of Environmental policy and the study of van den Bos on decisions deemed important for the Netherlands.

The current analysis overcomes at least some of the limitations of previous research and combines many of its advantages in a single framework. Like the content analyses of ministerial agendas (van Schendelen 1996; Gomez and Peterson 2001; Hayes-Renshaw and Wallace 2006) and Council documents (Andersen and Rasmussen 1998), the study relies exclusively on documentary evidence, ensuring the reliability of measures. Like the studies by Andersen and Rasmussen (1998) and by van den Bos (1991), the study traces proposals over time, guaranteeing that each proposal is counted only once as a committee or ministerial decision, respectively. In this way, the study omits the problems caused by 'false' A-points. Finally, similar to the work by Hayes-Renshaw and Wallace (2006), the study covers a range of different policy areas to allow for comparisons and to produce a general description. Thus, the descriptive analysis in this study improves on existing research in several respects. While the studies discussed in this section offer descriptions of the extent of committee

Existing research on Council decision-making 35

decision-making, they do not propose general explanations to why certain decisions are made by committee members. In the remainder of this chapter, I discuss how far other research on Council committees and Council decision-making can inform the explanatory analysis of this study.

Committee communication and co-operation patterns

A number of quantitative studies examine the communication and co-operation patterns in working parties and senior committees. The seminal studies in this respect were conducted by Beyers and Dierickx (1997, 1998). Based on standardised interview data, they studied the communication networks of members of 13 working parties. The main finding in Beyers and Dierickx (1998) is that working party members form a rather centralised network. The representatives of the large Member States, Germany, France and the UK, and the representatives of the institutional actors, the Presidency, the Commission and the Council Secretariat, form the core of this network, while the representatives of the smaller countries are located at the periphery. They also concluded that this finding holds regardless of the current workload of the working party, the formal decision-making rule in the Council, or the meeting frequency of the working party. Another major finding of the study by Beyers and Dierickx (1998) is the existence of a division between northern and southern Member States. This north–south cleavage has subsequently been confirmed by many other authors using very different methodological techniques (Mattila and Lane 2001; Selck 2004; Thomson *et al.* 2004; Kaeding and Selck 2005; Zimmer *et al.* 2005). Beyers and Dierickx discuss several interpretations of this division, including an interpretation based on the cultural proximity of Member States.

In an earlier published follow-up analysis, Beyers and Dierickx (1997) investigate whether factors related to individual negotiators rather than Member States also have an effect on the communication behaviour of working party members. The empirical results indicate that members with supranational attitudes are more likely to communicate with any other working party member, regardless of that member's network position or attitudes towards European integration. The results also show that negotiators tend to contact peers that they perceive to be influential. While officials from the supranational institutions and the larger Member States are contacted regardless of their influence esteem, officials from smaller Member States can increase their status in the communication network if they are able to increase their influence esteem. Note that Beyers and Dierickx (1997) do not find evidence for an impact of left–right ideological positions of negotiators or of the perceived professional qualities of peers on the communication behaviour of working party members.

Other network studies only partly support the findings by Beyers and Dierickx (1997, 1998). Elgström *et al.* (2001) research co-operation patterns of Swedish officials in EU committees. The authors find strong indications for a preference of Sweden's representatives to co-operate with their Nordic neighbours. This finding

36   *Part I: Introduction and background*

is in line with Beyers and Dierickx' (1998) claim that a north–south division exists among the members of Council working parties. Elgström *et al.* also interpret this dimension as representing differences in cultural affinities among Member States and they do not detect an effect of left–right ideology on co-operation behaviour. However, in contrast to Beyers and Dierickx (1997, 1998), Elgström *et al.* do not find evidence that attitudes towards European integration influence esteem, or that the size of Member States affects the co-operation behaviour. When directly asked about the reasons for contacting other committee members, respondents in their study consider the position held by other committee members and the committee members' knowledge about the policy issues at hand as most influential factors. Apparently, nationality and language preferences do play a far less important role.

Finally, the most recent work by Naurin (2007; 2010) investigates co-operation patterns in working parties as well as in senior committees of the Council. The study clearly confirms Beyer and Dierickx' (1998) finding of the higher network status of larger Member States. Like earlier studies, Naurin (2007) finds a clear division between northern and southern Member States. Based on post-enlargement data, Naurin (2007) also identifies a new cleavage separating the eastern European Member States from both the northern and southern bloc of old Member States. Both the results of a multivariate regression analysis and the stability of the geographical divisions over time and across policy areas support the interpretation that the conflict lines are a result of cultural factors rather than economic interests. The north–south–east pattern is confirmed by the study of Mattila (2009), which analyses Council voting records.

Taken together, the studies of co-operation and communication networks in Council committee indicate that the supranational institutional actors such as the Commission and the Presidency, as well as the larger Member States play the most vital roles in committee deliberations. The studies also indicate that divisions in the working parties occur mainly along geographical lines between northern and southern Member States. The studies give very insightful descriptions of the recurrent conflict dimensions, of the general social structure of working parties, as well as the factors influencing the standing of individual representatives within this structure. At the same time, the findings are very stable across working parties with very different institutional and policy characteristics. Thus, the studies do not point to any factors that could potentially explain variation in the extent of committee decision-making within or between individual committees.

Committee member socialisation

Another body of literature investigates the role perceptions of bureaucrats representing Member States in meetings of Council committees. The standard method of data collection for these studies is a survey with a standardised questionnaire. In general, the results of the studies support the notion that committee members hold supranational role perceptions that complement their identities as government representatives (Beyers 1998; Egeberg 1999; Trondal 2001, 2002; Beyers and Trondal 2003; Egeberg *et al.* 2003; Beyers 2005). The findings in Egeberg (1999) and Trondal (2001, 2002) also corroborate the view that supranational role perceptions are the result of socialisation that occurs through the interaction in committees at the European level.

For example, Egeberg (1999) finds that allegiances to the EU committee are positively related to the number of committee meetings attended by the official. Egeberg *et al.* (2003) also show that the attendance of EU committees fosters positive views about European integration. Similarly, Trondal (2001) detects a positive relationship of supranational allegiances among officials with the number of informal meetings arranged with other committee members. In another study, Trondal (2002) shows that supranational attitudes are correlated with a number of indicators measuring different aspects of the intensity of interaction in EU committees. This study also shows that supranational attitudes are strong when domestic policy co-ordination mechanisms are weak. Despite these apparent socialisation effects, loyalty shifts seem to be generally rather marginal (Egeberg 1999). Even though supranational role perceptions are present, Council working group members still see themselves and other group members mainly as government representatives (see also Trondal 2001; Egeberg *et al.* 2003).

In contrast to the studies discussed so far, the results by Beyers (1998; see also 2003, 2005) indicate that national factors play a more prominent role in shaping the attitudes of officials towards the EU than the social interaction at the European level. In particular, the organisational self-esteem of national officials seems to play a major role in explaining supranational role perceptions. Negative views about the national political system foster pro-European attitudes. Attitudes of working party members towards the EU also seem to reflect general elite attitudes in their home country (Beyers 2005). However, the degree of federalism and the size and geographical location of the Member State are not related to the degree of supranationalist attitudes held by national officials (Beyers 1998). Most interestingly, supranational role perceptions show no relationship with several different indicators measuring the amount of interaction in working parties. Supranational role perceptions are also not related to the extent of previous international professional experiences (Beyers 2005).

In general, the existing literature suggests that members of Council committees see themselves mainly as government representatives. However, many committee members complement this role perception with a supranational role perception. The existing studies disagree about whether differences in the degree of supranational role perceptions of committee members can be attributed to socialisation in the Council committees themselves. Nevertheless, the literature suggests that committee members' role perceptions might change as a result of the exposure to European norms and values when interacting in Council committees. The literature discussed in the next section sheds more light on the question whether we should expect more or fewer committee decisions as a result of such a change in role perceptions.

Committee interaction styles

Based on qualitative case studies and interviews with practitioners, a number of researchers argue that the complementary adoption of supranational role perceptions leads to a distinct decision-making style in Council committees. Drawing on case studies of decision-making in Coreper, Lewis (1998, 2003b, 2005) argues that committee members develop process and relationship interests as well as a sense of collective responsibility for ensuring the functioning of the Council as a whole. According to this account, interactions in Coreper are not only governed by the logic of consequences, but also by the logic of appropriateness (Lewis 2005: 942). The result of several informal norms regulating Coreper negotiations is a generally more co-operative decision-making style. Juncos and Pomorska (2006) argue that a similar code of conduct is operating in working parties in the Common Foreign and Security Policy (CFSP) area. However, Juncos and Pomorska (2006) also suggest that working party members have not internalised these rules but rather follow them for strategic reasons. Reh (2007) studies the role of the Group of Government Representatives in the preparation of the Amsterdam and Nice Treaties. The study finds evidence that the insulated and dense interactions during the pre-negotiations resulted in an efficient and co-operative negotiations style similar to the one found in Coreper. Fouilleux *et al.* (2005) have also noted that the interactions in working parties are structured by a dense net of rules and norms.

Some of these sociological accounts of committee decision-making also detect a requirement to justify negotiation positions as an important feature of the committee negotiation style (Lewis 2005). In this view, demands without justifications are not acceptable. Member State representatives are expected to give reasons for their positions and to change their minds in light of a more convincing argument. Naurin (2010) presents results of the first large-scale quantitative analysis of reason-giving in Council committees. Based on telephone interview data of members of several committees, Naurin (2010) shows that delegates almost always give reasons for the positions they represent in Council committees. When asked about why they give reasons for positions, slightly more representatives state that they give reasons to convince other committee members than claim that they give reasons to clarify their position. Interestingly, no differences in either the occurrence of arguing or the reasons stated for arguing exist between formal meetings and informal contacts. However, the propensity to argue seems larger in policy areas in which unanimity constitutes the decision-rule and in policy areas co-ordinated through soft law rather than legally binding acts. The classic community policy areas under the qualified majority voting rule are most prone to bargaining.

The literature on committee interaction styles points to two factors that might be relevant for explaining committee decision-making. First, some studies assert that committee members are socialised into supranational norms and values which lead to a more co-operative negotiation style. The absence of hard-headed intergovernmentalist bargaining should make committee decisions more likely.

Second, the formal decision-making rule seems to have an influence on the discussion style in the Council committees. Given the veto of each individual Member State under the unanimity rule, committee members seem to resort more often to arguments in an effort to persuade their counterparts of the advantages of their position. This finding indicates that the need to secure the agreement of every Member State makes it more difficult to reach a committee decision. So far, I have discussed existing studies directly concerned with Council committees. However, the wider literature on Council decision-making could also yield some insights about the explanatory factors of committee decision-making.

Policy outcomes of Council decision-making

Beginning in the early 1990s, a number of formal game-theoretic models have been proposed to explain the outcome of EU decision-making processes and the influence of individual actors on this outcome. Schneider *et al.* (2006) distinguish two broad classes of models: procedural models and bargaining models. Given the common foundation of these models in the rational choice approach, policy positions or preferences of actors play a prominent role in both types. Besides the preferences of actors, procedural models treat formal institutional features of the decision-making process as another major explanatory factor (Steunenberg 1994; Tsebelis 1994; Crombez 1996, 1997). The proposal-making and amendment powers of actors, the voting threshold for collective decisions in the Council and the EP, and the sequence of moves in which actors act during the formal legislative procedure play particularly important roles in procedural models. Formal features of the decision-making process are not necessarily completely neglected in bargaining models. However, bargaining models put more stress on other explanatory factors, like the power resources of actors and the importance actors attach to an issue (e.g. Pierce 1994: 10–11; Arregui *et al.* 2004; Arregui *et al.* 2006). Formal aspects of the decision-making process also enter into bargaining models, but more indirectly: the legislative procedure determines which actors are considered to be of relevance for shaping the negotiation outcome and the voting weights of Member States are usually used to operationalise their bargaining power in the Council.[3]

The large majority of formal models of EU decision-making do not ascribe a role to the Council's committee system. The only exceptions are the models by König and Proksch (2006a, b). These models mix features of a bargaining model with features of a procedural model. More precisely, the authors combine a model of resource exchange with a spatial voting model. However, their main purpose is to predict decision-making outcomes. Although the authors justify crucial assumptions in their models with reference to the Council's committee system, they do not model the role of those committees explicitly. The models do not

---

3 Usually, the voting weights do not enter the analysis directly, but in the form of values of a voting power index (e.g. Arregui *et al.* 2006: 137).

40   *Part I: Introduction and background*

allow for the possibility that decisions are made at different levels of the Council hierarchy. As they do not make any predictions about the conditions under which decisions are expected to be reached at the committee level, the models are not helpful in deriving potential explanatory factors for committee decision-making.

In general, the formal theoretical literature on Council decision-making yields little insights for committee decision-making. The large majority of theoretical models completely neglect the role of committees, and the few models that refer to committees do not consider the reasons why some legislative decisions are made by committees and others by ministers. The discussion in the previous chapter has clearly demonstrated the empirical relevance of committees in Council decision-making. Thus, theoretical models neglect crucial characteristics of the Council decision-making process when they neglect the role of committees. In the next section, I discuss whether the empirical literature on process characteristics of Council decision-making fares better in this respect.

Process characteristics of Council decision-making

The theoretical models discussed above are mainly concerned with predicting the outcome of collective decision-making and with determining the degree of influence of individual actors. A more empirically oriented type of literature is concerned with procedural aspects of Council decision-making, especially speed and voting behaviour. The studies on decision-making speed examine mainly the impact of formal institutional characteristics, like the voting rule in the Council and the rights of the EP in the legislative process. Most of the studies also detect a non-negligible influence of these rules. Golub (1999, 2007), Golub and Steunenberg (2007), Schulz and König (2000), König (2007), and Hertz and Leuffen (2011) find that the involvement of the EP prolongs the decision-making process considerably. Some studies also investigate the effect of political conflict among Member States on decision-making efficiency. Most of these studies also suggest that preference divergence between Member States slows down decision-making (for less conclusive results, see Hertz and Leuffen 2011). In general, the literature on decision-making speed identifies preference divergence, the voting rule and EP involvement as consequential influence factors.

The finding of a stable effect of the voting rule is somewhat surprising, especially in comparison to the results of studies on voting behaviour (Mattila and Lane 2001; Heisenberg 2005; Hayes-Renshaw *et al.* 2006; Mattila 2009; Plechanovová 2011). These studies show that explicit voting is the exception rather than the rule in Council decision-making. Even in areas where the Council can take decisions through a qualified majority of votes, about 75–80 per cent of the decisions are still adopted unanimously. Furthermore, if a Council decision is contested, the group of countries contesting a Council decision is usually very small; often much smaller than needed to reach the required voting threshold (Mattila and Lane 2001; Mattila 2009). In the large majority of contested Council decisions, only one or two countries oppose the majority. In contrast to the findings of studies on decision-making speed, the findings of voting behaviour studies point to a rather consensual decision-making style in the Council and question the relevance of the voting rule. However, the voting behaviour studies also show that the extent of explicit voting varies considerably across different policy areas. Thus, if Council decision-making is really governed by a norm of consensus (Heisenberg 2005), then this norm is not a constant, but varies with specific characteristics of policy sectors. The committee structure in the different Council formations might be one of these factors. Unfortunately, neither the literature on Council decision-making efficiency nor on voting behaviour has considered any potential effects of organisational features of the committee system on voting or decision-making speed.

Summary of the literature review

In this chapter, I reviewed the existing literature on Council decision-making that is directly or indirectly related to the research questions of this study. I started with a discussion of earlier attempts to measure the extent of committee decision-making. This discussion identified several shortcomings in previous studies that potentially led to biased results. Most likely, the existing research overstates the relevance of Council committees to some extent. I argued that the measurement approach pursued in the current study overcomes at least some of the main problems of earlier work and results in a more valid description of the extent of committee decision-making.

In the remaining part of the chapter, I reviewed studies with the potential to shed some light on the factors determining why certain decisions are made by committees and others by ministers. First, I examined studies that focused directly on characteristics of committees or their members as their independent variables. The studies on communication and co-operation patterns in Council committees indicated that committee members' networks are very similar regardless of their member composition and policy area context. According to these network studies, the way committee members communicate and coalesce does not vary with committee characteristics. Therefore, the studies do not identify any factors that might explain differences in decision-making behaviour across committees. In contrast, the literature on supranational role perceptions and decision-making styles in Council committees pointed to the degree of socialisation as an important factor for explaining the behaviour of committee members. Committee members are supposed to adopt more co-operative negotiation styles once they internalised the supranational norms and values governing committee interactions. Thus, the role of socialisation for committee decision-making deserves a more detailed theoretical elaboration in the next chapter.

After the committee literature review, I turned to a survey of the literature on Council decision-making outcomes and process characteristics. For the most part, this discussion demonstrated the lack of attention to committees in existing empirical and theoretical research on the Council. Although committees play a

42 Part I: Introduction and background

crucial role for the functioning of the Council as a whole, the existing studies on different aspects of Council decision-making did not consider any committee characteristics as explanatory factors in their analyses. Thus, the existing research on Council decision-making does not point to any crucial characteristics of committees that might influence the decision-making behaviour of their members. However, given that the literature on Council decision-making outcomes and process characteristics purports to explain aspects of Council decision-making, and given that Council decision-making corresponds in practise largely to decision-making in Council committees, the factors identified as explanatory factors in studies of Council decision-making should also be of relevance to the study of committee decision-making.

Preference divergence and institutional rules are two factors whose effects were regularly studied in previous research on Council decision-making. Actors' preferences and institutional rules entered into all formal theories of Council decision-making and were also subject to much empirical examination in the studies on Council decision-making speed. Although studies on voting behaviour established that voting occurs relatively rarely in the Council, the studies on decision-making speed still showed that the voting rule has a substantial impact on the time it takes to reach a decision in the Council. Thus, although explicit voting is relatively rare, the possibility of taking a vote nevertheless seems to affect the negotiation behaviour of Member States. The studies on Council decision-making speed also showed that the introduction of a veto right for the EP slowed down decision-making. Finally, these studies identified the divergence of preferences among Member States as a factor decreasing decision-making speed. In the next chapter, I discuss the theoretical rationales underlying these factors and the committee socialisation argument in more detail. I also discuss potential explanatory factors invoked for similar political phenomena. These factors are derived from a general theory of delegation.

4 Theoretical perspectives on committee decision-making

The literature review in the previous chapter pointed to formal institutions, preference divergence and socialisation as factors that are potentially of relevance for explaining committee decision-making. In this chapter, I discuss the theoretical arguments underlying these factors in more detail. I also address the potential influence of policy uncertainty and political salience. Both factors are derived from a general theory of delegation applicable to the types of social situations studied here. In this chapter, my goal is to identify and describe potential explanatory factors based on a variety of existing theories. These factors then guide the quantitative analysis and also inform the qualitative case studies.

I begin with a discussion of the role of generic factors that are supposed to influence policy stability in any type of collective decision-making body, including Council committees. These factors include divergent views among the members of the decision-making body as well as the institutional rules determining how decisions are to be made and who participates in decision-making. Thus, this discussion elaborates on the effects of institutional rules and preference divergence on committee decision-making. Then I discuss how committee members are thought to be socialised into supranational norms and values and the conditions under which we would expect such socialisation to have an effect on committee decision-making. Up to this point, the theoretical discussion focuses on committee characteristics that are supposed to influence the difficulty of reaching an agreement within the committee.

The remaining two factors are based on a very different theoretical perspective. Based on delegation theory, I derive the conditions under which ministers are more or less likely to refer decision-making authority to their representatives in Council committees.[1] First, I discuss how uncertainty about the practical consequences of policy provisions influences the choice of principals to delegate decisions to better-informed experts. Second, I elaborate on the role of political

---

1 Of course, ministers usually do not take a collective, formal decision in the Council on whether a proposal should be decided by a working party or senior committee. The referral of decision-making authority to national officials is often more implicit, as when ministers decide to not get involved in the development of the national negotiation position and also do not show an interest in the progress of negotiations in the Council committees.

44   Part I: Introduction and background

salience in determining the amount of attention ministers decide to devote to a certain issue. The discussion of each explanatory factor concludes with the derivation of a hypothesis. I subject these hypotheses to empirical testing in the subsequent quantitative and qualitative empirical analyses.

Preferences, institutions and policy stability

In order to explicate the logic of why and how committee decision-making should be affected by institutional rules and preferences, I rely on tools and concepts from social choice theory. This branch of formal theory has a long tradition in the study of how individual preferences are aggregated into group decisions. A major advantage of the formal social choice framework is that it is explicit about the assumptions on which an argument relies, and that it offers a precise language as well as clearly defined concepts for theory development and explication. In the following, I illustrate the effects of the voting rule, preference divergence and the veto right of the EP on committee decision-making through this framework.

To keep the illustration simple, I assume that a Council committee consists of seven members. Each member has a most preferred position or ideal point in a multi-dimensional policy space. Furthermore, each member prefers policies closer to his or her ideal point to policies further away from it. The committee members know each others' ideal points as well as the location of the existing policy. The existing policy is also called the status quo policy. If decisions can be taken by a qualified majority of votes, I assume that the consent of five out of seven members is sufficient to adopt a decision.[2]

In line with previous research on EU decision-making (Tsebelis and Yataganas 2002; König and Bräuninger 2004), I use the core as a concept for the stability of policy decisions. The core contains all points in the policy space that cannot be defeated by any other policy proposal in a pair-wise comparison. The proportion of votes needed to defeat a policy depends on the decision-making rule.[3] Due to the assumption that committee members are fully informed about each others' preferences and the location of the status quo policy, committee members reach a decision instantly in this model. If the status quo policy is located inside the core, the committee will not be able to agree to a new policy alternative. At least one member of any winning coalition would be made worse off by changing the policy to a location outside the core. In contrast, if the status quo policy is located outside the core, the committee will change the policy to a location somewhere inside the core. All members of a winning coalition will be made better off by such a move.

---

2 An extension to include all Member State representatives and to consider weighted votes would not change the general logic of the model. All hypotheses stated below can also be derived from such a more complicated model.

3 The use of the terms vote and voting to describe the mechanics of the model does not mean that actors are assumed to vote explicitly. In the context of these models, voting in favour of a policy proposal just means that actors indicate their agreement to the proposal in some way; the indication of agreement does not necessarily have to occur through a formal vote.

Theoretical perspectives on committee decision-making 45

In principle, the size of the core does not determine whether a collective body agrees to a change in policy or not. In each individual case, the agreement on policy change depends solely on whether the status quo policy is located within or outside the core. However, over a large number of cases, the size of the core determines the probability that the status quo policy is located within it. Under the assumption that status quo policies are distributed uniformly across the policy space, larger cores are more likely to include the status quo policy than smaller cores. By implication, committees with larger cores are then less likely to reach an agreement than committee with smaller cores. The following discussion relies on this additional assumption about the distribution of status quo points to derive testable hypotheses relating the size of the core to the propensity of a committee decision.

Unfortunately, the core does not generally exist in situations where decisions over more than one policy dimension have to be made by simple majority rule. However, this problem does not preclude the usefulness of the core as a concept of policy stability for the purposes of this study. The Council's decision-making rules prescribe that legislative agreements have to be reached by unanimity or by qualified majority voting. In the former case, the core is equivalent to the actors' Pareto-set and exists regardless of the dimensionality of the policy space. In the latter case, the adoption of a proposal requires the agreement of Member States holding about 71 per cent of the votes.[4] As Schofield *et al.* (1988) have shown, the core is more likely to exist in high-dimensional policy spaces the larger the majority required to make a decision. In particular, the qualified majority threshold of 62 out of 87 votes guarantees that a core still exists in two dimensions regardless of the configuration of preferences and that at least some preference configurations allow the construction of a core even in three dimensions.[5] Either way, only the prediction about the effect of preference divergence under qualified majority voting is affected by the potential problem of the non-existence of the core. The unanimity rule and EP involvement predictions benefit from the fact that the setup includes actors with veto power. Under this condition, a core always exists (Schofield *et al.* 1988).

Voting rule

Having discussed the general modelling tools, I now turn to the first substantial hypothesis. Graphical representations are helpful for understanding the mechanics of the models. Figure 4.1 illustrates a preference configuration of the seven member committee in a two-dimensional policy space. As discussed above, the core contains all points in this space that cannot be beaten by any other point. Furthermore, whether a point can be beaten or not depends crucially on the

---

4 The discussion refers to the pre-Nice voting system in force between 1995 and 2004 (Hayes-Renshaw and Wallace 2006: 264), which covers the largest part of the time period under study here.

5 The voting threshold that guarantees a core in three dimensions would be 66 out of 87 votes. Given that individual Member States have up to ten votes at their disposal, the requirement to gather 62 votes might result in many cases in an automatically oversized majority of 66 or more votes.

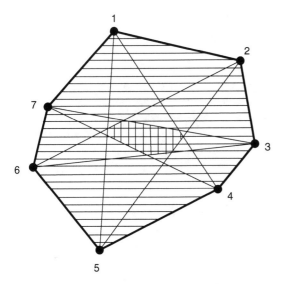

Figure 4.1 Unanimity and qualified majority core.

Note: The qualified majority rule requires the agreement of five out of seven committee members. The unanimity core is the area bounded by the heptagon 1234567. The qualified majority core is the cross-hatched area within the unanimity core.

decision-making rule. The figure indicates both the unanimity and the qualified majority core. The core can be constructed by drawing lines connecting the ideal points of members so that a majority of ideal points are located on one side of each line or on the line itself.[6] The core is then the polygon generated by the intersection of these lines.

The figure indicates both the unanimity and the qualified majority core. The unanimity core is the whole heptagon 1234567. The qualified majority core is the cross-hatched area within the heptagon. All other things equal, the qualified majority core is always smaller than the unanimity core. In order to see this, note that the qualified majority core is the intersection of the unanimity cores of all winning coalitions. Each unanimity core of a five-member winning coalition is necessarily smaller than the unanimity core of the full seven-member committee. Given that each unanimity core of a winning coalition contains only a subset of the points contained in the unanimity core of the whole committee, the intersection of the unanimity cores of all winning coalitions, that is the qualified majority core, must then be smaller than the unanimity core of the full committee. This expectation leads to the first hypothesis about the effect of the voting rule on committee decision-making:

Hypothesis 1: A committee decision is more likely under qualified majority rule than under unanimity rule.

---

6 In more than two dimensions, the lines are replaced by planes and hyperplanes.

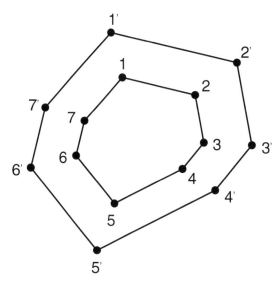

Figure 4.2 Small and large preference divergence unanimity cores.

Note: The small preference divergence unanimity core is the heptagon 1234567. The large preference divergence unanimity core is the heptagon 1'2'3'45'6'7'.

Preference divergence

The effect of preference divergence on the core is not as straightforwardly determined as the effect of the voting rule. In the one-dimensional case, the core consists simply of the line segment between the two decisive actors. In the case of the unanimity rule, the two decisive actors are simply the actors with the most extreme ideal points. In the case of qualified majority voting, the decisive actors are the actors with ideal points such that their ideal point and the number of ideal points of committee members located on one side of their ideal point form a qualified majority of members. Either way, if one of the decisive actors moves further away from the other, the preference divergence increases and the core increases as well. However, in the multi-dimensional case, the situation is more complicated. Here, preference divergence depends on the relative positions of all ideal points. However, one can easily imagine keeping constant the relative positions of the ideal points and magnifying or shrinking the entire preference configuration of committee members. This process is illustrated in Figure 4.2 for the unanimity core.

All other things equal, increasing preference divergence by enlarging the original heptagon 1234567 to the new heptagon 1'2'3'4'5'6'7' yields a larger unanimity core. The converse is true when shrinking the heptagon. The same procedure arrives at equivalent results for the qualified majority core. Thus, increased or decreased preference divergence affects unanimity and qualified majority decision-making in similar ways: the more diverse preferences, the larger the core; and under the assumption of a uniform distribution of status quo policies, larger cores are more likely to include the status quo policy. These relationships imply the following hypothesis:

48 Part I: Introduction and background

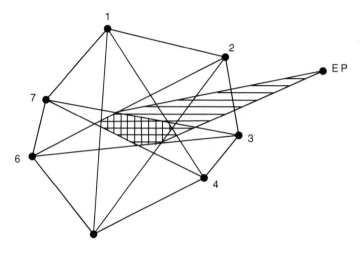

Figure 4.3 Qualified majority committee core and co-decision core.

Note: The qualified majority rule requires the agreement of five out of seven committee members. The co-decision core is the hatched area and includes the qualified majority core of the committee. The qualified majority core is the cross-hatched area. The abbreviation EP refers to the European Parliament.

Hypothesis 2: A committee decision is more likely the less the preferences of committee members diverge.

Veto right of the European Parliament

Besides the voting rule and the preference configuration, the legislative procedure should also influence committee decision-making. A committee decision should be harder to reach under the co-decision procedure. The co-decision procedure essentially empowers an additional player, the Parliament, with a veto right. Thus, the Member States have to take the views of an additional actor into account in order to reach an overall agreement on EU legislation. Although the EP does not take part directly in Council deliberations, the EP exerts indirect influence. During recent years, the Council and the EP have made more and more efforts to reach an early agreement during the first reading of the co-decision procedure. These inter-institutional negotiations usually take place at the level of working parties and senior committees. Furthermore, while the EP representatives usually negotiate on a clear mandate in the form of the report of the responsible standing committee of the EP, the Council side can enter the inter-institutional negotiations even before Member States have resolved all disagreements among themselves. In effect, the Parliament then becomes an additional negotiation partner in Council negotiations. Thus, committee decision-making should clearly be affected by the veto right of the Parliament. Figure 4.3 shows the change in the size of the core when the committee has to take account of the views of the EP.

The figure illustrates the most common situation, in which the co-decision procedure applies in combination with the qualified majority voting rule in the Council. The predictions are qualitatively the same in the case where the committee has to reach decisions by unanimity. I assume that the EP can be treated as a unitary actor. As discussed above, the EP delegation usually negotiates with the Council on the basis of a clear mandate given by the formally adopted report of the responsible EP committee. Thus, the EP can reasonably be considered to have a single ideal point by the time it engages in negotiations with the Council. Fortunately, the hypothesis stated below does not depend on this assumption. The same hypothesis can also be derived from a model in which the EP is treated as a collective actor (see, e.g. Tsebelis and Yataganas 2002), but the illustration is made much clearer through the unitary actor assumption. Unless the EP's ideal point is located within the core of the committee members, the veto right of the EP results in a co-decision core that is larger than the committee core. Assuming that the EP's ideal point is more often located outside than inside the committee core and that status quos are uniformly distributed in the policy space, we can state the following hypothesis:

Hypothesis 3: A committee decision is more likely under the consultation procedure than under the co-decision procedure.

In summary, the formal literature on collective decision-making argues that the stability of policies depends on the preferences of actors and the institutional rules in place. Applying this reasoning to committee decision-making in the Council, this section has shown that a committee decision should be easier to reach in cases where committee members' preferences converge, the EP is in effect excluded from decision-making, and the qualified majority voting rule applies in the Council. In the next section, I discuss to what extent we should expect international socialisation to also have an effect on policy stability in committee decision-making.

Committee socialisation

A growing field of research considers the socialising effects of international institutions (Johnston 2001; Checkel 2003; Hooghe 2005). As the literature review has shown, this field is also one of the few areas where research has directly focused on Council committees and their members. Quantitative studies have mainly focused on an analysis of the extent to which committee members invoke supranational role perceptions and in how far these role perceptions can be attributed to the interaction in committees. The general argument is simple: working in the EU institutions exposes people to supranational norms and thus makes them more prone to accept these norms as valid guidelines for their behaviour. Even if we accept the validity of this statement, the question remains how and under which conditions we would expect international socialisation to matter not only for the self-image of national officials but also for the difficulty of reaching a collective agreement in committees. I elaborate on these points in the remainder of this section.

50   Part I: Introduction and background

Socialisation is the process by which individuals internalise the norms and rules of a group in which they interact. The transfer and adoption of norms can occur through a variety of mechanisms, including normative suasion, social mimicking, shaming and communication (Hooghe 2005: 865). At any point in time, individuals are members of several groups, possibly at different levels of aggregation. For example, a Dutch national official seconded to the permanent representation to the EU is a member of the embassy in Brussels, but at the same time also a member of his or her sectoral ministry in The Hague. At a higher level of aggregation, the official is a member of Dutch as well as Belgian society. Furthermore, individuals' group memberships vary during their lifetime. Young people are primarily affiliated with an educational institution. After finishing their education, people enter work organisations like companies, bureaucracies or non-governmental organisations. Over time, people may move between different units within organisations, between different organisations of the same type, and between organisations of totally different types and functions. Given multiple and changing group memberships, individuals are exposed to a number of socialisation processes concurrently and sequentially. At any point in time, the type and extent of norms internalised by an individual is then a result of past and current membership in different groups.

Thus, the degree to which an official holds a supranational role perception is not only expected to be a function of the time spent working in an EU institution, but also of the prior time spent interacting with people in other groups promoting similar norms (Beyers 2005; Hooghe 2005). People might have developed supranational role perceptions because of earlier experiences even before they entered the European institutions, gained for example through international student exchanges or the work in other international organisations. In short, the degree of socialisation into supranational norms is an attribute of individuals and, given the idiosyncratic life histories of national officials, expected to vary considerably across individuals. As the extent to which committee members hold supranational role perceptions is expected to vary considerably, the consequences of holding such broad role perceptions for collective decision-making are hard to predict.

Committees composed of members with a heterogeneous degree of supranational role perceptions are not likely to sustain supranational norms as guides for appropriate behaviour. Supranational role perceptions are supposed to foster a commitment to joint problem-solving and to reduce the propensity to pursue individualist state interests. If only some of the members of a committee hold a high degree of supranational role perceptions, their willingness to compromise would be exploited by the other members with a lower degree of supranational role perceptions. In the long run, the committee members with a high degree of supranational role perceptions clearly lose out in comparison with the committee members with a low degree of supranational role perceptions. As a result, the committee members with a high degree of supranational role perceptions will eventually either start disregarding the norms calling for compromising behaviour or their superiors at home will replace them by less socialised officials. Without reciprocity, norms that demand flexibility in the positions of committee members'

Theoretical perspectives on committee decision-making 51

positions are not likely to be sustained. This discussion points to the limitations of general supranational role perceptions to influence collective decision-making in Council committees.

Rather than very abstract norms that form part of general supranational role perceptions, such as 'Promote European integration!', specific norms about how to conduct negotiations are more likely to affect collective decision-making in committees. Lewis (2000: 273), for example, stresses the relevance of performance norms in Coreper negotiations. These norms include tangible guidelines aimed at maintaining the efficiency of decision-making in the committee, such as 'Find a solution!', 'Abstain rather than veto!' and 'Do not be a demander all the time!'. Committee norms give relatively straightforward directions on how to behave in a specific situation. Thus, the norms' practical implications are not as open to inter-pretation as the implications of more abstract norms. More importantly, most committee members adhere to these norms to a similar degree. The norms are specific to the committee, so the national officials do not enter the committee with different degrees of pre-socialisation. Members of the committee internalise the norms purely on the basis of their interactions within the committee, which should influence all members in a similar way. The homogenous exposure of all committee members to committee norms means that these norms are not affected by the free-rider problem of the more abstract norms discussed above.

So far, I have discussed which types of norms are likely to affect committee decision-making in systematic ways. I argued that any norm inducing more co-operative negotiation behaviour can only be sustained when most committee members adhere to it to a similar degree. I also maintained that specific norms relating directly to the performance of the committee rather than to more abstract processes of European integration are more likely to satisfy this requirement. Next, I describe in more detail how such committee-specific performance norms affect collective decision-making in a committee. Figure 4.4 illustrates a committee with three members who decide by unanimity over a policy in a two-dimensional issue space.[7] The current status quo policy is located within the unanimity core of the three committee members. As outlined in the previous section, we do not expect any policy change to occur under this condition. If committee members care only about policy, no proposal can muster the required majority of votes to change a status quo policy located within the core. However, the presence of performance norms changes the incentives faced by committee members. A failure to agree on a new policy now imposes costs on the committee members, which creates additional scope for finding a collectively acceptable agreement.

In order to illustrate this effect, the introduction of additional concepts is useful. The preferred-to-SQ set of an actor is the set of points that the actor prefers to the status quo policy. The borders of the preferred-to-SQ sets of actors are delineated

---

7 A similar example could be constructed for a committee with more members deciding by qualified majority voting. The hypothesis derived below is not affected by the number of committee mem-bers, the voting rule, or the dimensionality of the policy space.

52 Part I: Introduction and background

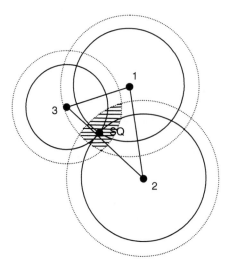

Figure 4.4 Performance norms winset of socialised committee members.

Note: The unanimity core is the triangle 123. The performance norms winset is the hatched area. The standard indifference curves are drawn with solid lines; the performance norms indifference curves are drawn with dotted lines. The abbreviation SQ refers to the status quo policy.

by so-called indifference curves. When committee members are purely motivated by policy concerns and have Euclidian preferences, the indifference curves are circles around actors' ideal points that cross through the status quo point.[8] In Figure 4.4, these standard indifference curves are drawn as solid lines. The winset contains all points in the intersection of the preferred-to-SQ sets of the actors.[9] In substantial terms, the winset contains all policy alternatives that the required majority of committee members prefers to the status quo policy. In Figure 4.4, the winset is empty. This observation is in line with the fact that the status quo policy is located inside the core. The committee members cannot normally agree to move policy to another location under such circumstances. In the presence of performance norms though, committee members do not only consider policy benefits when they decide about accepting or rejecting a new policy proposal; they also take into account that the failure to agree on a new policy results in a costly violation of the performance norms. The larger these norm violation costs, the more a committee member is inclined to accept a new policy position even if it is further away from his or her ideal point than the status quo policy. Thus, the larger the norm violations costs, the more incentives committee members have to compromise.

---

8 The indifference curves are spheres in the case of higher-dimensional settings.
9 In the case of qualified majority voting, the construction of the winset is more complicated. First, one creates a winset for each winning coalition by intersecting the preferred-to-SQ sets of the actors contained in the coalition. In a second step, the overall winset is created by taking the union of the winsets of all winning coalitions.

Theoretical perspectives on committee decision-making 53

Note that the norm violations costs are modelled as integral parts of the committee members' utility function. In theoretical terms, this modelling approach captures the argument that socialisation leads to the internalisation of norms, which then form an integral part of the committee members' decision-making considerations. The model differs therefore fundamentally from liberal institutionalist models of interaction in international institutions that stress the anticipation of repeated interaction as a factor generating co-operative behaviour. In the latter type of models, international institutions do not affect the actors themselves. They just provide an environment that induces actors to also consider the long-term repercussion of their actions and not only their immediate consequences. In game-theoretic terms, the prospect of future interaction changes the structure of the game but not the characteristics of the players. In such models, co-operation can arise even when players' utility functions include only policy motivations. Conceptually, one major difference between the two perspectives is that the socialisation perspective explains co-operative behaviour as a result of past experiences while the liberal institutionalist perspective explains it as a result of the anticipation of future behaviour. Empirically, the effects of the two perspectives might be hard to delineate, but theoretically the underlying arguments are clearly distinct. Given its prominence in the literature on Council committees, this study focuses on an examination of the socialisation perspective.

Norm violation costs result in enlarged preferred-to-SQ sets of actors. To distinguish the corresponding indifference curves and winset from the standard indifference curves and winset that are solely based on policy considerations, I call them performance norms indifference curves and performance norms winset, respectively. The dotted circles in the figure indicate the performance norms indifference curves of actors and the hatched area demarcates the performance norms winset. The figure shows that a performance norms winset exists even in cases when the status quo is located in the core and the standard winset is empty. Thus, the socialisation of committee members into committee-specific performance norms allows for policy change even in cases where purely policy oriented actors could not agree to any change. This observation leads to the following hypothesis:

Hypothesis 4: A committee decision is more likely if committee members are socialised into committee-specific performance norms than if committee members are purely policy-oriented actors.

Note that this view of the effects of socialisation is conceptually distinct from a change in policy preferences, which would result in a simple movement of the ideal points of the actors. The result of committee socialisation is not a change in specific policy positions, but a change in the standards according to which different negotiation outcomes are evaluated. The norm violation costs introduced above are a very simple way to model the additional considerations that socialised committee members take into account when negotiating in the Council and to ponder their consequences for collective decision-making in committees.

54   *Part I: Introduction and background*

The theoretical perspectives discussed so far led to several expectations about the ability of bureaucrats to reach agreement at the committee level, but the focus on the attitudes and interaction of committee members completely neglected the role of their political superiors. The delegation approach takes a different view and discusses the conditions under which politicians are willing to delegate decision-making authority to bureaucrats rather than examine legislative proposals themselves. Although this approach has not been applied to Council decision-making yet, the basic tenets of its theoretical arguments are transferable to this setting.

Policy uncertainty, salience and delegation

Delegation theories point out that the uncertainty about the practical consequences of legal provisions is an important reason for principals to transfer decision-making authority to agents that are better informed about these consequences (Bendor *et al.* 2001). Delegating a decision to better-informed agents might result in a policy outcome that the principal actually prefers to the policy outcome that would have been realised through the principal's own, uninformed decision. In the case of the Council, ministers that are uncertain about the practical consequences of policy measures should therefore have incentives to transfer decision-making authority to better-informed committee members. In the following, I adapt the general game-theoretic model of delegation developed by Bendor and Meirowitz (2004a) to describe the basic logic underlying this argument.[10]

The model consists of two actors, a minister and a bureaucrat. I consider the delegation decision to be a decision of individual Member States, not of the Council as a whole. On the one hand, this setup reflects the reality of decision-making in the Council. The discretion of committee members is usually not collectively determined by a decision of ministers in the Council, but ministers decide unilaterally on how much leeway to grant to their representatives. On the other hand, the focus of the model on an individual minister's decision to delegate precludes a direct exploration of the consequences on collective decision-making in committees. Such an exploration requires the additional assumption that the model represents a typical delegation situation that is the same in all Member States for a certain policy proposal. The theoretical arguments relate mainly to characteristics of the policy itself, which affects all Member States equally. Given that the public services of Member States are structured along similar principles, the relationships between national officials and ministers should be quite comparable across countries as well. Thus, the assumption that the model depicts a typical delegation situation that is very alike in all Member State governments does not seem to be too far-fetched.

---

10 For a more formal and complete treatment, see model A' in Bendor and Meirowitz (2004a).

Theoretical perspectives on committee decision-making   55

The formal structure of the model is as follows: the minister and her official have ideal points in a multi-dimensional policy and outcome space.[11] Both actors have Euclidean preferences; they like outcomes closer to their ideal points more than outcomes further away. The minister's ideal point is located at zero.[12] Uncertainty about the practical consequences of policies is represented by an additive random disturbance term that perturbs the policy after its adoption to produce the final outcome.[13] The distinction between policies and outcomes captures the differences between the letter of the law and its practical consequences. The value of the random shock is drawn from a symmetric distribution around zero. The uninformed minister moves first: she decides whether or not to delegate decision-making authority. If the minister does not delegate, she chooses a policy herself. The chosen policy is then perturbed by the random shock to generate the actual outcome. If the minister delegates, the national official first observes the random shock's realisation and then picks a policy. Thus, the national official is completely informed about how policy maps into practical outcomes by the time he makes a decision.

Given the minister's knowledge about the distribution of outcomes for a certain policy choice, she can calculate her expected utility resulting from deciding about policy herself. Because more than one outcome can result from any selected policy, this expected utility is always less than the utility she would receive when she was able to implement her ideal outcome with certainty (Bendor and Meirowitz 2004a: 299). This setup assures that delegation might be beneficial at least under some circumstances. The minister anticipates the behaviour of the national official resulting from the conferral of decision-making authority to him. The minister knows that the national official is informed about the size of the random shock and that he will therefore simply choose the policy that produces his ideal position as the outcome.[14] Effectively, the minister's delegation decision involves choosing between the policy that maximises her expected utility and the policy that is most favoured by her national official. Bendor and Meirowitz (2004a, b) prove the existence of what they call certainty equivalents in outcome space. These certainty equivalents are a set of outcomes with the property that the minister is indifferent between maximising her expected utility and getting such an outcome for sure. The certainty equivalents delimit what Bendor and Meirowitz (2004a: 299) call the delegation set. The minister delegates decision-making authority to the national official if and only if the agent is located within her delegation set. Given that utility is monotonic in Euclidean distance, the minister's certainty equivalents all have the same distance from her ideal point.

---

11 To ease the exposition of the model, I refer to the minister with female pronouns and to the national official with male pronouns. This choice is essentially arbitrary.
12 This assumption about the location of the minister's ideal point does not have any substantial effect other than allowing for a clearer illustration of the consequences of increased uncertainty.
13 In mathematical terms: Outcome = Policy + Random Shock.
14 That is, the national official will choose Policy = Ideal Point − Random Shock.

56 Part I: Introduction and background

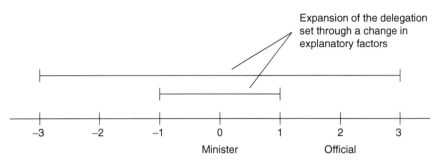

Figure 4.5 The delegation set of the minister in a one-dimensional policy space.

Note: See the main text for further details on the structure of this model.

To illustrate this setup, let us consider a special case of the model in which the policy under discussion can be represented in a one-dimensional space and in which the minister has a tent-shaped utility function.[15] The minister's ideal point is located at zero and the distribution of the random shock specifies that the random shock equals either −1 or 1 with equal probability. The national official's ideal point is located at 2. This situation is depicted in Figure 4.5. If the minister delegates decision-making authority, the national official will select the policy that results in his ideal point. If the random shock equals 1, the national official will select policy = 2 −1 = 1. If the random shock equals −1, the national official will select policy = 2 + 1 = 3. In either case, the final outcome will correspond to the ideal position of the national official at 2. Anticipating the behaviour of the official, the minister evaluates whether the certain outcome of 2 resulting from delegation to the national official is better or worse than the uncertain outcomes resulting from her own decision.

Given that the minister is not sure whether the random shock is −1 or 1, her best guess when making the decision herself is to select the policy that results in outcomes with the highest average utility. One such policy is her ideal point.[16] If the minister sets policy to zero, the outcome will be located at −1 with probability 0.5 or at 1 with probability 0.5. In both cases, the outcome will be one unit away from her ideal point. Thus, on average, the minister will incur a utility of −1. In this situation, the minister prefers to make the decision herself, since the average utility of −1 is higher than the utility of −2 received from delegating to the national official. However, the situation would be different if

---

15 More precisely, the utility function takes the following form: $U = -|p + r|$, where p stands for the policy and r for the random shock.
16 The minister chooses a policy p that maximizes her expected utility $EU = \text{Prob}(r = 1)U + \text{Prob}(r = -1)U = -0.5|p + 1| - 0.5|p - 1|$. Any $p \in [-1, 1]$ maximises this equation, resulting in an expected utility $EU = -1$.

the views of the national official were closer to the views of the minister. If the ideal point of the national official was located at 0.5 for example, delegating would result in a utility of –0.5 and would be preferred to not delegating which results in a utility of –1. In general, any ideal point of the national official located between –1 and 1 results in a delegation payoff larger than –1 and is preferred by the minister to making the decision herself.

Having outlined and illustrated the general model, I now turn to different factors that influence the delegation decision of the minister. In formal terms, these factors influence the delegation decision of ministers by changing the size of the ministers' delegation set.

Uncertainty

A major rationale for delegation to experts is the politician's uncertainty about the practical consequences of policy provisions. In the model, uncertainty can be varied by increasing the variability of the random shock around its mean. The minister's ideal point is assumed to be located at zero, which is also the mean of the distribution of the random shock. A mean-preserving spread of the distribution means that the tales of the distribution get fatter. In substantial terms, the result of a mean-preserving spread of the distribution is that outcomes far away from the minister's ideal point have now a higher probability of being realised than before. The higher probability that more distant outcomes are realised through an uninformed decision by the minister decreases her expected utility of not delegating. In contrast, the national official knows the realisation of the random shock before he selects a policy. Thus, the increased variability of the random shock does not affect his capacity to choose a policy that leads to his most preferred outcome. In summary, the increase in the variability of the random shock does not affect the utility the minister receives from delegating decision-making authority to the national official, but it decreases the minister's expected utility from making a decision herself. As a result of the increased variability of the random shock, the minister's delegation set increases and the delegation option becomes more valuable.

In the example illustrated in Figure 4.5, an increase in the variability can be represented by increasing the size of the random shock. Instead of –1 and 1, consider a random shock that takes the values –3 and 3 with equal probability. Selecting her ideal point as policy is still an optimal choice when the minister makes the decision herself. But due to the increased variation, not delegating will then result in a utility of –3, which is clearly lower than the utility from delegation of –2. The figure shows the expansion of the delegation set ensuing from this increase in uncertainty. While the original delegation set ranged from –1 to 1, the delegation set under increased uncertainty ranges from –3 to 3. The new delegation set includes the ideal point of the national official. Thus, delegation becomes the preferred option of the minister in this case. In general, an increase in uncertainty either does not affect the delegation decision of the

58   *Part I: Introduction and background*

minister or sways the minister's decision towards delegation, depending on the precise location of the policy most preferred by the national official. We should be able to observe a positive average effect of policy uncertainty on committee decision-making over a large number of cases, even though an increase in uncertainty strictly speaking constitutes only a necessary condition for delegation. This expectation can be represented by the following hypothesis:

Hypothesis 5: A committee decision is more likely the larger the degree of uncertainty about the practical consequences of policy provisions.

Salience

Besides the lack of expertise, organisational and natural resource constraints of politicians are also reasons for delegation. Law-makers have only a certain amount of time available that they can devote to scrutinising and discussing legislation (Cox 2006). Even in cases where the practical implications of a policy are clear, drafting legislation takes time and effort that cannot be spent on other purposes (Huber and Shipan 2002: 79). Initial uncertainty about the preferences of other legislators rather than the policy outcome might also be of relevance in this respect. The very process of decision-making, that is, building coalitions and reaching agreements, becomes rather costly when the views of the other legislators on a policy issue are not apparent (Cox and McCubbins 2006: 306). Extending the size of the legislature to overcome these resource constraints is also not an option, at least not in the short run (Epstein and O'Halloran 1999: 44). Therefore, legislators are expected to prioritise. Politicians are likely to focus their attention on the dossiers that promise them the highest return on the investment of their time and to delegate decision-making authority on other dossiers to parliamentary assistants or public servants (Epstein and O'Halloran 1999: 47; Franchino 2004).

The importance or salience of a dossier as perceived by the political actors involved in the decision-making process is often a result of the dossier's consequences for core constituencies, powerful organised interests, or the public in general. In the context of the Council, ministers are expected to focus their attention on dossiers that might impose significant costs on influential domestic groups and companies as well as the administration of the state itself. In more politicised policy areas like Justice and Home Affairs or Economic and Financial Affairs, issues might also be considered important because they touch on core-ideological commitments of government parties. Regardless of the reasons for which a dossier is considered important, ministers should be more likely to concern themselves with politically salient dossiers and delegate decision-making authority on more routine legislation to their representatives in the Council committees.

The effect of salience on the minister's delegation decision can also be illustrated through the model described above. I assume that ministers incur additional costs when they waste their time on dossiers that are not relevant for the implementation of their most important policy concerns or for improving their re-election chances. Ministers have a limited time budget, and spending time on largely inconsequential legislation reduces the time that can be spent on the more salient dossiers. When the minister decides about delegating or deciding on the proposal herself, these costs reduce only the expected utility of the no-delegation option. Obviously, the minister does not bear costs in terms of time and attention when she delegates the decision on the dossier to the national official. As in the case of policy uncertainty, the consideration of the costs of considering low-salience dossiers tilts the minister's decision-making balance towards the delegation option. These costs decrease the expected utility of the minister's no delegation option while the utility of the delegation option remains the same. Again, the result is an increase of the delegation set as illustrated in Figure 4.5. All other things equal, an increase in the costs of attending to low-salience dossiers results either in a choice for delegation or in no effect on the outcome of the minister's decision. The minister will select the delegation option when the enlarged delegation set includes the ideal point of the national official. However, assuming a uniform distribution of ideal points of national officials over a large number of cases, we should expect a negative relationship between salience and committee decision-making. Thus, the following hypothesis about the effect of salience can be stated:

Hypothesis 6: A committee decision is more likely the less salient a policy proposal.

The theoretical arguments in brief

The literature discussed in the previous chapter pointed to several factors potentially of relevance for the study of committee decision-making. The research on role perceptions of national officials and decision-making styles in Council committees pointed to the importance of international socialisation for the outlook and behaviour of committee members. In research on Council decision-making in general, the voting rule, actors' preferences, and the involvement of the EP were often hypothesised to have an impact on the process and outcome of decision-making. In this chapter, I first discussed the theoretical rationale for the impact of these factors on committee decision-making in more detail. In addition to these actor- and institution-related factors, I also discussed the possible impacts of different characteristics of the policy itself. Delegation studies have a long tradition in theorising the factors influencing the decision of principals to confer decision-making authority to their agents. I argued that the uncertainty about the practical consequences of a certain policy proposal and its political salience should be of particular relevance for ministers when deciding about delegating a decision on a legislative proposal to their representatives in Council committees. I used a general delegation model to study the effects of these factors on the delegation choice of ministers.

To illustrate the effects of preferences and institutional rules on the ability of committee members to agree on a change in policy, I relied on the core as a

60   *Part I: Introduction and background*

theoretical concept capturing policy stability in collective decision-making bodies. I showed that the existing policy in place tends to be harder to change when decisions have to be reached by unanimity, when the divergence in the views of committee members is large, and when the EP can be considered to be an additional veto player in committee decision-making. Each of these factors tends to increase the size of the core, which in turn increases the probability that the status quo policy is located within the core. Given that a policy located within the core cannot be beaten by any other policy alternative, a larger probability of the status quo policy being located inside the core corresponds to a larger probability that committee members will not be able to agree to a change in policy.

In substantial terms, the unanimity voting rule requires the assent of more committee members to adopt legislation than the qualified majority voting rule. Thus, it seems reasonable to expect that gridlock will occur more often in committees under the unanimity rule than under the qualified majority voting rule. Note that this expectation does not imply that committee members vote explicitly to make a decision; it just requires that committee members accept a proposal as agreed once the required majority of members support it. The involvement of the EP has a similar effect on committee decision-making as the voting rule. In effect, the co-decision procedure adds an additional veto player to legislative decision-making in the EU. Since the inception of the co-decision procedure, informal negotiations between representatives of the EU institutions to reconcile their views more efficiently have become more and more common. These inter-institutional negotiations often occur concurrently to the intra-institutional negotiations within the Council. Furthermore, most of these inter-institutional negotiations are managed at the committee level on the Council side. Thus, the EP involvement should in many cases directly affect decision-making in Council committees. The possibility of early agreements in the first-reading stage of the co-decision procedure in effect transforms the Council decision into a collective decision of the Council members and the Parliament.

An increased divergence of committee member's preferences should also make an agreement to change policy less likely. The further dispersed the preferences of committee members, the less likely will a required majority of committee members perceive a new proposal to be a mutually beneficial improvement over the existing status quo policy. Whereas the theoretical arguments underlying the effects of the voting rule, preference divergence, and the EP involvement assume that committee members are purely policy oriented, the research on international socialisation suggested that national officials might also internalise supranational norms. I argued that only committee-specific norms shared by all members are likely to affect committee decision-making in systematic ways and that, in line with the empirical findings of previous research, these committee-specific norms are likely to be performance norms. These performance norms should in turn lead to committee members gaining additional value from the very act of reaching an agreement to change policy, regardless of how the new policy looks like. As a result, committees whose members have internalised performance norms can agree on policy change even in situations where purely policy-oriented committee members would not be able to do so.

The voting rule, preference divergence, EP involvement and committee socialisation are expected to make it more or less difficult for committee members to agree to a change in policy. The remaining two hypotheses about the effects of policy uncertainty and political salience of the proposal were derived from a very different theoretical perspective. Rather than policy stability within committees, these factors are expected to influence the decision of ministers to delegate decision-making authority to committee members. If a minister lacks the expertise to evaluate the practical consequences of a policy proposal, the minister and the national official might both be better off when the better-informed official chooses the new policy than when the minister makes an uninformed decision. The more uncertain the link between policy provisions and the practical outcome, the more beneficial it is for ministers to leave the selection of the new policy to the policy experts in committees.

Political salience has the opposite effect on the minister's delegation decision. The more salient a dossier, the more ministers should be interested in dealing with the dossier themselves. I argued that ministers have a limited time budget and that they aim to focus their attention on those proposals most relevant with respect to their core ideological goals and re-election chances. Any time spent on proposals not furthering these central goals imposes costs on ministers. Thus, ministers are expected to be more likely to delegate decision-making authority to committee members if they perceive a dossier to be of little importance for achieving their essential policy and office goals.

The discussion of political salience concluded the discussion in this chapter of factors potentially influencing committee decision-making. Next, the actual relevance of these factors as explanatory variables is first examined through a quantitative large-N analysis. Following up on the correlational results of the statistical analysis, qualitative case studies are then used to further investigate the validity of the indicators used to measure the theoretical concepts, to refine these concepts as necessary, and to shed more light on the precise causal processes at work. In addition, the case studies are used to discover additional explanatory factors not yet identified in existing research.

Part II
Quantitative analysis

5 Sample selection

In Part II of the study, I describe the design and the results of the quantitative analysis.[1] Chapter 6 describes the number of Council decisions made at different hierarchical levels. This chapter gives at least a partial answer to the descriptive question of what proportion of Council decisions are made by committees. Chapter 7 presents the setup and the results of the explanatory analysis. I discuss the operationalisation of the variables, the empirical model, as well as the results of the statistical analysis. But before proceeding to the presentation of the descriptive and explanatory analysis, I first discuss the selection of the sample of cases on which both of these analyses are based.

Selection criteria

The study focuses on the role of Council committees in the standard legislative procedures through which internal policies are adopted in the EU. Thus, I limited the sample to legislative proposals regulating the content of domestic EU policies and having been decided through the classic Community method. This limitation entails the exclusion of external policy decisions, non-legislative acts, Member State initiatives, as well as administrative, budgetary, and institutional acts. Arguably, this selection results in a sample of decision-making cases most typical for the adoption of internal EU policies. At the same time, the result of this selection procedure is a relatively homogenous sample. A homogenous sample reduces the need to introduce additional control variables (Miller 1999; Achen 2002). For example, the consideration of proposals initiated by Member States rather than the Commission would have required an additional control variable in the multivariate analysis. In light of the frequent claim that Member States' initiatives are biased towards the interests of their proposers, an argument can be made that committees have more problems agreeing on such dossiers than on more balanced Commission proposals. Given that the effects of Member State initiatives are not a primary concern of this study and given their relatively

---

1 The quantitative analysis presented in Part II relies in parts on Häge (2007a).

66 *Part II: Quantitative analysis*

low number among all legislative proposals, I decided to exclude these proposals from the sample rather than to further complicate the statistical model by adding another control variable.[2]

In addition to these theoretically and methodologically justified selection standards, I employed two more criteria for mainly practical reasons. First, I consider only proposals transmitted to the Council between 1 July 2000 and 1 January 2004. This criterion delimits the sample along the temporal dimension. The focus on these years assures that the information necessary to conduct the analysis is publicly available. The observation period ends one year after the sample period, on 1 January 2005. The longer observation period ensures that the fate of a proposal can be followed for at least one year after its introduction by the Commission. This possibility reduces the problem of censored observations. Second, the sample includes only decision-making processes that resulted in an explicit first-reading decision of the Council by 1 January 2005. I do not consider proposals that were withdrawn by the Commission or proposals on which no Council decision has been made during the study period.

The loss of the cases without a Council decision is unfortunate but unavoidable, given that information on the value on the dependent variable is missing. Particularly the descriptive results might be affected by the exclusion of censored cases. Decision-making is likely to take longer on average in the censored than in the non-censored cases. Also, ministers should be more likely to get involved in Council decision-making the longer the process takes. Thus, the descriptive analysis based on the sample might underestimate the actual involvement of ministers in the population of acts deemed relevant.

The exclusion of proposals withdrawn by the Commission is also justified on practical grounds. The data indicate that the withdrawal of a proposal by the Commission is usually not a result of the Commission's discontent with the direction that the Council negotiations are taking. Almost all withdrawn proposals included in the original dataset were withdrawn as a result of periodic reviews of pending proposals conducted as part of the Commission's initiative to produce 'better regulation'. This finding indicates that the withdrawal of a proposal is not a result of the Commission executing its de facto veto right during Council negotiations. If the Commission wanted to prevent the Council from adopting an amended proposal, we should expect to see proposals being withdrawn individually at different points in time, not en bloc as part of general reviews.[3] Therefore, the withdrawals must have occurred due to other reasons, most likely because they were blocked in the Council by some of the Member States.

---

2 Note that including relevant third variables in a statistical model can do just as much harm to the validity of the results as omitting them, as long as we do not know and include all of the third variables affecting the independent variable (Clarke 2005). In practice, a researcher can hardly identify and measure all relevant third variables influencing the phenomenon under study.

3 For an example of such a review, see Commission (2005): Better regulation. MEMO/05/340, 27 September 2005, Brussels.

In such cases, the timing of a Commission decision to withdraw a proposal is not directly connected to the negotiation progress on the specific dossier. Thus, the date of withdrawal of a proposal by the Commission is not associated with the date at which the negotiations on the dossier stopped in the Council. This lack of association is unfortunate, as the PreLex database includes only information about the date at which the Commission withdrew a proposal, not about the date at which the proposal was actually rejected in the Council. Therefore, I cannot link the withdrawn proposals to any specific group of ministers responsible for blocking them. Since such information is necessary to examine one of the main hypotheses of this study, that the preference divergence of ministers affects committee decision-making, it is not useful to include these cases in the sample.

An argument could also be made that the cases in which the Commission withdrew the proposal are in fact censored observations and should be treated as such. The Commission can always reintroduce failed proposals after the views or the composition of the Council has changed. According to this interpretation, information about the highest level involved in Council negotiations is simply missing and cannot even be obtained in principle. Either way, no alternative exists to the exclusion of withdrawn Commission proposals from the sample.

Selection procedure

Having outlined the selection criteria, I describe the practical process of selecting the sample in this section. The starting point for identifying the sample of cases is the Commission's database PreLex. PreLex is an online database with information retrieval capabilities.[4] The database's purpose is to monitor the inter-institutional decision-making process in the EU. The entries in the database consist of webpages. Each webpage describes the progress of a Commission document that has been transmitted to one of the other EU institutions. The webpages describe mainly characteristics of the document (e.g. title, type of document, policy area and treaty basis) and formal aspects of the decision-making process (e.g. type of legislative procedure, dates of Commission, EP, and Council decisions, and procedural outcomes of meetings of these institutions). Monitored documents include proposals for binding and non-binding legal acts, but also communications, staff working papers, and reports.

The identification of the sample of cases involved several steps. First, I downloaded all PreLex webpages describing the progress of Commission documents adopted by the Commission between 1 July 2000 and 1 January 2004. Second, I extracted the information contained in those webpages and brought it into a format that can be read by data analysis software. To automate the first two steps, I wrote an Excel macro in Visual Basic for Applications. The web addresses of the PreLex webpages contain a unique identifier. The identifier is simply a running

---

4 The database is freely accessible online at: http://ec.europa.eu/prelex/apcnet.cfm?CL=en (accessed 21 August 2011).

68 Part II: Quantitative analysis

number indexing the webpages. I used this feature of the web addresses to download the webpages. The Excel macro looped through all the identification numbers related to Commission documents transmitted during the indicated time period. In a first step, the macro downloaded the webpage, checked whether it contained any relevant information and, if it did, saved the webpage as an Excel spreadsheet.[5] Because the content of the webpages is structured in html tables, the conversion into the Excel spreadsheet format did not pose any problems. In a second step, the Excel macro opened the webpage in its new spreadsheet format and extracted the relevant information through a number of search procedures. Because the PreLex webpages do not have a completely standardised structure, I conducted several trials to develop a comprehensive set of procedures that extract all the relevant information contained in the webpages.

All extraction procedures followed the same template. First, the procedure searched for an entry indicating a certain event, for example the formal adoption of a proposal by the Council. Then it copied all information related to that event from the spreadsheet containing the webpage content to the spreadsheet containing the dataset. The cell structure of Excel spreadsheets was very helpful in this respect. Like any standard statistical dataset, the rows of the dataset spreadsheet indicate different cases and the columns different variables. Each decision-making process constituted one case in this setup. In the example of the Council adoption event, the procedure copied the date of the adoption by the Council, the type of agenda item (i.e. A- or B-item), the session number, and the name of the Council formation from cells of the webpage spreadsheet into cells of the dataset spreadsheet. Each of these pieces of information was recorded in a variable in a separate column in the dataset spreadsheet. This process was repeated for all events of interest and all webpages. The result of this procedure was a data matrix with 3,607 cases and 288 variables. Following the information extraction and the rearrangement of the information into a classic dataset format, I converted the Excel spreadsheet into a Stata dataset file to code the raw information into variable values. In most cases, the recoded variables still did not enter the analysis directly. The variables formed only the basis for the construction of variables more useful for narrowing down the sample and for representing the theoretical constructs in the statistical analysis.

Overall, the macro extracted information on the decision-making process of 3,607 Commission documents transmitted to the other EU institutions during the time period under consideration. The focus on binding acts such as Directives, Regulations and Decisions led to the deletion of 1,747 cases, resulting in a dataset size of 1,860 cases. I deleted a further 1,049 cases to restrict the sample to co-decision and consultation files. These selection procedures reduced the sample to 809 legislative proposals. I excluded further cases from the analysis either because the Council did not adopt a decision during the study period or because the proposal did not fall within the scope of the study. The former category

---

5 Each identification number is connected to a webpage, but many webpages are empty.

included 26 proposals that were withdrawn by the Commission and 96 proposals that were still pending in the Council by 1 January 2005. The latter category included all dossiers dealing with foreign policy, administrative, institutional or budgetary issues, as well as proposals initiated by Member States.

The exclusion of acts decided through the assent procedure excluded already many foreign policy decisions. In order to ensure an exclusive focus on internal policy, I also discarded all remaining proposals that indicated in their title that their purpose was the conclusion of an international agreement (76 proposals). Furthermore, I deleted all proposals that were handled by the Development (10 proposals) or External Relations Council (15 proposals). Because the General Affairs Council is mostly concerned with administrative and institutional issues and not with substantive matters of policy, I removed all dossiers handled by this Council formation as well (44 proposals). For a similar reason, I excluded proposals discussed in the Budget Council formation (10 proposals). I also dropped all dossiers considered to be of a non-legislative nature (58 proposals), as indicated in the Summary of Council Acts. Finally, as part of the focus on decision-making through the Community method, I excluded all proposals introduced by a Member State rather than the Commission (35 proposals).

The final result of this selection procedure is a sample of 439 legislative decision-making cases. This sample represents only a small fraction of the overall decision-making activity in the EU during the period studied. At the same time, the sample represents a relatively homogenous set of cases that is of direct interest to the research question pursued in the current study. Arguably, the sample of cases also corresponds most closely to the type of decisions scholars of legislative politics usually have in mind when they devise and test theories of law-making. In any case, the selectivity of the sample should be borne in mind when interpreting the findings of the descriptive and explanatory analyses I present in the following two chapters.

6 Describing the extent of committee decision-making

In this chapter, I describe the extent of committee decision-making. In essence, this description answers the question of how many legislative Council decisions are made by committees. Before describing the results of the descriptive analysis in the second section, I first discuss some issues regarding the classification of Council decisions into ministerial and committee decisions, respectively.

Measuring committee decision-making

The descriptive analysis is based on the 439 legislative decision-making cases identified through the sample selection procedure described in the previous chapter. Being explicit about the underlying sample of cases is necessary to reach valid descriptive inferences about the involvement of different hierarchical levels in Council decision-making. The following figures do not relate in any way to Council decision-making in general. The exclusion of non-legislative, non-binding and foreign policy acts certainly biases the current sample in favour of stronger ministerial involvement. Thus, the following statistics describe the involvement of different Council levels only for standard Community legislation on the substance of internal policies. This restricted sample focuses on a homogenous selection of cases most relevant for testing theories of legislative politics.

Although the description is deliberately limited in terms of the types of Council decisions covered, the methodology employed to measure the involvement of ministers for this limited sample has an important advantage compared with the techniques used in earlier studies. Previous research relied mainly on the agendas and minutes of ministerial meetings to discern whether a proposal was discussed by ministers or not (van Schendelen 1996; Gomez and Peterson 2001; Hayes-Renshaw and Wallace 2006). This approach does not trace proposals over time, which results in a systematic understatement of the actual ministerial involvement. The formal adoption of a Council decision occurs almost always through the A-point procedure without any ministerial discussion. Even if Member States reached the final agreement in a ministerial meeting in which ministers discussed the dossier as a B-point, the ministers do not formally adopt the Council decision until the text has been checked and translated by the

Council's legal-linguistic experts (Häge 2008: 548). After this screening and translation process, ministers adopt the act formally as an A-point. If a proposal is not traced over time through all relevant ministerial meetings, each type of agenda item is counted independently for each meeting. In the aggregate, the 'pseudo' (de Zwaan 1995: 136) or 'false' A-point (van Schendelen 1996: 540) for the mostly irrelevant meeting in which ministers formally adopted the dossier then neutralises the B-point count for the earlier meeting in which minister reached the actual agreement. The result is a bias overstating the extent of committee decision-making. Thus, although the approach pursued in the current study describes ministerial involvement for a narrower range of types of decisions, the description for this subset of decisions is more valid than the descriptions provided by previous studies.

Tracing proposals over time also requires deciding which Council decisions should be considered to be the most relevant. In this study, I examine only first-reading decisions of the Council. In cases where the consultation procedure applies, the EP can only give a non-binding opinion and the Council's first-reading decision coincides with the adoption or rejection of the proposal. In contrast, the co-decision procedure grants far-reaching amendment and veto rights to the EP and allows for up to three readings on the proposal by both institutions. In this case, the Council's first-reading decision corresponds to a rejection of the proposal or to the adoption of a so-called common position. The Council's common position then forms the basis for the EP's deliberations in the second reading and for possible negotiations between the two institutions in the third reading. The Council can only adopt a proposal in its first reading if it accepts all of the EP's first-reading amendments. I focus on first-reading decisions of the Council because the legislative process after the first reading is mainly about resolving the conflict between the Council as a collective actor and the EP, not about reaching an agreement within the Council. The first-reading stage under the co-decision procedure is the point at which Member States collectively adopt a Council position. In this respect, the Council's first-reading decision under the co-decision procedure is most comparable to a Council decision under the consultation procedure.[1] The view that the Council reaches its main internal agreement in first reading is also reflected in the fact that Coreper and working parties almost exclusively manage co-decision dossiers after the Council has

---

1 In recent years, the EU institutions reach more and more legislative decisions in the first- or second-reading stage of the co-decision procedure. The attempts to reach an early agreement involve trilateral negotiations, so-called trilogues, between representatives of the Commission, the EP and the Council (Farrell and Héritier 2003, 2004; Häge and Kaeding 2007). Sometimes, these inter-institutional negotiations start even before the Member States have fully agreed to a common point of view in the Council. In cases where the institutions envisage a first-reading agreement or a second-reading adoption by the EP, the first-reading decision by the Council does not only reflect the collective position of the Member States, but also a compromise agreement with the EP.

72   *Part II: Quantitative analysis*

agreed to a common position. Ministers hardly get involved in second-reading discussions or conciliation committee negotiations (Bostock 2002).[2]

Besides the focus on certain types of Council decisions and on a certain stage of the decision-making process, I also focus in the quantitative analysis on the division between ministers and national officials in general. I neglect the distinction between senior committees and working parties. The main reason for this limitation is a practical one: in order to examine the involvement of senior committees separately from working parties, the decision-making process for each individual proposal would need to be reconstructed through an extensive analysis of Council documents. No single document or database exists that allows relatively efficient access to this kind of information. In contrast, I obtained information about the involvement of ministers relatively easy and reliably from the Commission's PreLex database. Gathering data on the involvement of different types of committees is impractical, at least for a large number of cases. I consider the division between working parties and committees in more detail through the case studies.

Although the lack of information on the involvement of different committee types is regrettable, the focus on the division between ministers and committees in general does not substantially diminish the value of the quantitative study. From a normative perspective, the distinction between ministers and bureaucrats in general is certainly more relevant than the division between different layers of committees. Much of the democratic legitimacy of Council decision-making hinges on the link between government representatives and national parliaments; and ministers are more directly accountable to parliament than their civil servants, regardless of whether the latter are diplomats in Coreper or policy experts in working parties. From an empirical point of view, previous studies also indicate that the middle layer of the Council might not be very relevant in terms of actual decision-making. Coreper only makes about one-fifth of the Council's legislative decisions; the remaining proposals are either decided by working parties or ministers (van den Bos 1991; Häge 2008). In summary, the following description of committee decision-making concentrates on legislation concerned with substantial internal policy proposals initiated by the Commission and decided through either the co-decision or consultation procedure. The description also focuses on first-reading decisions of the Council and the division of legislative decision-making between ministers and committee members in general.

Results of the descriptive analysis

In Table 6.1, I present the results of the descriptive analysis. The table indicates the number of proposals discussed or decided by ministers as well as the number of exclusive committee decisions for different Council formations. Overall, committees exclusively discussed about 37 per cent of all proposals. In another 15.7 per cent of

---

2 With regard to the sample used in the current study, ministers discussed only one of the proposals they had not discussed in the first reading during later stages of the co-decision procedure. In practical terms, the focus on first-reading decisions has no substantial effect on the dependent variable and therefore does not affect the results of the descriptive or explanatory analysis.

Describing the extent of committee decision-making 73

Table 6.1 Decision-making level by Council formation

Council formation	Ministers			Committee	Total
	Discussion	Decision	Total		
Culture	0	1	1	5	6
	0	(16.7)	(16.7)	(83.3)	(100.0)
Education and Youth	0	7	7	2	9
	(0.0)	(77.8)	(77.8)	(22.2)	(100.0)
Agriculture	6	35	41	48	89
	(6.7)	(39.4)	(46.1)	(53.9)	(100.0)
Fisheries	6	11	17	20	37
	(16.2)	(29.7)	(46.0)	(54.0)	(100.0)
Economic and Financial Affairs	3	14	17	32	49
	(6.1)	(28.6)	(34.7)	(65.3)	(100.0)
Environment	5	24	29	7	36
	(13.9)	(66.7)	(80.6)	(19.4)	(100.0)
Justice and Home Affairs	9	11	20	17	37
	(24.3)	(29.7)	(54.0)	(46.0)	(100.0)
Transport and Telecommunications	17	48	65	4	69
	(24.6)	(69.6)	(94.2)	(5.8)	(100.0)
Industry and Energy	6	10	16	2	18
	(33.3)	(55.6)	(88.9)	(11.1)	(100.0)
Research	3	7	10	2	12
	(25.0)	(58.3)	(83.3)	(16.7)	(100.0)
Internal Market, Consumers and Tourism	9	20	29	23	52
	(17.3)	(38.5)	(55.8)	(44.2)	(100.0)
Employment and Social Affairs	3	12	15	2	17
	(17.7)	70.6)	(88.2)	(11.8)	(100.0)
Health	2	6	8	0	8
	(25.0)	(75.0)	(100.0)	(0.0)	(100.0)
Total	69	206	275	164	439
	(15.7)	(46.9)	(62.6)	(37.4)	(100.0)

Source: Own data based on information from PreLex and Council documents.

Notes: The numbers in brackets indicate row percentages. The sample is restricted to legislative proposals that regulate internal EU policies and were introduced by the Commission between 1 July 2000 and 1 January 2004. See text for the precise sample selection criteria. Minister discussion indicates proposals that were only discussed by ministers, but decided at the committee level. Minister decision indicates proposals on which the final decision was made by ministers. Such proposals might or might not have been discussed by ministers in an earlier meeting. The fourth column gives the total number of proposals discussed or decided by ministers. Committee indicates the number of proposals exclusively dealt with at the committee level.

the proposals, a committee made the final decision although ministers had previously discussed the dossier. Finally, ministers made the final decision on a dossier in 46.9 per cent of the cases. Overall, ministers discuss or make a decision on more

74   *Part II: Quantitative analysis*

than 60 per cent of all proposals. This proportion differs strongly from prominent previous estimates indicating that ministers deal only with 10-15 per cent of all Council decisions (Hayes-Renshaw and Wallace 1997: 40, 78). The higher figures for the involvement of ministers are probably due to a combination of both a more focused sample and an improved measurement approach.

The table also indicates that these aggregate figures have to be interpreted with care. A comparison of the rows in Table 6.1 shows marked differences in the extent of committee decision-making across Council formations. Agriculture, Fisheries, Justice and Home Affairs, Internal Market, and particularly Economic and Financial Affairs are Council formations in which committees play a disproportionately important role. In contrast, ministers are disproportionately involved in discussing and deciding legislative proposals in the areas of Environment, Industry and Energy, Research, Employment and Social Affairs, and especially Transport and Telecommunications.[3] Indeed, the extreme values of the proportion of exclusive committee discussions range from 65.3 per cent in Economic and Financial Affairs to only 5.8 per cent in Transport and Telecommunications. The variation in committee involvement also does not exhibit any obvious pattern. Both groups of Council formations include relatively settled and relatively new EU policy areas; and although areas in which the consultation procedure is still the standard legislative procedure, such as Agriculture, Fisheries and Justice and Home Affairs, are concentrated in the group that shows less minister involvement, this group also contains the Internal Market formation, in which most legislation is adopted through the co-decision procedure.

Thus, the descriptive analysis yields two main conclusions. First, the involvement of ministers is considerably stronger than suggested by previous research on Council decision-making. The results challenge the received wisdom in the field. At least with respect to the population of Council decisions considered in the current study, ministers are much more directly involved in the decision-making process than often suggested. Second, the usefulness of any single aggregate measure for committee decision-making is limited. The analysis shows a large variation between different Council sectors. The variation also does not involve any pattern pointing to a possible explanation. The fact that proposals are discussed in different Council formations does not by itself represent a theoretically satisfying explanation for the differences in committee decision-making among Council formations. The lack of any pattern across Council formations points to the importance of considering individual decision-making processes rather than aggregate figures to investigate the reasons why a certain proposal is discussed by ministers rather than exclusively handled by national officials. In the next chapter, I empirically examine several candidate explanations for the propensity of a proposal to be exclusively discussed at the committee level.

---

3 I do not comment on decision-making levels in the areas of Culture, Education and Youth, and Health. The number of cases in these Council formations is too small to allow any reliable inferences.

7 Explaining the variation in committee decision-making

The descriptive analysis in Chapter 6 showed considerable variation between different Council formations in the extent of committee decision-making. In this chapter, I inspect possible causes of this variation through a multivariate statistical analysis. More precisely, I examine whether the explanatory factors identified in Chapter 4 show a statistical relationship with the involvement of ministers in Council decision-making. Like the descriptive analysis, the statistical analysis considers the decision-making process only up to the first-reading decision of the Council and concentrates on the distinction between the bureaucratic and ministerial level. In the next section, I describe the operationalisation and the data sources of the dependent and the independent variables. In the second section, I present the results of the analysis. In the third section, I discuss preliminary conclusions about the implications of the results of the explanatory quantitative analysis.

Operationalisation of variables

The quantitative analysis concentrates on first-reading decisions and on the divide between the political and bureaucratic levels in the Council. But even with these restrictions, measuring the level at which the Council decided on a certain proposal is not straightforward. Different Council bodies may discuss a proposal several times and may refer the proposal up and down the hierarchy repeatedly. The goal of this study is to examine the factors that influence committee decision-making. Two natural candidates exist as indicators for whether or not a committee reached the agreement on a certain piece of legislation. One measure indicates whether a committee made the final decision on the proposal, the other measure indicates whether the proposal was exclusively discussed at the committee level.

The measure indicating whether a committee reached the final decision is problematic. How much influence the committee actually exerted on the content of the agreement is often not clear in those cases. The types of committee decisions made after ministerial discussions can range from agreements on substantially important, still outstanding issues to mere finalisations of the precise wording of compromises essentially reached by ministers. Although both of these instances would classify as a final decision by committee, the actual influence of

76   *Part II: Quantitative analysis*

the committee on the content of the agreement varies widely. In contrast, the coding of cases with no direct ministerial involvement as instances of committee decisions is based on a clear threshold of the actual influence of different Council levels. Either committee members exclusively discussed the proposal or ministers had some direct influence on the agreement. Technically, this variable is reliably measured through a dichotomous indicator. I classify a dossier that shows no direct involvement of ministers as being decided by a committee and therefore code it as one. If ministers discussed a proposal at some stage during the Council decision-making process, I code it as zero. I extracted the information to generate this variable from PreLex.

The committee decision variable forms the dependent variable in the statistical analysis. The independent variables are based on the discussion of explanatory factors in Chapter 4. As outlined earlier, I expect preference divergence, involvement of the EP and high salience to decrease the chances of a committee decision. In contrast, qualified majority voting, committee socialisation, and uncertainty should make a committee decision more likely. In order to examine the explanatory power of these factors empirically, they need to be translated into measurable indicators. In Table 7.1, I list all the indicators and their data sources. The indicator for EP involvement is a dichotomous variable indicating whether the EP made any amendments under the co-decision procedure or not. Thus, the variable measures not only the formal powers of the EP under the co-decision procedure, but also takes into account whether the EP actually made use of these powers. I extracted data on the applicable legislative procedure and the actual EP involvement from PreLex. I collected information on the voting rule from the 'Monthly Summary of Council Acts' published by the Council. When such information was not available, I identified the voting rule through the legal base of the proposal in conjunction with the appendix in Hix (2005). This appendix lists the voting rule and the legislative procedure prescribed by different EU treaty articles.

The preference divergence variable is based on data on the party composition of government cabinets and the parties' positions on different policy issues. I employ the party position data from the Chapel Hill 2002 expert survey (Hooghe *et al.* 2005). In contrast to other party position data sets (e.g. Benoit and Laver 2006; Klingemann *et al.* 2006), the Chapel Hill indicators are specifically constructed to provide party positions on EU policy issues. I collected information on the cabinet composition in Member State governments from various editions of the Political Data Yearbook of the *European Journal of Political Research*. I then linked the party affiliation of government ministers and the corresponding policy positions to the different Council formations. Table 7.2 indicates that the correspondence between Council formations and policy positions is not one-to-one. Policy-specific party positions are only available for the main EU policy areas. Therefore, I use the party positions on the internal market also as proxies for the party positions on Transport and Telecommunications as well as Industry and Energy. Similarly, I use party positions on the social left–right dimension to measure positions on Education and Youth as well as Culture.

Explaining the variation in committee decision-making   77

Table 7.1 Description of variables and data sources

Name	Description	Sources
Committee decision-making	Dichotomous variable: 0 = Discussed by ministers 1 = Never discussed by ministers	PreLex[a] and Council documents[b]
Preference divergence	Distance between most extreme policy positions of ministers' parties	Cabinets: Political Data Yearbooks, *European Journal of Political Research* 1999–2005; Policy positions: Hooghe *et al.* (2005)
Qualified majority voting	Dichotomous variable: 0 = Unanimity 1 = Qualified majority voting	Monthly Summary of Council Acts;[c] appendix in Hix (2005: 415)
EP involvement	Dichotomous variable: 0 = Consultation or no amendment under co-decision 1 = Co-decision and amendment	PreLex
Committee meeting density	Average number of meeting days per month between 1 January 2000 and 31 December 2004	Calendars of working party meetings maintained by the Council Secretariat,[d] Council documents
Comitology committee	Dichotomous variable: 0 = No provision for committee 1 = Provision for committee	Commission proposals
Policy areas	Dichotomous variable: 0 = One policy area 1 = More than one policy area	PreLex
Salience	Number of recitals	Commission proposals

Notes

a See the PreLex website at: http://ec.europa.eu/prelex/apcnet.cfm?CL=en (accessed 27 August 2011).

b See the Council's public register of documents at: http://www.consilium.europa.eu/documents/access-to-council-documents-public-register.aspx?lang=en (accessed 27 August 2011).

c See the 'Monthly Summary of Council Acts' on the Council's website at: http://www.consilium.europa.eu/documents/legislative-transparency/monthly-summaries-of-council-acts.aspx?lang=en (accessed 27 August 2011).

d The calendars were obtained through a request for access to Council documents; see the Council's website at: http://www.consilium.europa.eu/documents/access-to-council-documents-public-register/submit-a-request-for-access-to-council-documents.aspx?lang=en (accessed 27 August 2011).

In cases where several ministers of one government occupied portfolios that could all be related to a certain Council formation, I employed the average party position of these ministers as the country's position. Similarly, if I could not identify a specific minister, I used the average position of the cabinet as a whole as the country's position. Otherwise, I used the minister's party position to represent

78   *Part II: Quantitative analysis*

Table 7.2 The linkage of Council formations with party policy positions

Council formations	Party position on policy dimensions
Culture	Social Left–Right
Education and Youth	Social Left–Right
Agriculture	Agricultural Spending
Fisheries	Agricultural Spending
Economic and Financial Affairs	Internal Market
Environment	Environmental Policy
Justice and Home Affairs	Common Policy on Asylum
Transport and Telecommunications	Internal Market
Industry and Energy	Internal Market
Research	Internal Market
Internal Market, Consumers, Tourism	Internal Market
Employment and Social Affairs	Employment Policy
Health	Employment Policy

Note: The Council formations are based on the organisation of the Council as of June 2000, excluding General Affairs and External Relations, Budget and Development formations (see text for further details). Data on the party positions on the policy dimensions are taken from the Chapel Hill 2002 expert survey (Hooghe *et al.* 2005).

the country's position. Unfortunately, using the average party position of ministers in cases where none or where several portfolios can be related to a certain Council formation creates measurement error. However, information on which minister was primarily responsible for handling a certain dossier is generally not available without going into the details of each specific case. Thus, collecting such information for a large sample was not a feasible option. Still, the average party position should be the best approximation of the true party position in cases where the responsible minister could not be identified with certainty.

For each Council formation, I calculated the preference divergence variable as the maximum difference between the countries' policy positions. Although party positions are measured as constants over time, the aggregated preference divergence measure varies both between and within Council formations. Obviously, the variation between Council formations is due to the different party positions of government ministers on different policy issues. Even if the agriculture minister and the environment minister of a given government have the same party affiliation, their preference scores will usually be different simply because the agriculture minister's score represents the party's support of EU agricultural policy, while the environment minister's score represents the party's support of EU environmental policy. In contrast, the variation within Council formations over time is due to changes in the composition of government cabinets. Such changes over time occur through the reshuffling of minister portfolios among the coalition parties of an existing government or through the complete or partial replacement of the existing government after it resigned or lost the election. In short, any

Explaining the variation in committee decision-making 79

change in the party affiliation of a minister in any Member State government has the potential to change the preference divergence score.[1]

I measured the degree of exposure to supranational norms and values in committees by the average number of days a committee met per month between 1 January 2000 and 31 December 2004. I derived information on the number of committee meetings from the calendar of Council meetings maintained by the Council secretariat. Some of the committees meet on a regular basis several times per month and deal with all issues in a certain policy area (e.g. the environment committee), while others are highly specialised and meet only when the need arises to discuss a specific proposal (e.g. many working parties dealing with the common agricultural policy). To reflect the structural differences among committees rather than short-term fluctuations in their workload, I averaged the number of meetings over the whole time period rather than over months or over presidency periods. The socialisation arguments usually presume a direct causal chain from the amount of time spent on committee work through the values and norms bureaucrats hold to the type of behaviour bureaucrats consider to be appropriate in committee negotiations. This implies that no data on the attitudes of individual bureaucrats is needed to examine socialisation as an explanatory factor for committee decision-making.[2]

As a measure for the uncertainty surrounding the practical consequences of a dossier, I employed a variable indicating whether or not the proposal provides for the establishment of a Comitology committee. Comitology committees do not only assist and advise but also control the Commission in implementing EU legislation. Previous research argued that the need for post-hoc control of implementation tasks is stronger when legislators have diverse preferences (Franchino 2004). Thus, the establishment of a Comitology committee could be an indicator for both the complexity of the policy matter as well as the political conflict among legislators. However, the statistical analysis controls for a possible effect of political conflict through the inclusion of the preference divergence measure as a control variable. Thus, the Comitology indicator should yield valid estimates of the effect of uncertainty in the multivariate analysis. Nevertheless, I repeat the analysis with an alternative indicator for uncertainty. This variable indicates whether the proposal has implications for one or for several policy areas. The variable is based on the number of policy fields mentioned in the PreLex database. Anticipating the consequences of legal provisions that affect several policy areas should be more difficult than anticipating the consequences of legal provisions that affect only a single policy area.

---

1 Because the preference divergence score for a certain Council formation is calculated as the distance between the two most extreme party positions of ministers, the actual impact of a change in the party affiliation of a minister depends on whether it results in a change of one of the two extremes of the distribution of minister's party positions.
2 Unfortunately, this operationalisation does not allow for a clear differentiation between effects of the socialisation through past experiences and effects of the strategic anticipation of future interactions. Still, a negative finding of no effect of this variable would clearly reject the socialisation hypothesis.

80   *Part II: Quantitative analysis*

I assessed the salience of a dossier through the number of recitals contained in the proposal. Recitals outline and list the reasons for adopting a certain dossier.[3] This measure is based on the assumption that the importance of a piece of legislation varies with the number of reasons given for its adoption. The higher the importance of a dossier, the larger should be the number of justifications given. Actors are likely to value policy issues to different degrees, since actors are more or less affected by decisions on these policy issues. Considering that the Commission drafts the initial proposal, the salience variable represents the valuation of the Commission rather than some external, independent judgement of the importance of a dossier. However, the Commission is generally regarded as the promoter of European integration and the guardian of the common European interest. Thus, the measure should yield a good approximation of the importance of a proposal in the overall European legal order.

Results of the statistical analysis

I performed a logistic regression to examine the relationships between the independent variables and the Council decision-making level. The results of the analysis are presented in Table 7.3. A positive relationship in Table 7.3 indicates that a higher value of the independent variable increases the likelihood of a committee decision. Models 1 and 2 show the basic specifications based purely on the theoretical considerations discussed in Chapter 4. In Models 3 and 4, I added dummy variables for different Council formations to control for any unaccounted effects inherent to policy-making in a specific area.

The results of the statistical analysis are mixed. The preference divergence variable does not show a statistically significant effect in any of the models. Political conflict among Member States does not seem to influence the level at which a decision is taken in the Council. In contrast, the variable for EP involvement shows a rather strong and clear relationship in the expected direction. EP amendments under the co-decision procedure make a decision at the committee level less likely. The results regarding the voting rule variable are somewhat ambiguous. Although the coefficient of the voting rule variable shows the expected sign in all models, the relationship is only statistically significant in the models including the dummy variables representing different Council formations.

The data analysis does not support the committee socialisation hypothesis. The coefficient of the socialisation variable indicates a statistically significant negative relationship in the models excluding Council formation controls. This finding is clearly contrary to expectations. While the coefficient changes its sign when

---

3 European Communities (2003): *Joint practical guide of the European Parliament, the Council and the Commission for persons involved in the drafting of legislation within the Community institutions.* Luxembourg: Office for Official Publications of the European Communities, p. 31.

Table 7.3 Determinants of committee decision-making

Independent variable	Model 1	Model 2	Model 3	Model 4
Preference divergence	−0.19	−0.17	0.49	0.49
	(1.51)	(1.36)	(1.36)	(1.32)
Qualified majority voting	0.43	0.39	1.52***	1.59***
	(1.15)	(1.02)	(2.81)	(2.91)
EP involvement	−0.84***	−0.95***	−1.07**	−1.18***
	(2.66)	(2.95)	(2.47)	(2.62)
Committee meeting density	−0.17***	−0.19***	0.25	0.24
	(2.91)	(3.21)	(1.26)	(1.20)
Uncertainty:				
Comitology committee	0.51*	−	0.60*	−
	(1.89)		(1.95)	−
Policy areas	−	0.71***	−	0.97***
	−	(2.69)	−	(3.20)
Salience	−0.20***	−0.18***	−0.21***	−0.20***
	(7.52)	(7.75)	(7.27)	(7.48)
Council formation controls:				
Culture	−	−	1.84	2.38
	−	−	(1.02)	(1.30)
Education and Youth	−	−	−0.30	0.05
	−	−	(0.20)	(0.03)
Agriculture	−	−	0.07	0.39
	−	−	(0.05)	(0.29)

(Continued)

Table 7.3 (Continued)

Independent variable	Model 1	Model 2	Model 3	Model 4
Fisheries	–	–	–0.78	–0.42
	–	–	(0.58)	(0.30)
Economic and Financial Affairs	–	–	3.31***	3.61***
	–	–	(3.47)	(3.73)
Environment	–	–	–1.84	–1.75
	–	–	(0.99)	(0.93)
Justice and Home Affairs	–	–	2.57***	3.14***
	–	–	(2.68)	(3.21)
Transport and Telecommunications	–	–	–1.60	–1.44
	–	–	(1.44)	(1.26)
Research	–	–	–0.03	0.30
	–	–	(0.02)	(0.26)
Internal Market, Consumers and Tourism	–	–	2.58***	2.78***
	–	–	(2.76)	(2.94)
Health, Employment and Social Affairs	–	–	–1.27	–1.16
	–	–	(0.88)	(0.78)
Constant	2.62***	2.44***	–1.96	–2.56*
	(4.80)	(4.38)	(1.48)	(1.90)
Likelihood Ratio Chi^2	161.38***	165.26***	226.81***	233.73***
Pseudo R^2	0.28	0.28	0.39	0.40
Adj. Count R^2	0.42	0.37	0.53	0.49
BIC	–2209.67	–2213.55	–2208.17	–2215.09

Notes: The table reports logistic regression results; absolute value of z-statistics in parentheses, * significant at 10%, ** significant at 5%, *** significant at 1%, two-sided tests, $N = 439$. The dependent variable is a dichotomous variable indicating whether the dossier was only discussed at the committee level (1) or also by ministers (0).

Explaining the variation in committee decision-making 83

dummy variables for Council formations are introduced, the relationship is still not statistically significant. In contrast, uncertainty about the practical consequences of a proposal seems to have the expected effect on committee decision-making. Models 1 and 3 indicate a substantial increase in the likelihood of a committee decision when the dossier includes a provision for the establishment of a Comitology committee. Models 2 and 4 reproduce this result with the alternative measure of uncertainty. This measure indicates whether a proposal concerns one or several policy areas. The salience of the dossier is also of importance for determining at which level the Council reaches a decision. The variable measuring the salience of a dossier demonstrates a strong negative and statistically significant relationship with the dependent variable. The more salient a dossier, the less likely is a committee decision.

In order to control for any unaccounted effects specific to policy-making in certain areas, I include dummy variables for the different Council formations in models 3 and 4. Because of the small number of proposals in the Health Council formation, I merged the Health with the Employment and Social Affairs formation. The ministers discussed all eight Health proposals adopted during the study period. Thus, a dummy variable for the Health Council formation would have completely determined the value of the dependent variable and resulted in the exclusion of the Health formation observations from the statistical analysis. The European Council decided to merge these formations in the real world from summer 2002. Thus, decision-making in these two areas seems sufficiently similar to justify a common indicator.

Although the theoretically justified independent variables account for a considerable part of the variation in the propensity of committee decision-making, the substantially and statistically significant results for the Council formation dummies in Model 3 and 4 indicate that unexplained differences across policy sectors still exist. The results of the significance tests indicate that a committee decision is more likely in the areas of Economic and Financial Affairs, Justice and Home Affairs, and Internal Market, Consumers and Tourism. However, these tests have to be interpreted with care. The statistical significance of all Council formation dummy variables depends crucially on the chosen reference category. Given its relatively average position in terms of committee decision-making, I used the Industry and Research Council formation as the reference category in the models presented in Table 7.3. However, the coefficients of other Council formation variables would have been statistically significant when compared to a different reference category. In this respect, the direction and relative sizes of the coefficients of the Council formation dummy variables are more informative than their statistical significance. When considering the sizes and signs of coefficients, the Council formations of Culture, Environment, Transport and Telecommunications, and Employment, Social Affairs and Health stand out for decreasing the likelihood of a committee decision. The differences in committee decision-making between some of the Council formations and the substantial increase in the overall fit of the models when Council formation controls are included indicate that further unobserved factors connected to

84   *Part II: Quantitative analysis*

characteristics of Council formations influence committee decision-making. Thus, the inclusion of these control variables is warranted.

In Table 7.4, I illustrate the substantial effects of the statistically significant estimation results. The table is based on the best-fitting specification of Model 4, which includes the variable indicating the number of policy areas affected as a measure of uncertainty as well as Council formation indicators as control variables. In the table, I present the changes in the probability of a committee decision resulting from a change in the value of one independent variable, keeping all other independent variables constant at a specified value. The table shows the effects of qualified majority voting, EP involvement, uncertainty and salience given four different combinations of values of the independent variables. I present the values to which the independent variables are set in the lower part of the table. Each of these combinations of values of the independent variables corresponds to proposal features that are characteristic of a certain Council formation.

I selected four Council formations to cover a wide range of values of the independent variables: Agriculture, Environment, Justice and Home Affairs, and Internal Market, Consumers and Tourism. These four Council formations also represent some of the busiest EU policy areas in as far as legislative decision-making is concerned (see Table 6.1). In order to generate proposals that are 'typical' of a certain Council formation, I set continuous independent variables to their Council formation specific median values and dichotomous independent variables to the value that is more frequently observed in proposals of the Council formation. I set all dummy variables for the different Council formations to zero, except for the dummy variable that indicates the formation for which I calculated the effect.

For example, the typical Agricultural dossier is characterised by a relatively strong preference divergence, a rather low number of monthly committee meetings, a very moderate degree of salience, qualified majority voting, no involvement of the EP, and no uncertainty surrounding the consequences of the dossier in question. I describe these characteristics more precisely in the lower half of the second column of the table. Given these default values for the independent variables, the upper half of the second column of Table 7.4 indicates that a change from unanimity to qualified majority voting increases the predicted probability of a committee decision by 0.38. In contrast, a change from no EP involvement to EP involvement results in a 0.29 decrease in the predicted probability. Adding uncertainty increases the predicted probability of a committee decision by 0.17, while an increase in the salience variable from 3 (5th percentile) to 30 recitals (95th percentile) decreases the probability of a committee decision by 0.81. Overall, Table 7.4 indicates a relatively consistent pattern regarding the effect sizes of different variables. Salience is the most important predictor of committee decision-making, followed by the voting rule, EP involvement and uncertainty. All effects are of substantial size. Even the smallest effect leads to a 0.09 change in the predicted probability of a committee decision.

Table 7.4 Effects of changes in the explanatory variables

Changes in predicted probabilities	Council formation			
	Agriculture	*Environment*	*Justice and Home*	*Internal Market*
Qualified majority voting	0.379	0.119	0.340	0.366
EP involvement	−0.285	−0.218	−0.259	−0.230
Uncertainty	0.168	0.090	0.230	0.239
Salience	−0.810	−0.625	−0.829	−0.871
Variable settings:				
Preference divergence	5.09	3.55	2.75	2.33
Qualified majority voting	Yes	Yes	No	Yes
EP involvement	No	Yes	No	Yes
Committee meeting density	1.23	9.95	1.87	0.84
Uncertainty	No	Yes	No	Yes
Salience	7	14	12	12.5

Notes: The cell entries in the upper part of the table give the change (i.e. the first difference) in the predicted probability that a decision is made by a committee as a result of a change in an independent variable. I calculated the figures based on model 4 in Table 7.3. In the case of salience, the independent variable changes from 3 (5th percentile) to 30 (95th percentile) recitals. All other variables are dichotomous and change from the absence to the presence of the measured characteristic. I present effect sizes for different combinations of proposal characteristics that are typical for four Council formations. To generate 'typical' proposals, I set the continuous variables to their median values and the dichotomous variables to the value that is more common in a Council formation. I set all Council formation dummy variables to zero, except for the dummy variable concerning the formation for which I calculated the effects. In the lower part of the table, I give details on the precise values I set the other variables when calculating the effect of one of the independent variables.

86   *Part II: Quantitative analysis*

Summary and discussion

In the statistical analysis, I investigated the conditions under which legislative decisions are made by Council committee members rather than ministers. I used the theoretical perspectives on Council committee decision-making identified in Chapter 4 to guide the empirical analysis. An original data set of 439 legislative dossiers dealing with different policy matters formed the basis for the statistical inquiry. The analysis yielded mixed results. In the following, I briefly discuss these results and draw preliminary conclusions based on the quantitative analysis.

The empirical findings are not consistent with two of the theoretical arguments. The analysis gives no support to the notion that committee socialisation has an effect on whether or not a decision is made at the committee level in the Council. The rejection of the committee socialisation hypothesis does not necessarily mean that committee members do not share supranational norms and values or negotiate in a reciprocal and co-operative manner. But the rejection of the hypothesis does indicate that such co-operative negotiation behaviour is not a result of the direct socialisation in EU committees. In this respect, the finding is consistent with other recent research indicating that the direct socialising effects of international institutions are at best weak (Beyers 2005; Hooghe 2005). The results also indicate that preference divergence among Member States does not influence the level at which a decision is reached in the Council. This finding is somewhat surprising, given that ministers discuss only proposals on which no agreement can be found at lower levels in the Council hierarchy. Together with the large effect of salience identified in the analysis, this result might indicate that the importance Member States attach to an issue is of more relevance for explaining the internal working of the Council than the Member States' positions on the issue.

In accordance with the theoretical expectations, the findings indicate that the involvement of the EP in the co-decision procedure makes it more difficult to conclude negotiations at the committee level. Essentially, the involvement of the EP under the co-decision procedure adds an additional negotiation partner with veto power. The Member States have to take the views of the EP into account in order to pass legislation. Attempts of the Council and the EP to reach an early agreement during first reading have most likely a negative effect on reaching a decision at the committee level. Even if the institutions do not attempt a first-reading agreement, the Member States' anticipation of the future effects of the EP position on the outcome of subsequent inter-institutional negotiations could adversely affect the negotiations on a common position in Council committees.

Although the size of the voting rule effect depends on the inclusion of controls for different Council formations, the possibility of qualified majority voting seems to increase the probability of a committee decision. Existing accounts of Council decision-making give few indications that voting actually occurs at the committee level, but the sole prospect of a vote being taken by ministers seems to foster more compromising attitudes in committee negotiations. The analysis also identifies the expected effect of uncertainty about the practical consequences of legislative proposals. If a dossier demands more specialised knowledge to understand its consequences, the dossier is more likely to be decided at the committee level. Finally, the single most powerful predictor for committee decision-making is the salience of a dossier. Ministers can only devote a limited amount of time to Council decision-making. Thus, ministers focus their attention on the most sensitive proposals and leave less important dossiers for bureaucrats to decide.

In general, the results of the statistical analysis yield a rather favourable picture regarding the democratic legitimacy of Council decision-making. Although a considerable proportion of legislative decisions are indeed made by diplomats and national officials, the study finds no evidence that supports the view of government representatives 'going native' in Brussels as a result of participating in committee negotiations. Also, few commentators would argue against the merits of experts deciding on proposals that demand a good understanding of highly complex matters. Ministers have time constraints and cannot deal with each and every proposal personally. But the analysis demonstrates that the most important dossiers do not go through the Council machinery without the direct involvement of ministers. Thus, the quantitative analysis indicates that government ministers are more in control of Council decision-making than frequently suggested. In the next part of the study, I further investigate the validity of these findings through a number of detailed case studies.

Part III
Qualitative analysis

8 Methodological issues

In Part III of the book, I describe and compare six case studies of Council decision-making. Like the quantitative analysis, the case studies contribute to answer both the descriptive question about how many and the explanatory question of why certain issues are decided at the committee level. The research design allows for within-sector as well as between-sector comparisons. In each of the next three chapters, I describe two instances of legislative decision-making in a certain Council formation. Chapter 9 deals with the field of Agriculture, Chapter 10 with Environment and Chapter 11 with Economic and Financial Affairs. Every chapter ends with a within-sector comparison of the involvement of different Council levels and a discussion of the relevance of potential explanatory factors. In Chapter 12, I conclude the qualitative analysis with a summary of the results of the within-sector comparisons and an investigation of whether these results also hold up in a comparison across the different Council formations.

Before beginning with the case study descriptions, I discuss some methodological issues in this chapter. First, I outline the added value of case studies to the study of committee decision-making. Then I discuss whether 'nesting' a qualitative study within an earlier quantitative study is advisable. In particular, I discuss how far the empirical results of the quantitative study should factor into the case selection criteria of the qualitative analysis. Based on this discussion, I then present the case selection criteria and introduce the selected decision-making processes. Finally, I describe the methods used to collect the data and discuss the presentation of the results.

The complementarity of quantitative and qualitative research

The quantitative analysis of committee decision-making relied on whole proposals as the unit of analysis. The analysis only considered whether or not a committee agreed on all provisions contained in a proposal. But even if ministers discuss or reach the final decision on a dossier as a whole, many individual provisions in this dossier will have been decided by committees before. The quantitative analysis did not examine the relative number or the importance of those provisions.

92   Part III: Qualitative analysis

The case studies provide further insights in this respect. Thus, the consideration of specific provisions within a proposal is the main contribution of the case studies to answer the descriptive question about how many decisions committees make. In addition, the narrative form of qualitative case descriptions can illustrate how committees reach their decisions. Given the lack of systematic descriptions of committee negotiations in the Council, descriptions of the process through which committees reach agreements are also valuable contributions to the literature on Council decision-making.

However, the case descriptions are also useful for evaluating and developing theory. On the one hand, the plausibility of existing theories can be assessed by investigating the presence of the causal mechanisms posited by those theories. Statistical analyses only examine the co-variation between variables. The detailed analysis of individual cases is helpful for examining whether and how the change in an independent variable causes a change in the dependent variable. At the very least, case studies can be used as plausibility checks for the causal mechanisms suggested by the correlational results found in the statistical analysis. On the other hand, case studies can also positively contribute to theory development. Case studies are often of a rather exploratory nature. Usually, the goal of case study research is to explain the outcome of a case as comprehensively as possible rather than to test a specific theory. Case studies following this outcome-oriented approach are very useful for identifying hitherto neglected explanatory variables or for discovering complex causal structures such as equifinality or conjunctural causation. In this respect, case studies do not only serve as a plausibility check of statistical results, but also aid the development of more appropriate and sophisticated theories.

Advantages and disadvantages of a nested design

The case selection is based on both theoretical considerations as well as empirical results of the quantitative study in Chapter 7. No consensus exists in the literature on mixed-method research on how best to combine quantitative and qualitative research. With regard to qualitative follow-up studies of quantitative analyses, Lieberman (2005) distinguishes two possible combinations: if the statistical model fits the data well, the researcher should use case studies to further check the validity of the statistical results; if the model fits the data badly, the researcher should use case studies to improve the model specification. In the first situation, Lieberman (2005: 444) recommends to select cases with widely varying values on the central independent variables but well predicted outcome scores. This procedure allows for an investigation of the robustness of a particular causal argument across a wide range of values on the independent variables. In the second situation, Lieberman (2005: 445) suggests to select at least one case that is not well predicted by the statistical model. The study of cases with badly predicted outcomes is useful for identifying omitted variables and thus for improving the theoretical specification. Because the goal of these studies is to improve the explanation for the variation in the outcome, Lieberman (2005: 445) also stresses the need to select cases with widely varying values on the dependent variable.

Methodological issues 93

As Rohlfing (2008) demonstrates, the nesting of qualitative studies within quantitative studies generates a serious methodological and logical problem. If the researcher uses case selection criteria that are based on the results of a quantitative study, the researcher implicitly assumes that the results of the quantitative study are correct. However, if the results of the quantitative analysis are known to be correct, there is no need for further investigations through qualitative case studies. If doubts exist about the validity of the results of the quantitative analysis, any selection criteria whose calculation is based on the model estimates is as flawed as the model specification itself. Thus, using results of a badly specified statistical model as the basis for selecting cases in the qualitative part of the study is ill-advised. As a solution to this problem, Rohlfing (2008) proposes to discard the results of the quantitative analysis when the model appears to be misspecified and conduct a 'case study-based nested analysis' instead. This procedure reverses the 'nesting', starting with an exploratory small-N analysis to identify an empirically plausible model specification and proceeding to further analysis and diagnostic tests through large-N methods.

Although the quantitative analysis in Chapter 7 was guided by the relevant theoretical literature, my regression analysis was still largely empiricist in nature. In the statistical model, I assumed a linear additive relationship between the independent variable and the dependent variable. While the assumption of a linear additive relationship of the explanatory variables with the outcome variable has the virtue of simplicity, such a connection is not necessarily the most natural one to expect. Given that only little prior research exists that is directly related to committee decision-making in the Council, I might have omitted important explanatory variables as well. Similarly, the inclusion of variables in the model that are in fact irrelevant for explaining committee decision-making might also have distorted the results. Finally, some of the indicators I employed are probably only imperfect reflections of their underlying concepts.

Of course, none of the model diagnostics indicated the presence of non-linear relationships or other specification problems. I also based the selection of independent variables firmly on the theories presented in the existing literature. Model misspecification and unreliable measures are a potential problem for any type of regression analysis. In this respect, the quantitative study presented in Chapter 7 is not in any way exceptional. Indeed, the quantitative study constitutes an insightful initial analysis of committee decision-making in the Council. However, a reliance of further research on the full set of assumptions made in this analysis is neither needed nor advisable. At the same time, essentially discarding the results of the analysis in favour of a reversed nested analysis as suggested by Rohlfing (2008) is not useful either. Instead, I take an intermediate approach. Rather than selecting cases based on how well or how badly the statistical model predicts the value on the dependent variable, the case selection takes into account only the most robust empirical relationships discovered through the quantitative analysis. These relationships do not depend on the functional form of the model or the number and type of variables included in the specification. In this way, the qualitative study still builds on the results of the

94   *Part III: Qualitative analysis*

quantitative analysis, but only on those results that do not depend on possibly questionable modelling assumptions.

Case selection criteria

The salience of a proposal proved to be the single most important predictor of whether or not a Council decision was reached at the committee level. Indeed, a simple logistic regression of the Council decision-making level against the salience of an act results in a remarkably high model-fit statistic (i.e. a pseudo R-squared of 0.24). This simple model correctly predicts the outcome of three out of four cases (i.e. the count R-squared is 0.75).[1] Most importantly, the negative relationship between salience and committee decision-making is not only strong but also highly robust. The relationship is not sensitive to changes in the model specification. The finding is not affected by the inclusion or exclusion of other variables in the model or by some of the most common monotonic transformations of the functional form (i.e. logarithmic and exponential) of the relationship. In short, the negative effect of the salience of an act on the probability of a committee decision is what Achen (2002: 441) calls a 'reliable empirical generalisation'.

Slightly simplified, this empirical generalisation states that proposals of low salience are almost certainly decided by a committee, while proposals of high salience are almost certainly decided by ministers. Thus, in order to identify additional factors besides salience that influence the level of decision-making in the Council, we should either select proposals with a medium degree of salience or proposals that contradict this pattern. Proposals with a medium degree of salience are neither so unimportant that anything other than a committee decision would be surprising, nor so politicised that the involvement of ministers is necessarily expected. Proposals of low salience that were decided by ministers and proposals of high salience that were decided by committees yield even more leverage to identify additional explanatory factors affecting the level at which a decision is made in the Council. Therefore, a first criterion for the case selection is to choose cases that exhibited either a medium degree of salience or cases that were decided at an unexpected Council level given their degree of salience.

Another robust empirical result derived from the quantitative analysis concerns the wide variation in committee decision-making across different Council formations. Despite the inclusion of a number of substantially important explanatory variables with the potential to also tap cross-sector variation, significant differences between Council formations remained detectable. Thus, one main dimension of comparison in the case study analysis is cross-sectoral. Given limited resources, the case studies focus on three Council formations: Agriculture, Environment, and Economic and Financial Affairs. I selected

---

1 These results are based on the following logistic regression estimates (z-values in brackets): 1.79 (0.26) $-0.20 \times$ Salience (8.88).

these three formations because of the differences in their internal committee structures. In Agriculture, the SCA prepares the meetings of ministers and oversees the work of more than 100 working parties, most of which meet only occasionally.[2] The meetings of Environment ministers are prepared by the deputy permanent representatives in Coreper I. Coreper I in turn supervises the work of the two working parties in the field of Environment. The Working Party on International Environmental Issues deals with all external and the Working Party on the Environment with all internal measures of EU environmental policy. Finally, the permanent representatives in Coreper II prepare the meetings of Economic and Financial Affairs ministers. Coreper II also co-ordinates the work of the eight working parties in this Council formating

Assuring a large cross-sector variation in the committee structure of Council formations is useful for probing the generalisability of causal mechanisms identified through the within-sector comparisons. In contrast, the selection of proposals for the within-sector comparison aims at keeping as many proposal characteristics as possible constant within a certain policy sector. At the same time, the selection of cases within sectors should ensure variation on the value of the outcome variable. This procedure resembles Mill's Method of Difference. For each Council formation, I selected two proposals: one that was decided at the committee level and one that was discussed by ministers. Regarding the selection of proposals within Council formations, my goal was to match proposals on the following characteristics: the working party dealing with the proposal, the time at which the Council started negotiating, the legislative procedure, the voting rule, the type of legal instrument, and the status of the proposed legislative act. The status of a legislative act indicates whether the proposal suggests an amendment of existing or the creation of new legislation. In principle, if two cases with different values on the outcome variable differ only in one explanatory factor, then the outcome variable must be causally related to this explanatory factor. Of course, in practice, more than one potential explanatory factor varies across cases, no matter how well the cases are matched on possibly relevant characteristics. Thus, although a careful case selection can rule out many potential explanations, others must be examined through within-case methods such as process tracing and the method of congruence (George and Bennett 2005: 178–179).

In summary, the case selection procedure followed the following guidelines: select proposals as to minimise variation of proposal characteristics within Council formations and select Council formations as to maximise variation in committee structure characteristics. Finally, ensure that the proposals exhibit either a medium degree of salience or an unexpected value on the outcome variable given their degree of salience. Keeping many proposal characteristics within a Council formation constant makes it easier to identify further explanatory factors. The impact of additional explanatory factors should also be most visible in cases where the degree of salience of a proposal is contrary to expectations

---

2 The following figures about the number of working parties include subgroups, see Table 2.1.

Table 8.1 Characteristics of selected cases

Selected Council formations	Agriculture		Environment		Economic and Financial Affairs	
Sector characteristics						
Senior committee	SCA		Coreper I		Coreper II	
Number of working parties	Large		Small		Medium	
Selected proposals	Geographical Indications Regulation[a]	Leaf Tobacco Regulation[b]	Ambient Air Directive[c]	Batteries Directive[d]	Parent-Subsidiary Directive[e]	Mergers Directive[f]
Outcome variable						
Decision level	Committee	Ministers	Committee	Ministers	Ministers	Committee
Other characteristics						
Legislative significance	Medium (14)	Low (7)	Medium (14)	High (24)	Medium (12)	Medium (18)
Working party	Geographical Indications	Tobacco	Environment	Environment	Direct Taxation	Direct Taxation
Commission transmission date	Nov. 2001	Nov. 2001	July 2003	Nov. 2003	July 2003	Oct. 2003
Legislative procedure	Consultation	Consultation	Co-decision	Co-decision	Consultation	Consultation
Voting rule	QMV	QMV	QMV	QMV	Unanimity	Unanimity
Legal instrument	Regulation	Regulation	Directive	Directive	Directive	Directive
Status of act	Amendment	Amendment	New	New	Amendment	Amendment

Notes: SCA stands for Special Committee on Agriculture and Coreper for Committee of Permanent Representatives.

a Commission (2002): Proposal for a Council Regulation amending Regulation 2081/92/EEC of 14 July 1992 on the protection of geographical indications and designations of origin for agricultural products and foodstuffs. 15 March 2002, COM/2002/139.

b Commission (2001) Proposal for a Council Regulation fixing the premiums and guarantee thresholds for leaf tobacco by variety group and Member State for the 2002, 2003 and 2004 harvests and amending Regulation 2075/92/EEC. 21 November 2001, COM/2001/684.

c Commission (2003): Proposal for a Directive of the European Parliament and of the Council relating to arsenic, cadmium, mercury, nickel and polycyclic aromatic hydrocarbons in ambient air. 16 July 2003, COM/2003/423.

d Commission (2003): Proposal for a Directive of the European Parliament and of the Council on batteries and accumulators and spent batteries and accumulators. 21 November 2003, COM/2003/723.

e Commission (2003): Proposal for a Council Directive amending Directive 90/435/EEC on the common system of taxation applicable in the case of parent companies and subsidiaries of different Member States. 29 July 2003, COM/2003/462.

f Commission (2003): Proposal for a Council Directive amending Directive 90/434/EEC of 23 July 1990 on the common system of taxation applicable to mergers, divisions, transfers of assets and exchanges of shares concerning companies of different Member States. 17 October 2003, COM/2003/613.

given a certain Council decision-making level or where the degree of salience takes a medium value. I present the results of the selection procedure in Table 8.1.

Unfortunately, I could not match all the within-sector cases on all criteria. In particular, I could not identify two Agriculture proposals that were discussed by the same working party, were similar with respect to other characteristics, and exhibited variation on the dependent variable. The lack of similar Agriculture proposals is mainly due to the high specialisation of working parties in this area. Many Agriculture working parties discussed no or only one proposal during the time period considered. In the case where a working party discussed several proposals, the working party was either one of the few Agriculture working parties that reports to Coreper rather than the SCA, the proposals involved trivial dossiers, or the proposals belonged to a single policy package. In the end, I chose two Agriculture dossiers that are similar in all specified characteristics except for the working party dealing with the dossier. Given the level of salience, the Council decision-making level is exactly contrary to expectations. Thus, factors other than salience should have had a major influence on Council decision-making in these cases. Apart from slight differences in the dates of the transmission of the proposal from the Commission to the Council, I was able to match the proposals for the other Council formations on all specified characteristics. In the case of the Economic and Financial Affairs formation, the salience pattern also corresponds to the case selection guidelines. In the case of the Environment formation, the proposal decided by ministers unfortunately exhibits a relatively high degree of salience. This selection is again a result of a trade-off between different criteria. I could not identify another pair of proposals in the field of Environment that were so closely matched on all other selection criteria and exhibited the required salience pattern as well.

In terms of their content, the two proposals selected in the field of Economic and Financial Affairs, that is the Merger and the Parent-Subsidiary Directive, are most closely related. Both Directives deal with the taxation of cross-border financial transactions of companies within the single European market. The contents of the matched proposals in the other two Council formations are less similar. In the field of Environment, the Ambient Air Directive sets air quality standards and regulates the monitoring of hazardous substances in the air. In contrast, the Batteries Directive lays down provisions for the production, collection, and recycling of different types of batteries. In Agriculture, the Geographical Indications Regulation provides for the registration and protection of geographical names for food products whereas the Leaf Tobacco Regulation determines the amount of subsidies granted for tobacco producers. In general, the exceptions in the matching of case characteristics have to be taken into account when comparing the cases and drawing inferences.

Across sectors, the cases vary considerably in terms of their institutional features. With respect to the voting rule, qualified-majority voting was a possibility in the Agriculture and Environment cases. The unanimity rule applied only in the Economic and Financial Affairs Council formation. Regarding the legislative procedure, the consultation procedure was applicable in the Agriculture and the

98   Part III: Qualitative analysis

Economic and Financial Affairs cases, and the co-decision procedure in the Environment cases. Thus, the cases cover all empirically relevant configurations of the voting rule and the legislative procedure. Cases where the co-decision procedure applies together with the unanimity decision-rule in the Council are extremely rare in reality. The type and the status of the legal instruments also vary across sectors. In Agriculture, the legal instruments are Regulations; in the other two sectors, the legal instruments are Directives. The Regulations in Agriculture and the Directives in Economic and Financial Affairs amend existing laws, whereas the Directives in Environment constitute new European legislation. The fact that two sectors always exhibit one characteristic in common allows at least for some level of control in pair-wise comparisons of decision-making in different sectors.

Data sources and collection

Information on the different cases was drawn from three different sources: primary documents of the EU institutions, particularly of the Council, interviews with public officials who participated in the negotiations in the Council, and contemporary newspaper reports. In a first step, the relevant primary documents were examined. The Council's new transparency rules allow the public access to a wide variety of documents related to the Council's decision-making process. These documents include the legislative proposal of the Commission, agendas and progress reports of working parties and senior committees, Presidency compromise proposals, I/A-item and A-item notes, agendas and minutes of ministerial meetings as well as press releases summarising the outcomes of ministerial meetings. In some instances, room documents of varying content, which are distributed before or during meetings to aid the discussion, are also available. If possible, I downloaded the Council documents directly from the Council's public register of documents website.[3] If the register did not contain a document known to exist because it was mentioned in another document or the register denied access to a document, I obtained the documents through a formal request for access to Council documents.[4]

The examination of these documents allowed a relatively detailed reconstruction of the process as well as the content of Council discussions. Many of the Council documents contained cross-references to earlier or accompanying documents. The documents also referred to specific meetings with specified dates. The meeting agendas of Council bodies in turn mentioned the documents on which discussions were supposed to be based during the meeting. These cross-references

---

3 The Council's register of documents can be accessed online at: http://www.consilium.europa.eu/documents/access-to-council-documents-public-register.aspx (accessed 22 August 2011).

4 Requests for access to Council documents can be made online at: http://www.consilium.europa.eu/documents/access-to-council-documents-public-register/submit-a-request-for-access-to-council-documents.aspx?lang=en (accessed 22 August 2011).

made double-checking the completeness of the document record for a certain case possible. In instances where documents turned out to be missing, I filed a new request for access to these documents with the Council secretariat. Unless a document concerned a legal opinion, the Council Secretariat granted all these requests. Through the cross-references between documents, I could reconstruct the formal aspects of the negotiation process in considerable detail with a high degree of confidence in the accuracy and completeness of the description.

The reports of working parties and senior committees were particularly useful for examining the content of negotiations. These reports mention the issues contested during a meeting and usually also note the positions and demands of dissenting delegations. I could trace the progress of discussions by comparing the content of reports over time. In order to trace the developments on individual issues, I manually coded all documents with the aid of qualitative content analysis software. This procedure allowed the identification of contested issues, the timing at which an issue was first raised, the nature of the disagreement, the time and the Council level at which an issue was resolved as well as the final decision-making outcome in terms of policy substance.

Thus, the analysis of Council documents forms the backbone for the case narratives I present in the following chapters. Although these documents present a wealth of information about the negotiation process in the Council, they also have some shortcomings. First, the documents often lack information on developments happening before and between formal meetings. Second, in line with the Council's guidelines for producing documents, the reports also focus on those issues on which agreement is still outstanding after a meeting rather than on how committee members resolved issues during a meeting.[5] Third, the documents do not always state the reasons for objections by delegations.[6] Fourth, Council documents neglect much of the history of the proposal and the context of the decision-making process. Finally, some of the issues are technically complex and insufficiently explained in the documents.

For these reasons, I complemented the data from the document analysis with information gained from expert interviews and newspaper reports. The expert interviews were semi-structured in that they aimed at answering a similar core set of open questions for each case. However, I also used the interviews to supplement the information gained from the primary documents. I used them to fill gaps in the document trail and to ask for clarifications of technically complex matters. In general, the interviews mainly served the purpose of exploration and information-gathering. My goal was to interview representatives of the most central actors in the decision-making process. Beyers and Dierickx (1998: 299) found that the Commission, the Council Secretariat and the Presidency are the most central

---

5 Council (2003): Guide for producing documents for the Council and its preparatory bodies. N. d., SN 1430/03 Rev. 1.
6 The lack of reasons in a report is at least sometimes due to the fact that delegations simply did not give any reason for their position (Interview F).

100 Part III: Qualitative analysis

actors in the communication networks of working parties. Thus, I contacted representatives of these institutions who were involved in the Council negotiation process in the selected cases. If the proposal was decided through the co-decision procedure, I also approached a member of the EP delegation representing the Parliament's position in negotiations with the Council. This selection procedure resulted in 20 potential interview partners.

Unfortunately, I could not interview all of these experts. The selected decision-making processes all date back several years. Many potential interview partners had changed their job positions within Brussels or moved back to national administrations. Some of the organisational structures within the EU institutions had also changed in the meantime. As a result, I could not determine the current location and contact details of one of the selected interview partners. In addition, resource constraints restricted the possibilities to interview former EU officials in their home countries. I could not interview five of the seven experts who were not working in Brussels anymore. Four experts explicitly refused an interview. One of the experts who declined an interview mentioned confidentiality concerns, the others referred to their heavy workload. However, in other instances, not only one but several representatives of the same institution agreed to an interview. Overall, I conducted 14 interviews in May and June 2007: 11 in Brussels and another three in different EU countries. Four of the interview partners were able to provide information on two of the selected cases. In Table 8.2, I list the interview partners for each case.

Because of the low number of interviews related to some of the decision-making cases, I do not mention the institutional affiliation of respondents to ensure their anonymity. Overall, five interviewees represented the Commission in negotiations in Council committees, five other interviewees were part of the Presidency delegations chairing the meetings of these committees, one interviewee was part of an EP delegation and three interviewees were affiliated with the Council's General Secretariat. Table 8.2 shows that the number of interviews per case varies quite considerably. I was able to conduct at least one interview for each case. The reliance on only one interview for the cases in Agriculture is somewhat unfortunate. However, the more comprehensive press coverage of policy-making in this policy area compensates to a large extent for any lack of information gained from interviews. In contrast to the other policy areas considered, news reports about Council negotiations in the field of Agriculture contain quite detailed accounts of the state of play of negotiations and the different views of Member States even when the dossier is still under discussion at committee level.

In general, I used newspaper reports as a third source of information for the case studies to complement the information gained from the primary documents and the expert interviews. The newspaper reports were particularly valuable for obtaining some insights into the broader context of the decision-making process at the time. I used the Factiva database as source for the news reports. The Factiva database provides access to the full-text of thousands of news sources, including

Table 8.2 List of case study interviews

Case and interviewee	Interview date
Geographical Indications Regulation	
Interview A	Brussels, 14 May 2007
Leaf Tobacco Regulation	
Interview B	Brussels, 15 June 2007
Ambient Air Directive	
Interview C	Brussels, 18 June 2007
Interview D	Member State, 8 June 2007
Batteries Directive	
Interview E	Brussels, 18 June 2007
Interview F	Brussels, 15 May 2007
Interview G	Brussels, 14 May 2007
Interview H	Member State, 1 June 2007
Mergers Directive	
Interview J	Brussels, 13 June 2007
Interview K	Brussels, 13 June 2007
Interview L	Brussels, 21 June 2007
Interview M	Brussels, 21 June 2007
Interview N	Brussels, 13 June 2007
Interview O	Member State, 4 June 2007
Parent-Subsidiary Directive	
Interview J	Brussels, 13 June 2007
Interview K	Brussels, 13 June 2007
Interview L	Brussels, 21 June 2007
Interview M	Brussels, 21 June 2007

key newswires and many internationally renowned newspapers.[7] The database also covers the major news providers specialising in EU politics, such as Agence Europe, European Voice and Europolitics. For each of the decision-making cases, I performed an English-language search in the database. I chose the search terms as to maximise the comprehensiveness of the search results rather than their precision. I restricted the time coverage to the period starting a month before the transmission of the Commission proposal and ending a month after the Council decision. In a second step, the articles produced by the search were manually screened for their relevance.

I used the information gained from primary documents, interviews and newspaper reports to reconstruct in detail the negotiation process in the six Council decision-making cases. The presentation of the qualitative analysis is divided into three chapters according to policy area. In each chapter, I begin by briefly describing the background and history of EU policy-making in the policy area and by outlining the organisational structure of the Council formation. Subsequently,

7 A description of the database can be found at http://www.dowjones.com/factiva/ (accessed 22 August 2011).

102 *Part III: Qualitative analysis*

I present the negotiation process on each of the two dossiers in the policy area. In line with the exploratory character of the study, I describe each negotiation process chronologically. The chronological approach results in comprehensive narratives that form the base for the comparative analyses. Only such relatively detailed narratives provide the reader with the necessary data to judge the validity of the inferences drawn from the case studies. At the end of each policy chapter, I discuss the applicability of potential explanatory factors through a within-sector comparison. The within-sector comparisons allow only for limited examinations of factors that are constant within sectors. Thus, the qualitative analysis concludes with a chapter containing an inter-sectoral comparison of Council decision-making. In this chapter, I pay special attention to factors that vary only across Council formations.

9 Agriculture

The Agricultural policy field stands out for at least two reasons. First, Agriculture is one of the oldest policy fields regulated at the EU level. National approaches were integrated into the Common Agricultural Policy (CAP) already in the late 1950s and early 1960s. Second, the CAP was the largest expenditure item in the EU budget for a long time and is still one of the main spending areas even after recent reforms. Thus, decision-making on Agricultural policy is a major arena for explicitly distributive conflicts. Third, Agriculture is the internal policy area most intensely affected by European regulation (Nugent 2006: 388).

The intensity of European regulation in the field of Agriculture is also reflected in the organisation and the frequency of meetings of Council bodies in this area. Agriculture ministers meet almost every month. In addition, agriculture ministers have their own exclusive preparatory body, the SCA. Member States established the SCA in 1960 to relieve Coreper from the increasing workload generated by the establishment of the CAP. The SCA meets weekly and consists of senior officials from national Agriculture ministries, usually posted temporally to Member States' permanent representations. Besides Coreper, the SCA is the only preparatory body with a prerogative to put items directly on the agenda of ministers. However, the SCA does not have the exclusive right to prepare the meetings of Agriculture ministers. Coreper I prepares all agenda items for Agriculture ministers related to food safety and animal welfare issues. The working party system in Agriculture is also somewhat particular. With over 100 groups, the Agriculture Council formation includes by far the most working parties (see Table 2.1). Not surprisingly, most of these working parties are highly specialised. Many of them deal only with a specific group of agricultural products. The Agriculture working parties meet only irregularly. The groups usually consist of officials from national Agriculture ministries travelling to Brussels especially for the meetings.

In the remainder of this chapter, I describe and analyse the process leading to the adoption of two Council Regulations in the field of Agriculture. The first Regulation amended the existing European provisions on the protection of geographical indications for agricultural products. The second Regulation amended

104   *Part III: Qualitative analysis*

aspects of the organisation of the market in raw tobacco and set new premiums and guarantee-thresholds for the subsidisation of raw tobacco production. As was typical for decision-making in Agriculture, the Council passed the acts through the consultation procedure.[1] The Council decision-rule allowed for the adoption of the proposals by a qualified majority of Member States. In the case of the Leaf tobacco Regulation, the Working Party on Tobacco discussed the dossier. In the case of the Geographical Indications Regulation, the Working Party on Foodstuff Quality (Geographical Indications and Designations of Origin) was responsible.

One reason for the selection of the Geographical Indications Regulation was the absence of any minister involvement despite a moderately high salience level. The case constituted a good comparison case for the Leaf Tobacco Regulation, which exhibited a rather low value on the salience variable but was nevertheless decided by ministers. Unfortunately, the case study research revealed that ministers in fact also discussed the Geographical Indications Regulation. However, ministers did not make any specific decisions. Thus, actual ministerial influence was minimal. Committee members still made the final Council decision on all issues. In addition, comparisons can still be made at the level of individual issues within a proposal, even if the lack of variance does not allow comparisons at the level of proposals as a whole. Ministers discussed only a subset of conflictual points contained in a proposal. Thus, we can still investigate why ministers discussed certain conflictual issues while others were completely handled at lower Council levels. The lack of variation of the dependent variable at the proposal level is unfortunate but does not completely exclude an examination of possible explanations for committee decision-making in these cases.

Geographical Indications Regulation

Background and proposal content

The proposal amends a Regulation on the protection of geographical indications and designations of origin for agricultural products and foodstuffs, which the Council had adopted in 1992.[2] The original Regulation established legally binding provisions for the protection of geographical names of agricultural products. The new rules harmonised the protection of geographical names for all food products other than wines and spirits. Wine and spirits were already covered by other Community legislation. The Regulation gave producers and processors the opportunity to register geographical names at the Community level. Under the provisions of the Regulation, only undertakings that are actually active in the area carrying a registered name have the right to use the name for their products.

---

1 The Lisbon Treaty amendments have introduced the ordinary legislative procedure, formerly called co-decision, in the area of Agriculture.
2 Proposal for a Council Regulation amending Regulation 2081/92/EEC of 14 July 1992 on the protection of geographical indications and designations of origin for agricultural products and foodstuffs, 15 March 2002, COM/2002/139.

Agriculture 105

A major aim of the Regulation is to protect producers and consumers from practices and imitations that misuse geographical names.[3]

Several cases pending before the European Court of Justice underlined the importance of these provisions for producers of agricultural products. Member States as well as individual companies contested the exclusive right of foreign companies to use certain product names. In one instance, Denmark sued the Commission because the Commission granted Greece an exclusive right to produce Feta cheese.[4] In an earlier ruling in 1999, the Court had decided in favour of Denmark, but the Commission had sidestepped this decision by introducing new implementing legislation through the Comitology procedure.[5] In another case, Italian companies disputed the right of a British supermarket chain to slice and package Parma ham outside the Italian Parma region and the right of a French company to grate imported Parmesan cheese before selling it on the French market. The issue of protecting geographical indications also involved an international dimension. At the same time as the Council discussed the new proposal amending the Geographical Indications Regulation, the EU was promoting the worldwide protection of geographical product names through the establishment of a global registry in the framework of the Trade-Related International Property Rights (TRIPS) agreement of the World Trade Organisation (WTO).[6] Some less developed Asian and African countries co-sponsored such a registry, but especially the United States and Australia opposed the protection of geographical indications.[7] The United States and Australia are both large export countries of agricultural products. They challenged the EU Regulation on grounds that it discriminated against non-EU producers and therefore violated WTO rules.[8] The new Commission proposal included some amendments designed to alleviate such concerns.

The proposal amending the Geographical Indications Regulation did not challenge the general goal and approach of the original Regulation, but nevertheless suggested significant changes to the content of the legislation. More specifically, the Commission proposed the following changes to the original text of the Regulation:[9]

3 Commission (2002): Proposal for a Council Regulation amending Regulation 2081/92/EEC of 14 July 1992 on the protection of geographical indications and designations of origin for agricultural products and foodstuffs, 15 March 2002, COM/2002/139, pp. 2-4.

4 Smith, Jeremy (2003): EU's top court to rule May 20 on Parma food cases. 30 April 2003, Reuters News.

5 European Report (2002): Agriculture: One deal on table for final Spanish Presidency Farm Council. 26 June 2002; Dow Jones International News (2002): Denmark sues EU Commission over Greek Feta cheese ruling. 23 December 2002.

6 European Report (2002): EU/WTO: Union bids to extend trademark protection. 26 June 2002.

7 *Food and Drink Weekly* (2002): EU moves to protect geographic indications of food products. 1 July 2002.

8 Buck, Tobias, and Guy de Jonquieres (2003): Name-calling over Europe's delicacies. *Financial Times,* 5 May 2003.

9 Commission (2002): Proposal for a Council Regulation amending Regulation 2081/92/EEC of 14 July 1992 on the protection of geographical indications and designations of origin for agricultural products and foodstuffs. 15 March 2002, COM/2002/139.

106 *Part III: Qualitative analysis*

- The inclusion of wine vinegar in the scope of the Regulation.
- The exclusion of mineral and spring waters from the scope of the Regulation and the removal of already registered names related to such products from the register.
- The adoption of provisions on how to deal with identical names that designate different regions or places (so-called homonyms).
- The extension of the procedure regulating objections to applications for product name registrations to nationals of all WTO member countries.
- The adoption of provisions allowing for and regulating the cancellation of the product name registration by the original applicant.
- The extension of the Community application procedure for registering product names to products originating from non-EU countries.
- The abolishment of the simplified procedure used to grant Community status to names already protected in Member States.
- Change of the version of standard EN 45011 applicable to inspection bodies from the specific version mentioned in the original Regulation to a general reference to the 'latest' version of the standard.

Among the proposed changes, the only amendment that did not stir controversy among Member States during Council negotiations was the inclusion of wine vinegar in the scope of the Regulation. Neither the original Regulation nor the corresponding wine and spirits legislation covered wine vinegar. Thus, the inclusion of this product in the scope of the Regulation merely filled a gap in the existing product name protection provisions. Although several of the remaining amendments seem to be of a rather technical nature as well, all of them raised objections by one or more Member States during Council negotiations.

Negotiation process

The adoption process of the proposal amending the Geographical Indications Regulation took well over a year (see Table 9.1). The long duration of the process is quite remarkable, given the relatively limited scope of the proposal, the possibility to adopt the proposal by a qualified majority in the Council and the lack of veto power by the Parliament. Furthermore, the duration of the actual negotiation process, as measured from the day of the first Council meeting in which the dossier was discussed to the day on which the Council de facto reached an agreement, overlaps almost completely with the formal adoption process. Negotiations in the Council started just ten days after the transmission of the proposal by the Commission and the Council formally adopted the law just a week after the informal agreement. Further below, other case descriptions show that this close correspondence between the adoption and the actual negotiation process cannot be taken for granted.

In Figure 9.1, I illustrate the involvement of different Council bodies over time. The SCA conducted a large part of the negotiations. After the reception of the proposal, the SCA decided about how and by which working party the dossier will be handled. Subsequently, the SCA met seven times to discuss the dossier. The

Agriculture 107

Table 9.1 Geographical Indications Regulation: main decision-making events

Date	Collective actor	Event
15-03-2002	Commission	Adoption of proposal
15-03-2002	Commission	Transmission to Council and EP
25-03-2002	SCA	Decision about procedure
09-04-2002	WP	First reading of proposal
15-04-2002	SCA	Discussion of WP report
07-05-2002	WP	Discussion of WP report
21-05-2002	SCA	Discussion of WP report
27-05-2002	Agriculture Council (B-item)	Policy debate
31-05-2002	SCA	Discussion of SCA report
17-06-2002	SCA	Discussion of SCA report and Presidency proposal
18-07-2002	WP	Discussion of SCA report and Presidency proposal
05-12-2002	EP	Adoption of opinion
05-12-2002	Commission	Partial agreement on EP amendments
13-01-2003	SCA	Discussion of WP report
25-03-2003	SCA	Discussion of WP report
31-03-2003	SCA	Discussion of SCA report, de facto adoption of Regulation
08-04-2003	Agriculture and Fisheries Council (A-item)	Formal adoption of Regulation

Notes: EP = European Parliament, SCA = Special Committee on Agriculture, WP = Working party.

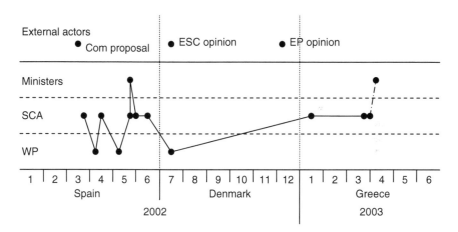

Figure 9.1 Geographical Indications Regulation: negotiation process.
Source: Data based on an analysis of Council documents.
Note: SCA = Special Committee on Agriculture, WP = Working Party.

Working Party on Foodstuff Quality (Geographical Indications and Designations of Origin) discussed the proposal three times, too. After each meeting, the working party reported back to the SCA about the progress made. The ministers discussed

108 Part III: Qualitative analysis

the proposal only once in the form of a general policy debate. But SCA members eventually reached the actual agreement. The Agriculture ministers then formally adopted the dossier through the A-point procedure.

The Commission adopted and transferred the proposal to the EP and the Council on 15 March 2003. Ten days later the SCA decided that the Working Party on Geographical Indications should first examine the dossier. The working party had its first reading on 9 April. Although the general reactions of delegations to the proposal were positive, the working party members identified a number of problematic issues during the meeting. One major point of controversy concerned the products covered by the Regulation. Mainly for practical reasons, the Commission proposed to exclude mineral and spring waters from the scope of the Regulation. Mineral and spring waters already registered would lose their protected status after a transition period of five years. The Commission argued that it was overwhelmed with applications for registering such products but that, at the same time, most names in question were not suitable for registration. In addition, the Commission claimed that other Community legislation already protected these products.[10] Germany doubted that other existing legislation adequately protected mineral and spring waters and strongly opposed their exclusion from the scope of the Regulation.[11] A large part of the mineral and spring waters registered under the existing provision were of German origin.[12] Thus, the exclusion of these products would have affected mostly German producers. To support specific regional industries, the French and Portuguese delegations felt that various additional products should be covered by the legislation. The French delegation asked for the inclusion of mustard paste and pasta and the Portuguese for the inclusion of wool fibres and wicker. Both countries insisted on the inclusion of sea salt. Similarly, Italy demanded that spirituous beverages should be covered.

Another contested point concerned the co-existence of protected geographical names and identical names traditionally in use but not covered by the scope of the Regulation.[13] The Commission proposal outlined several conditions to be met for the co-existence of a protected name and an identical non-registered name. These conditions formed the basis for the Commission decision to allow the use of the unregistered name. Even if the unregistered traditional name satisfied all the conditions for co-existence, the proposal suggested limiting the use of the unregistered name to at most 15 years. Member States questioned several aspects of these provisions. Delegations were most unhappy about the maximum time

---

10 Commission (2002): Proposal for a Council Regulation amending Regulation 2081/92/EEC of 14 July 1992 on the protection of geographical indications and designations of origin for agricultural products and foodstuffs. 15 March 2002, COM/2002/139, p. 2.

11 Council (2002): Report of the meeting on 9 April 2002 of the Working Party on Foodstuff Quality (Geographical Indications and Designations of Origin). 15 April 2002, 7779/02, p. 2.

12 European Report (2003): Food products: Designation of origin deal looming up. 11 January 2003.

13 Council (2002): Report on the meeting on 9 April 2002 of the Working Party on Foodstuff Quality (Geographical Indications and Designations of Origin), 10 April 2002, 7779/02, p. 4.

period for co-existence. Eight delegations (AT, BE, DE, IE, LU, NL, SE, UK) judged the 15-year limit as too short. But some delegations (AT, BE, DE, IE) also considered the criteria for co-existence to be too strict. Particularly the 25-year period of legal use of the unregistered name prior to the entry into force of the original Regulation in 1992 sparked opposition.

In principle, the Member States welcomed the introduction of provisions allowing the cancellation of the registration of names. However, the working party members agreed changes to clarify the obligation of the country requesting the cancellation. The change resulted in a clear requirement for Member States to evaluate applications for the cancellation of registrations before transmitting the applications to the Commission. In this context, Germany called for the inclusion of Community-wide standards for evaluating applications. The Commission and several delegations (BE, FR, NL, SE) argued against the need for such criteria. Another contested aspect concerned the entities and persons permitted to apply for the cancellation of registered names. Greece, Italy and Spain argued that, given the time that could elapse between the original application and a possible need to cancel the registration, any concerned person and not only the original applicant should be permitted to apply for the cancellation of a registered name. The United Kingdom suggested that the Member State concerned should also have the possibility to apply on its own initiative.

Most Member States accepted the extension of the provisions of the Regulation to products and residents of WTO member countries. Only Denmark opposed the inclusion of those amendments, preferring to await the outcome of the ongoing WTO negotiations on the TRIPS agreement before including such provisions in Community legislation. Denmark was particularly concerned about granting third countries the right to object to the registration of a name in the EU.[14] Denmark also doubted the sufficiency of Article 36 of the Treaty establishing the European Community (TEC) as a legal base for the proposal. As the extension of the Regulation to WTO member countries is an obligation resulting from international agreements, Denmark proposed a Common Commercial Policy treaty article (Article 133 TEC) as an additional legal base.

At the end of the first working party meeting, the Spanish Presidency concluded that the proposal required more detailed technical examination at the working party level. In the meantime, the Presidency would present a progress report to the SCA.[15] The SCA discussed the progress report of the working party at a meeting six days later on 15 April. With new instructions given by the SCA, the working party resumed its discussion of the dossier on 7 May. The Presidency made a proposal to redraft the provisions relating to homonyms to clarify their practical implementation.

---

14 European Report (2002): Farm Council: Decision on potato starch likely in short meeting on May 27. 25 May 2002.

15 Council (2002): Report of the meeting on 9 April 2002 of the Working Party on Foodstuff Quality (Geographical Indications and Designations of Origin), 10 April 2002, 7779/02, p. 7.

110   *Part III: Qualitative analysis*

During the course of the meeting, delegations agreed that not only the original applicant, but any legal or natural person with a legitimate interest should be able to apply for the cancellation of a registration. The UK delegation had requested that states should also be able to apply for cancellation on their own initiative, but other working party members did not support this suggestion. In the first meeting of the working party, the German delegation had asked for common criteria for Member States to evaluate applications for the cancellation of registrations. The German request had been opposed by several delegations as well as the Commission and was not repeated in subsequent sessions of the working party. The working party meeting did not result in much progress on the remaining issues. Thus, Member States still disagreed on the scope of the Regulation, the rules governing the co-existence of identical names, the extension of the provisions to third countries, and the legal base.

On 21 May, the SCA dealt with the proposal for the third time. By that time, Italy had dropped its demand for the inclusion of spirituous beverages in the scope of the Regulation. Regarding the other aspects related to the scope of the Regulation, Germany still fought the exclusion of mineral and spring waters. The German delegation stressed that the transition period of five years was far too short. The Commission stood by its initial position, but signalled that it was willing to compromise on the length of the transition period.[16] The Commission opposed the request of France and Portugal to include sea salt in the scope of the Regulation. The Commission argued that sea salt was not an agricultural product or foodstuff. The SCA agreed to consult the Council's legal service on the question of whether the legal base of the proposal would allow the inclusion of sea salt in the scope of the legislation. However, the Commission promised to consider the demands by Portugal and France to include wool fibre and wicker as well as mustard paste and pasta in the scope of the Regulation.

Again, the SCA made no progress on the rules governing the co-existence of registered and non-registered names. Delegations simply reiterated their earlier positions. The Commission defended its strict criteria for the co-existence of identical registered and non-registered names by pointing out that the right to the exclusive use of a registered name was the basic principle underlying the Regulation and that this right should not be undermined. The French delegation supported the Commission's position. Regarding the extension of the provisions of the original Regulation to third countries, the Commission gave an extensive explanation of the impact of the TRIPS agreement on the Regulation. This explanation convinced all delegations except Denmark about the benefits of adopting the proposal amending the Geographical Indications Regulation. Denmark insisted that it was preferable to wait for the outcome of the TRIPS negotiations before amending Community legislation. However, Denmark did not reiterate its related demand for an additional Common Commercial Policy treaty base. The

---

16 Council (2002): Outcome of proceedings of the meeting on 21 May 2002 of the Special Committee on Agriculture. 21 May 2002, 8906/02, p. 2.

Agriculture 111

UK repeated its request to allow Member States to apply for the cancellation of a registered name on their own initiative, but still none of the other delegations supported the request. The SCA provided a report on the proceedings of negotiations in the preparatory bodies for the Agriculture Council on 27 May.[17] The ministers were pleased with the reported progress and asked the SCA 'to press on with its work' so that the matter could be concluded after the EP submitted its opinion.[18] The ministers did not give any specific impetus or direction to the negotiation.

Following the meeting of ministers on 27 May, the SCA discussed the proposal again on 31 May and 17 June, before referring the proposal back to the working party. The next working party meeting took place on 18 July and was the only meeting chaired by the Danish Presidency. By that time, several delegations had dropped objections to certain provisions. For example, the United Kingdom did not ask for the possibility of Member States applying for the cancellation of registration anymore. After receiving the opinion of the Council's legal service, Denmark also no longer insisted on Article 133 as an additional legal base.

Regarding the remaining points, differences in opinion could not be completely resolved. Germany indicated that it would be able to accept a 25-year transition period for the exclusion of mineral and spring waters if the provision would not only apply to already registered names but also to names who are still in the process of being registered. The Commission again indicated its willingness to compromise on the length of the transition period. No change in positions occurred with respect to the demands made by France and Portugal for the inclusion of several other products. However, the two countries noted the opinion of the Council's legal service, which supported the Commission opinion that sea salt was not included in the treaty definition of agricultural products.

With regard to the co-existence rules, Germany and Ireland still disputed the maximum time period for co-existence proposed by the Commission. Ireland opposed any limitation of the time period for co-existence. Germany, supported by Austria, made a compromise proposal. Germany suggested that it would be able to accept a 25-year co-existence period in exchange for less strict requirements that traditional non-registered names have to fulfil to qualify for the co-existence provision. The Commission retained its position, arguing that only limited use should be made of the co-existence possibility. Given the stalemate on this point, several Member States (FR, ES, PT) questioned the value of a general co-existence clause and pointed out that it might be more useful to find a specific solution for the problem of Munster cheese.[19] Munster cheese was produced in

---

17 Council (2002): Outcome of proceedings of the meeting on 21 May 2002 of the Special Committee on Agriculture, 21 May 2002, 8906/02 + Add. 1.
18 Council (2002): Draft minutes of the 2428th meeting on 27 May 2002 of the Council (Agriculture), 9 July 2002, 9251/02, p. 5.
19 Council (2002): Report of the meeting on 18 July 2002 of the Working Party on Foodstuff Quality (Geographical Indications and Designations of Origin). 5 September 2002, 11156/02.

112 Part III: Qualitative analysis

Germany as well as Ireland and both countries wanted to retain the label. The change in the positions of a number of delegations should be noted here. At the start of negotiations, Belgium, Luxembourg, the Netherlands, Sweden and the UK had also supported a longer co-existence time period. However, at this stage, these delegations were apparently able to accept the Commission provisions. No changes occurred with respect to the remaining issues. Denmark still demanded to wait for the outcome of the TRIPS negotiations before deciding on the dossier.

Overall, nine out of the original 19 issues and sub-issues had been resolved by July 2002. However, the Member States had not settled any of the more serious disagreements. The Danish Presidency did not continue negotiations, either because of an obvious lack of interest to get the Regulation adopted or because the EP did not deliver its opinion until 5 December, just before the end of the Danish Presidency. The Greek Presidency took up the negotiations again at the beginning of 2003. The first SCA meeting under the chairmanship of Greece on 13 January 2003 was characterised by deadlock. Germany and Ireland still insisted on a longer transition period for the co-existence of identical names. Ireland even called for the deletion of the co-existence time limit. The Commission refused this request categorically. Based on the opinion of the Council legal service, the Commission also rejected the inclusion of sea salt in the scope of the Regulation. The legal service had argued that the inclusion of sea salt would require an amendment of the list of products regulated by the CAP as contained in annex 1 to the TEC.[20] Italy introduced another demand in response to newly erupted disputes of Italian producers with foreign companies about the packaging of registered products outside the region in which they were produced. Italy requested to allow regional producers to include the packaging within the region as part of the specification requirements of a registered product.[21] France, Spain and Portugal supported the Italian request.

The discussions during the next SCA meeting of 25 March resulted in a new compromise proposal by the Presidency. The SCA accepted this proposal in its meeting on 31 March. Regarding the scope of the Regulation, the committee accepted France's proposal to include mustard paste and pasta and Portugal's proposal to include wool fibres and wicker. Both delegations had also demanded the inclusion of salt in the scope of the legislation, but this request was not met. Interestingly, the SCA also incorporated several additional products suggested in the EP's opinion in the list of types of products covered by the Regulation. As proposed by the Commission but strongly opposed by Germany, the SCA decided to exclude mineral and spring waters from the Regulation's coverage. However, the Commission agreed to extend the transition period for already registered mineral and spring waters from five to ten years. Furthermore, the transition

---

20 Europe Agri (2003): Council debate on designations of origin bogged down. 31 January 2003.
21 European Report (2003): Council close to agreement on registered designations of origin. 2 April 2003.

period applies not only to already registered names, but also to names that are in the process of being registered.

The SCA also agreed to change the provisions on product specifications to allow for the possibility of requiring that a certain product is not only produced but also packaged in a region. This change was a direct result of demands by France, Spain, Portugal and particularly Italy. The SCA extended the application and objection procedures of the Regulation to also cover products of WTO countries, despite the objections of the Danish delegation. In a similar vein, the committee adopted the rules governing the co-existence of a registered name and an identical non-registered geographical name as proposed by the Commission, although several aspects of these rules were contested by a number of delegations. Particularly Germany and Ireland had been strongly opposed to the time limit set for the co-existence of identical product names. In the end, the SCA accepted the compromise proposal by a qualified majority of Member States. Denmark opposed the decision and the United Kingdom abstained. Officially, the two countries did not support the adoption of the proposal because they were opposed to extending the provisions of the Regulation to WTO countries before the TRIPS negotiations were finalised.[22] However, the newly adopted provision allowing for the inclusion of packaging within the region as a specification requirement for protected products was a direct result of an ongoing legal battle between the British supermarket chain Asda and Italian Parma ham producers. Asda was selling Parma ham which was imported from the Italian Parma region but sliced and packaged in the UK. Similarly, Denmark opposed the Regulation in general, since the Commission had ruled that Danish cheese producers could not call their goat cheese 'Feta' anymore. Thus, domestic pressures might have also affected the decision of the two governments to not support the new Regulation. In any case, ministers of the Agriculture and Fisheries Council formally adopted the legislative act without discussion on 8 April.

Leaf Tobacco Regulation

Background and proposal content

The proposal amending the Leaf Tobacco Regulation suggested premiums and guarantee-thresholds for leaf tobacco by variety group and Member State for the years 2002, 2003 and 2004. The proposal also included amendments of some provisions of the common organisation of the market in tobacco.[23] In May 2001, the Commission published a Communication on an EU strategy for sustainable development. In this Communication, the Commission committed itself to the adaptation of the CAP tobacco regime 'to reward healthy, high quality products

---

22 Agence Europe (2003): Council adopts new rules to protect geographic indications and appellations. 9 April 2003, Brussels.

23 Council Regulation 2075/92/EEC of 30 June 1992 on the Common Organisation of the Market in Raw Tobacco. 30 July 1992, OJ L215, p. 70.

114 *Part III: Qualitative analysis*

and practices rather than quantity'.[24] The Commission intended to introduce new legislation to fundamentally restructure the regime on the basis of an evaluation study, allowing for the phasing-out of tobacco subsidies and replacing them by measures to develop alternative sources of income for tobacco growers. As the Commission did not expect any results of the evaluation study before late 2002, the Commission could not initiate such legislation before early 2003. Thus, the proposal considered in this study constituted an interim solution to secure the continued operation of the raw tobacco regime for another three harvests until the Council could make a more fundamental decision on its reorientation. The main changes that the proposal suggested can be summarised as follows:

- Changes in the size of the premiums for the years 2002 to 2004.
- Changes in the size of the guarantee thresholds for the years 2002 to 2004.
- Extending the applicability of the auction system.
- Abolishing the national tobacco quota reserves.
- Changes to the activities funded by the Community Tobacco Fund.
- Increases in the size of the premium deductions used to finance the Community Tobacco Fund.

As in the previous case, Member States had diverging views on all of these issues. In addition, the medium- to long-term goal of abolishing tobacco subsidies became a highly contested topic. The Commission proposal included recitals referring to the 'new priority' of phasing-out tobacco subsidies and replacing them by measures to develop alternative means of employment and economic activity.[25] These purely programmatic statements proved to be major obstacles for reaching an agreement in the Council.

Negotiation process

The adoption process of the proposal amending the Leaf Tobacco Regulation shows some similarities with the adoption process of the proposal amending the Geographical Indications Regulation. In both cases, the formal adoption process is not much longer than the actual negotiation process (see Table 9.2). Furthermore, the SCA also dominated the negotiation process within the Council, just as in the case of the Geographical Indications Regulation (see Figure 9.2). The Working Party on Tobacco discussed the dossier only once at the beginning of Council negotiations. In contrast, the SCA dealt with the dossier on five occasions. Also

---

24 Commission (2001): A Sustainable Europe for a Better World: A European Union Strategy for Sustainable Development. 15 May 2001, COM/2001/264, p. 11.

25 See recital 5 and the reference in recital 6 of Commission (2001) Proposal for a Council Regulation fixing the premiums and guarantee thresholds for leaf tobacco by variety group and Member State for the 2002, 2003 and 2004 harvests and amending Regulation 2075/92/EEC. 21 November 2001, COM/2001/684.

Table 9.2 Leaf Tobacco Regulation: main decision-making events

Date	Collective actor	Event
21-11-2001	Commission	Adoption of proposal
22-11-2001	Commission	Transmission to Council and EP
04-12-2001	SCA	Decision on procedure
13-12-2001	WP	First reading of proposal
04-02-2002	SCA	Discussion of WP report
18-02-2002	Agriculture Council (B-item)	Policy debate
04-03-2002	SCA	Discussion of SCA report
12-03-2002	SCA	Discussion of SCA report
14-03-2002	EP	Adoption of opinion
14-03-2002	Commission	Refusal of EP amendments
19-03-2002	Agriculture Council (B-item)	Discussion of SCA report, political agreement on Regulation
25-03-2002	SCA	Finalisation of legal text
25-03-2002	Transport and Telecommunications Council (A-item)	Formal adoption of Regulation

Notes: EP = European Parliament, SCA = Special Committee on Agriculture, WP = Working party.

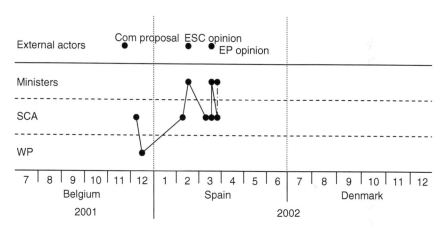

Figure 9.2 Leaf Tobacco Regulation: negotiation process.

Source: Data based on an analysis of Council documents.

Note: SCA = Special Committee on Agriculture, WP = Working Party.

similar to the Geographical Indications Regulation, ministers held a policy debate on the proposal relatively early during the negotiation process. However, the process also shows some marked differences. First, the whole adoption process took less than four months, almost nine months less than the adoption of the proposal amending the Geographical Indications Regulation. Second, ministers did not only hold a general policy debate on the proposal as in the case of the Geographical Indications Regulation, but actively negotiated the final agreement.

116 *Part III: Qualitative analysis*

The Commission adopted the proposal on 21 November 2001 and transmitted it to the Council on the following day. About two weeks later, on 4 December, the SCA decided that the relevant working party should first examine the dossier. Shortly afterwards, on 13 December, the Working Party on Tobacco discussed the dossier. The working party members identified already most of the contested issues in this meeting.[26] A major point of disagreement was the goal of eventually abolishing tobacco subsidies. A number of delegations (AT, BE, FR, EL, IT, ES, PT) demanded the deletion of the recital referring to this goal. This group included all tobacco-producing countries except Germany.[27] Several other delegations (DK, FI, DE, NL, SE, UK) supported the Commission's point of view. The Commission justified the phasing-out of tobacco subsidies by a reference to obligations under the TEC to assure that any Community legislation ensures a high level of health protection. Some delegations that supported the Commission argued that Community subsidies for a product that harms human health were not acceptable, particularly in the light of public opinion. The tobacco-producing countries argued that the reduction of subsidies would only have limited effects on tobacco consumption in the EU, much of which relied already on products imported from third countries, while having very negative social and economic consequences for regions relying heavily on tobacco production.

Regarding the size of premiums, the Commission suggested a reduction of the premiums by 10 per cent for the least profitable variety group V, the so-called 'Sun cured' variety. The Commission argued that such a reduction was necessary to set a real incentive for tobacco producers to switch to more profitable variety groups. Not surprisingly, the only two countries producing this type of tobacco, Greece and Italy, were opposed to this reduction. In contrast, Denmark and Sweden favoured more far-reaching measures in the form of a reduction of the premiums in all variety groups. A similar conflict constellation can be observed with respect to the size of the guarantee thresholds. The Commission suggested a two-step reduction: an initial reduction for the 2002 harvest and a further reduction for the 2003 and 2004 harvests. The goal of these reductions was to support depressed market prices by reducing supply. The Commission determined the precise distribution of the reductions across variety groups through a selective approach that suggested more rapid reductions for the least popular varieties. Many of the tobacco-producing countries (AT, EL, IT, ES, PT) opposed the suggested reductions and demanded the retention of the current rules until the results of the evaluation study were available. In contrast, Denmark and Sweden asked for larger and more rapid reductions.

Two other issues concerned aspects of the Community Tobacco Fund. In line with the goal of phasing-out tobacco subsidies, the Commission suggested reorienting the fund by changing the types of activities supported and to increase

---

26 Council (2002) Report of the meeting on 2 February 2002 of the Special Committee on Agriculture, 11 February 2002, 6069/02.

27 The eight countries receiving tobacco subsidies under the Regulation were Austria, Belgium, Italy, France, Germany, Greece, Portugal, and Spain.

the deductions used to finance the fund. With respect to the financed activities, the proposal suggested to replace research on healthier, more environment-friendly and economically sustainable varieties of tobacco and on alternative uses for raw tobacco with measures helping growers to switch to other crops or economic activities altogether. Most of the tobacco-producing countries (AT, FR, EL, IT, PT, ES) resisted such a change, making the case that a fund financed by tobacco producers should not exclusively be used to discourage tobacco production. However, the Commission argued that it was necessary to refocus the activities financed by the fund to make better use of its resources.

In order to increase the funds available for information measures on the health-risks associated with tobacco consumption and for initiatives to switch to other types of crops or economic activities, the Commission suggested a step-wise increase in the levies charged to finance the fund. More precisely, the Commission advocated increasing the levy from 2 to 3 per cent of the premium for the 2003 harvest, and from 3 to 5 per cent for the 2004 harvests. Finland, Sweden and the United Kingdom favoured even larger and more rapid deductions to promote conversions of tobacco producers. In contrast, many producer countries (AT, FR, EL, IT, PT, ES) opposed these increases. They argued that increases of the levies were not necessary because the current resources of the fund were already not exhausted.

The original Regulation had set up national quota reserves to encourage existing producers to restructure their holdings and to increase efficiency. The Commission argued that the national reserves had little effect on farm restructuring, while the management of the complicated system resulted in an excessive workload for national administrations. Therefore, the Commission proposed to abolish the national reserves. Some producer countries (BE, EL, PT) opposed this change as well. Belgium, Greece and Portugal suggested allowing the Member States the option to retain national quota reserves if they wanted to.

Despite these disagreements, the Belgian chairman of the working party concluded that there was broad approval of the proposal and that only some specific problems remained. In particular, the chairman stressed two issues that needed to be discussed by the SCA: the approach to the future development of the tobacco sector and the scope of the Tobacco Community Fund. For this reason, the chairman referred the proposal back to the SCA.[28] Under the Spanish Presidency in the first half of 2002, the SCA did not consider the dossier until 4 February 2002. Delegations outlined and justified their positions in more detail, but they did not make substantial progress towards a solution. On the contrary, the Italian delegation posed new demands regarding the flexibility of the auction system, although the chair of the working party had already reported that delegations were able to agree to the measures proposed by the Commission.

The Commission proposal sought to make the auction system for cultivation contracts provided for in the original Regulation more flexible and easier to

---

28 Council (2001): Report of the meeting on 13 December 2001 of the Working Party on Tobacco. 30 January 2002, 5452/02.

118   *Part III: Qualitative analysis*

operate for Member States. In order to receive premiums, producers had to enter into cultivation contracts with companies that first processed their tobacco products. The EU then paid premiums according to the amount of tobacco agreed to and transferred under these arrangements. The proposal introduced the possibility to apply the auction system to a single variety group and not only to the whole range of variety groups produced in a Member State. The Commission expected that such a provision would increase the use of the auction scheme and, as a result, would increase competition on the side of first processors. The higher level of competition would in turn result in higher market prices for raw tobacco. While all delegations preferred the Commission proposal to the status quo, Italy requested to provide for even more flexible arrangements by allowing to limit auctions not only to specific groups of tobacco varieties but also to only those producer groups that actually wished to participate.

The SCA agreed that the future development of the tobacco regime and the activities supported by the tobacco fund as well as its financing were essentially political questions.[29] Therefore, the SCA decided to ask the Council for guidance on these matters. The SCA also urged the Council for a rapid decision on the dossier, as the planting season was approaching. Two weeks later, on 18 February, the Council held a policy debate on the three political issues identified by the SCA. The Council asked the SCA to take the points raised during the discussions into account, to continue its work on the proposal, in particular on the more technical questions, and to report back to the Council after the opinion of the EP had been received in March.

The SCA subsequently considered the proposal in two meetings on 4 and 12 March without achieving much progress. With the exception of France, all delegations had at this stage accepted the changes proposed by the Commission regarding the activities sponsored by the Community Tobacco Fund. Given that agronomic research on tobacco could still be funded through the Community's general research budget, France indicated its willingness to also agree to a reorientation of the fund as part of an overall compromise solution. Thus, the SCA essentially decided this important issue.

However, the SCA did not find solutions for the other contentious points. Among the questions the SCA members considered to be of 'a more technical nature', Italy reiterated its demand for maximum flexibility regarding the auction system.[30] Belgium and Greece pleaded again for the optional maintenance of national quota reserves. Despite some difficulties, this demand was acceptable to most other Member States as part of an overall compromise solution. Only one delegation sided with the Commission in this case.[31] Among the other questions,

---

29 Council (2002): Report of the meeting on 2 February 2002 of the Special Committee on Agriculture. 11 February 2002, 6069/02.

30 Council (2002): Report of the meetings on 4 and 12 March 2002 of the Special Committee on Agriculture. 15 March 2002, 7120/02, p. 7.

31 Council (2002): Report of the meetings on 4 and 12 March 2002 of the Special Committee on Agriculture. 15 March 2002, 7120/02, p. 7.

Agriculture 119

Italy and Greece continued to object to the reduction of premiums for variety group V, but the Commission re-emphasised the need to set incentives for producers of this variety group to switch to other economic activities and rejected claims by the two Member States that premium reductions would actually lead to the opposite result. Despite attempts by the Presidency to reach a compromise solution, disagreements on the size of the guarantee threshold and the eventual phase-out of tobacco subsidies continued. Germany, the Netherlands, Finland and Sweden now joined Denmark and the UK in supporting the proposed reductions of the guarantee thresholds. However, the tobacco-producing countries still opposed these reductions.

Differences in opinion also remained on the two points with 'major political implications': the recitals stating the goal to eventually phase-out tobacco subsidies and the size of the levies for the financing of the Tobacco Fund.[32] Regarding the recitals, the Presidency suggested a rewording to focus the text more on the specific reasons for adopting the current proposal. As a compromise, the Presidency suggested referring to the goal of achieving a better balance between the orientation of the Tobacco Fund and the health protection requirements of Article 152 TEC. Additionally, a Commission statement could be inserted in the Council minutes pointing to the prospect of fundamentally reforming the tobacco market organisation in the near future. Most delegations, including all producer countries, were able to accept the Presidency proposal. In this context, the Greek delegation again stressed the need to come to an agreement before the start of the planting season. Denmark, Germany, the Netherlands and the UK also signalled their willingness to compromise, but they insisted on a wording that would more closely reflect the spirit of the original recital. Only Denmark and the Commission continued to oppose any solution involving the deletion of the goal of phasing-out tobacco subsidies.

The Presidency also made a compromise proposal to generate an agreement on the size of the levies used to finance the Tobacco Fund. The Presidency proposal allowed for an increase in the levies from 2 to 3 per cent in 2003, as suggested by the Commission, but it also envisioned freezing the deductions at this level rather than increasing them further to 5 per cent in 2004. While the Italian delegation still opposed any increase in the levies, most other producer countries (AT, BE, FR, EL, PT, ES) indicated that the Presidency proposal was acceptable to them. However, Denmark, Germany, Ireland, the Netherlands and Finland still backed the Commission's proposal on this point. Sweden and the UK favoured even higher levies.[33]

This situation characterised the state of play of negotiations after the SCA meeting on 12 March. Possible compromise solutions and the flexibility of Member States' positions had been explored, but substantial agreement was still

---

32 Council (2002): Report of the meetings on 4 and 12 March 2002 of the Special Committee on Agriculture. 15 March 2002, 7120/02, p. 2.

33 Council (2002): Report of the meetings on 4 and 12 March 2002 of the Special Committee on Agriculture. 15 March 2002, 7120/02, p. 5.

120   *Part III: Qualitative analysis*

lacking on almost all issues. The EP delivered its opinion two days later on 14 March, but there was still no prospect of reconciling the differences in positions in the SCA. Thus, the Presidency referred the dossier to ministers to be discussed during their meeting on 19 March. The ministers reached a political agreement on the dossier by a qualified majority, but only 'after lengthy discussions'.[34] Regarding the more technical issues, the compromise allowed for auction schemes to be set up not only for individual variety groups, but also for certain producer groups as requested by Italy. Belgium, Greece and Portugal also succeeded with their demand for the optional retention of national quota reserves. With respect to the more political issues, the ministers agreed to the reduction of the premiums for group V products as suggested by the Commission, although Italy and Greece had opposed them.

As was predictable from the outcome of the SCA negotiations, agronomic research was indeed eliminated from the activities financed by the Tobacco Fund and replaced by measures and studies supporting the conversion of tobacco producers to other economic activities. With respect to the question of how to finance the fund, the ministers found a compromise between the Presidency proposal made during SCA discussions and the original Commission proposal. The original Commission proposal suggested increasing the deductions automatically to 5 per cent of the premium in 2004. In contrast, the Presidency had proposed to freeze the size of the deductions at their 2003 value. Eventually, the ministers agreed that the Commission should report on the use of the Fund's resources by the end of 2003. This report may then be accompanied by a proposal to increase the deductions by up to 5 per cent.

Regarding the most contentious issue, the reference to the goal of phasing-out tobacco subsidies, the ministers agreed to a solution based on the approach taken by the Presidency in the SCA. However, the compromise also takes account of the additional demands voiced by Denmark, Germany, the Netherlands and the United Kingdom. As a result, the new recitals do not mention the abolishment of tobacco subsidies as a strategic goal anymore, but acknowledge that the EU should support the development of 'new sources of income and economic activity for the [tobacco] growers'.[35] Furthermore, the recitals mention that the TEC requires that all Community legislation conforms to high health protection standards. As Denmark, Germany, the Netherlands and the United Kingdom requested, this wording was closer to the thrust of the original Commission proposal. As proposed by the Presidency, the Commission decided to ask for the inclusion of a formal statement in the minutes of the Council meeting. The statement announced that the Commission intended, as part of its strategy on sustainable development, to adapt the tobacco regime after its review in 2002 to allow for

---

34 Council (2002): Press release on the outcome of the 2419th meeting on 18 March 2002 of the Council (Agriculture). 18 March 2002, 7097/02, p. 6.

35 Council Regulation 546/2002/EC of 25 March 2002 fixing the premiums and guarantee thresholds for leaf tobacco by variety group and Member State for the 2002, 2003 and 2004 harvests and amending Regulation 2075/92/EEC. 28 March 2003, OJ L84, pp. 4–7.

Despite several compromises, not all delegations could accept the final text of the proposal. From the very start of negotiations in the working party, Denmark and Sweden had demanded more encompassing reductions in premiums and larger cuts in the guarantee thresholds than proposed by the Commission. Together with Finland, Sweden and the UK had also asked for an even higher proportion of premiums to be deducted to finance the Tobacco Fund. In addition, these countries were staunch supporters of the Commission's strategy to eventually phase-out tobacco subsidies. Particularly Denmark was strongly opposed to the deletion of the recitals referring to those goals. Compared with the status quo legislation, the new Regulation moved the policy considerably towards the most preferred positions of Denmark, Sweden and the United Kingdom. Nevertheless, the United Kingdom abstained and Denmark and Sweden voted against the adoption of the Regulation.

Comparative analysis

In this section, I compare Council decision-making on the two Agriculture proposals. First, similarities and differences of the adoption processes are outlined. Then I discuss the varying degrees of involvement of different Council levels. Special attention is paid to the explanatory power of the factors outlined earlier and already examined in the quantitative analysis. However, I also identify additional factors that seem relevant but have not been discussed before.

Negotiation process

The negotiation processes of the two Agriculture proposals show some similarities. In both cases, the SCA dealt first with the dossier and decided about the 'procedure' through which the dossier was to be examined. The SCA decided whether the dossier would be discussed by a working party and which working party that would be. Although this decision is usually just a formality, it distinguishes the working method of the SCA from those of the two Coreper formations. The Working Party on Foodstuff Quality (Geographical Indications and Designations of Origin) met three times to discuss the Geographical Indications Regulation. The working party resolved a considerable part of the contested issues. Member States did not reiterate some less crucial suggestions made early during the negotiations when it became apparent that these suggestions were not supported by other delegations in the working party. Other suggestions were not

---

36 Although the thresholds for all countries were reduced as compared to the status quo figures of 2001, the reduction finally agreed to did not always correspond to the initial suggestions of the Commission. Compared with the Commission proposal, the agreed reductions were larger for Italy and Belgium, but smaller for Spain and Portugal.

122 Part III: Qualitative analysis

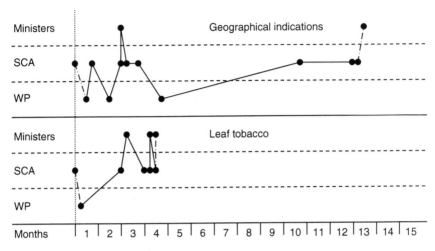

Figure 9.3 Agriculture: comparison of negotiation processes.
Source: Data based on an analysis of Council documents.
Note: SCA = Special Committee on Agriculture, WP = Working Party.

contested as most Member States could agree with the proposed provision. The opinion of the legal service also solved a contested issue. However, the SCA regularly received reports of the progress of negotiations in the working party and was actively involved in advancing the discussions on the dossier. In the case of the Leaf Tobacco Regulation, the Working Party on Tobacco met only once. The working party did not solve any of the contested issues in this case. The negotiation took place mainly in the SCA.

Another similarity concerns the early involvement of ministers. In both cases, the SCA asked ministers to have a general policy debate relatively soon after the beginning of the negotiation process. Whether these ministerial policy debates are characteristic for decision-making in Agriculture or rather for the way the Spanish Presidency led the negotiations in the Council is hard to judge. However, several indications suggest that both proposals were among the priorities of the Spanish Presidency. Spain held the Presidency in the first half of 2003. The Spanish Presidency had scheduled the adoption of the Leaf Tobacco Regulation for March and the adoption of the Geographical Indications Regulation for April. In the latter case, the Spanish Presidency even publicly voiced its annoyance over the delay caused by the late EP opinion.[37]

The main difference in the decision-making processes of the two proposals was their duration. The decision-making process on the Geographical Indications Regulation took almost three times as long as the negotiations on

---

37 European Report (2002): Farm Council: Decision on potato starch likely in short meeting on May 27. 25 May 2002.

the Tobacco Leaf Regulation. Two reasons are responsible for this difference in the length of negotiations. First, the EP delayed a decision on the Geographical Indications Regulation by about half a year. The EP set its internal decision-making process in motion rather late and did not deliver its opinion before December 2003. The Spanish Presidency had complained about this hold-up already in May. Note that the delay was not the result of an intentional strategy of the EP to get the Commission to adopt some of the EP's amendments.[38] The delay was simply due to a slow internal decision-making process on the part of the Parliament.

Second, the Leaf Tobacco Regulation needed to be adopted urgently, because the planting season for tobacco growers was approaching. Particularly the tobacco-producing countries were eager to get the Regulation adopted in order to provide their farmers with reliable guidelines. This urgency was the reason why Member States discussed the proposal in short sequence at a number of SCA and Council meetings during the first half of 2003. Thus, the large difference in the length of the adoption process was a result of both the delay of the Geographical Indications Regulation through the late opinion of the EP and the perceived need to adopt the Leaf Tobacco Regulation as quickly as possible.

Another difference concerns the conclusion of negotiations. In the case of the Geographical Indications Regulation, the SCA eventually adopted the proposal by a qualified majority of Member States' votes. Agriculture ministers only rubber-stamped the agreement as an A-item. Given the lack of actual decisions reached in the ministers' earlier policy debate, the overall substantial input of ministers to the negotiations must be judged to be rather modest. In the case of the Leaf Tobacco Regulation, the initial ministerial policy debate was not more fruitful. However, the SCA was also not able to make any further progress on the proposal. In the end, only Agriculture ministers were able to reach a final agreement after extensive negotiations.

Decision-making level

In Table 9.3, I present the number of issues decided at different Council levels. The table is based on a detailed analysis of contested points in the two decision-making processes. I indicate the level at which Member States resolved an issue as well as the type of final policy outcome. With regard to the type of policy outcome, 'proposal' means that the Council retained the provision as suggested in the original Commission proposal. If the Council decided to change the dossier to fully incorporate a suggestion of a Member State, I classified the issue as being an 'amendment'. Finally, if the final Council decision incorporated a solution that was different from both the original proposal text and the demands of Member

---

38 The Council can only adopt legislation after the EP has delivered its opinion. If the Commission is eager to get a piece of legislation adopted quickly, the EP can exploit this rule to receive some policy concessions. The EP can use the threat of delaying the adoption of its opinion to force the Commission to incorporate some of the EP's amendments.

124   *Part III: Qualitative analysis*

Table 9.3 Agriculture: types of negotiation outcomes by Council level

Outcome	Geographical Indications				Leaf Tobacco			
	WP	SCA	Ministers	Total	WP	SCA	Ministers	Total
Proposal	3	7	0	10	0	0	3	3
Amendment	4	4	0	8	0	0	2	2
Compromise	0	2	0	2	0	0	3	3
Total	7	11	0	20	0	0	8	8

Source: Data based on an analysis of Council documents. See the appendix to this chapter for more detailed information on the individual issues.

Note: SCA = Special Committee on Agriculture, WP = Working Party.

States, I coded the issue as a 'compromise'. I present the disaggregated data on which Table 9.3 is based in the appendix to this chapter.[39]

The table shows stark differences between the two cases. In the case of the Geographical Indications Regulation, ministers did not decide any of the issues. In contrast, ministers decided all issues in the case of the Leaf Tobacco Regulation. However, the latter finding might somewhat exaggerate the role of ministers. At least some of the issues retained until the last minister meeting were not really controversial and were probably left open for strategic reasons or simply because no need existed to incorporate those demands into the text earlier. In particular, the optional retention of national reserves as requested by Belgium and Greece as well as the further increase in the flexibility of auction schemes as demanded by Italy were not opposed by any of the other actors. These changes had no negative consequences on other Member States or for the achievement of the goals of the Regulation. Yet, the Presidency changed the text of the dossier only after the ministers had reached a complete compromise solution. Despite this caveat, the fact remains that ministers decided most issues of the Leaf Tobacco Regulation. In contrast, the working party and the SCA exclusively decided most issues in the Geographical Indications case. Interestingly, the SCA decided considerably more issues than the working party. Overall, these descriptive findings suggest that the characterisation of the Council as a filtering system might be too simplistic. If the Council structure acted as a filtering system, we would expect to see a decreasing number of issues decided at higher levels of the Council hierarchy. Table 9.3 gives no indication of any such pattern.

39 To generate the figures in the appendix, I identified all contested issues in a proposal and traced the length of their discussion over time. As a primary source of information, I relied on Council documents describing the progress of negotiations in different Council bodies. The figures indicate what the disagreements were about, at what time in point a certain issue was raised, how long it was discussed or at least mentioned as being unresolved, at which level the issue was closed and in what type of outcome the discussions resulted. Although the figures in the appendix present a wealth of information and are interesting in their own right, their detailed discussion is beyond the scope of this book. I present the figures in the appendix to be transparent about the generation of the aggregated comparison tables included in the main text of the chapter.

Agriculture 125

Preference divergence among Member States can by itself not explain why certain issues are discussed at higher Council levels and why others are not. Preference divergence of actors is a defining characteristic of all controversial issues. At least in the case of the Geographical Indications Regulation, the working party decided a number of issues on which Member State preferences diverged. However, no reason exists for a discussion at higher Council levels if actors agree on a certain course of action. Thus, preference divergence is a precondition for higher Council levels to discuss an issue, but it is not a sufficient factor.

Two other factors also seem relevant. First, the salience of issues is a major determining factor. In the case of the Geographical Indications Regulation, the SCA asked ministers to focus their discussion on those issues that had direct adverse consequences for specific groups of producers in different Member States. These issues included the exclusion of mineral waters from the scope of the Directive. Germany heavily opposed the exclusion of mineral waters from the scope of the Directive because a very large number of mineral water producers with registered names were located in Germany. Similarly, ministers discussed the requests by France and Portugal to have several additional products covered by the Directive. These products were especially prevalent in these countries. The other main issue concerned the co-existence of homonyms. The Commission had suggested a 15-year transition period for the co-existence of protected names and identical geographical names not covered by the Regulation but legally used for a long time. Several delegations opposed the requirement for an eventual abolition of traditionally used names, mostly because domestic companies were affected adversely by such a requirement.

Similarly, the first discussion of ministers in the case of the Leaf Tobacco Regulation focused on the eventual phase-out of tobacco subsidies as a medium-term policy goal as well as the financing of the tobacco fund and the types of activities supported by the fund. Direct consequences of the provisions for national interests were not the main factor making these issues salient. However, the suggestions by the Commission threatened to funnel the future decision on the EU's tobacco regime in a direction that countries with many tobacco-producing farmers strongly opposed. Thus, these issues threatened to have severe negative consequences for important national constituencies in the future. Still, the ministers eventually had to decide on all outstanding issues in the proposal, not only on the most salient ones. We can consider at least three potential explanations for the strong involvement of ministers. First, at least two of the other issues did not require any real discussions at ministerial level. These issues got pulled along with the more salient ones. Second, the remaining issues were quite important as well. For example, the sizes of premiums and guarantee-thresholds directly affected tobacco farmers' incomes. Thus, their discussion by ministers might not be so surprising after all. Third, the Presidency was eager to finalise the negotiations before the start of the tobacco-planting season. Rather than to go through a protracted negotiation process at the committee level, the Presidency might have figured that the chances of a quick adoption are highest at the level of ministers, who have the authority to agree to more far-reaching compromises. In the two compared cases, the effects of Presidency impatience on the one hand, and

126　*Part III: Qualitative analysis*

salience on the other, are hard to discern. But the possible effects of Presidency priorities are further investigated in the remaining case studies.

Regarding the effect of the voting rule, the empirical record is mixed. On the one hand, Member States discuss some issues at higher levels that are only contested by one or very few Member States without a blocking minority. In the case of the Geographical Indications Regulation, only individual Member States demanded the inclusion and exclusion of different products from the scope of the Regulation. Nevertheless, ministers discussed the issue and actually met some of the Member States' demands. On the other hand, many idiosyncratic requests regarding less salient issues seem to be simply dropped during negotiations at lower levels of the hierarchy when it becomes apparent that these requests will not gather enough support from other Member States to be adopted. The clearest evidence for an effect of the voting rule is the fact that the SCA made the final decision through a vote. The SCA did neither want nor need to refer the proposal to ministers to reach a more encompassing compromise. The first ministerial discussion in the case of the Leaf Tobacco Regulation involved only issues where two larger blocks of Member States opposed each other. This finding also supports the relevance of the voting rule. In the second meeting in the case of the Leaf Tobacco Regulation, ministers made the final decision on all issues. Still, Member States received only concessions in cases where they formed a blocking minority. The two rather uncontroversial demands to allow for the optional retention of national reserves and for a further increase in the flexibility of auction schemes formed the exception to this pattern.

The EP had virtually no effect on the level of decision-making in the Council. The late opinion of the EP surely delayed the Council decision-making process in the case of the Geographical Indications Regulation, but it did not affect the negotiations substantially. In both cases, the Council bodies did not even discuss the opinion of the EP. Any effect of uncertainty is hard to detect in a comparison of the two cases, mainly because the consequences of the provisions proposed in the dossiers were relatively clear. Both proposals made adjustments to legislation already in force for about a decade and the amendments proposed by the Commission had straightforward implications. The fact that the SCA is dominating Council negotiations in Agriculture to such a large extent might be in part a result of the absence of a larger information asymmetry between the SCA members and working party officials about the consequences of policy provisions. In contrast to Coreper, the SCA consists of policy experts. Thus, working parties in the field of Agriculture have a smaller informational advantage in relation to their senior committee than the working parties in other Council formations.

In summary, the working parties played a rather limited role in the two examined Agriculture cases. On the one hand, the low involvement of working parties is probably due to the salience of many of the contested issues. The salience of issues and the impatience of the Presidency are the main candidates for explaining the early ministerial discussions of the dossier in both cases as well as the final decision by ministers in the case of the Leaf Tobacco Regulation. On the other hand, the low involvement of working parties might also be caused by the lack of an information asymmetry between the working party members and the members of the SCA. The SCA has both more time and policy expertise than

Agriculture 127

the Coreper formations in other Council formations. As expected by theory, the EP had no influence on Council decision-making under the consultation procedure. The evidence regarding the effect of the voting rule is somewhat ambiguous, but tends towards corroborating the hypothesis that qualified majority voting makes an agreement at lower Council levels more likely.

Appendix: development of individual negotiation issues

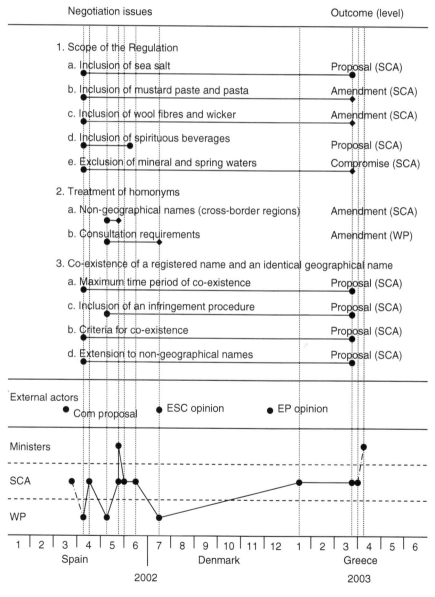

Figure 9.4 Geographical Indications Regulation: negotiation issues (continued over page).

Note: See footnote 39 on page 124 for further information on this figure and its data sources.

128 *Part III: Qualitative analysis*

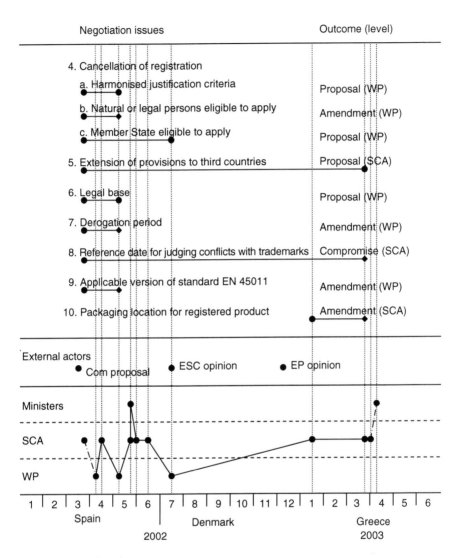

Figure 9.4 Continued.

Agriculture 129

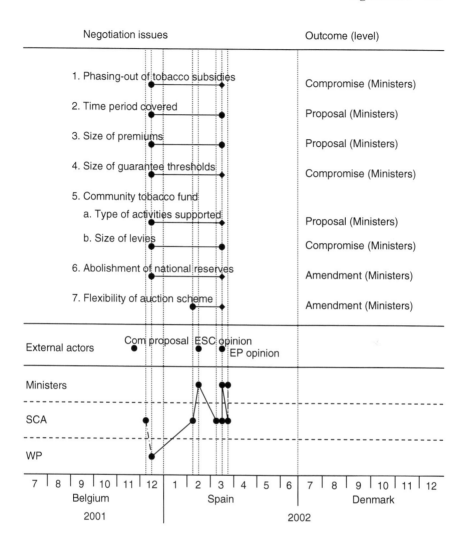

Figure 9.5 Leaf Tobacco Regulation: negotiation issues.

Note: See footnote 39 on page 124 for further information on this figure and its data sources.

10 Environment

In contrast to the field of Agriculture, which is a classic area of redistributive policy, the Environment field is predominantly governed through regulatory instruments. The European dimension of Environmental policy was formally recognised in 1986 through the adoption of the Single European Act. However, Environmental policy measures had already been adopted by the EU institutions since the early 1970s. Given the lack of an explicit legal base for EU Environmental policy, these early measures were often couched as instruments to remove non-trade barriers to the internal market (Lenschow 2005: 306–307). Compared to Agriculture, EU Environmental policy can be classified as moderately integrated (Nugent 2006: 388). As can be discerned from Table 6.1, Environmental policy is characterised by a considerable degree of legislative activity. The relatively large amount of legislation adopted in Environment, together with the fact that the co-decision procedure grants the EP powers equal to the Council's, has elevated membership in the Environment standing committee to one of the most prestigious posts in Parliament.

Environment ministers usually meet twice during a Presidency, once in the middle and once at the end of the half-year period. The deputy permanent representatives in Coreper I prepare the meetings of Environment ministers. Deputy permanent representatives in turn rely largely on the preparatory work of a single working party, the Working Party on the Environment. In terms of the number of working parties and their composition, the Environment formation is thus the extreme opposite of the Agriculture formation. A single working party discusses all issues related to internal environmental policy. The members of the working party are usually officials seconded from national environment ministries to the permanent representations in Brussels. Depending on the proposal discussed, different specialists from the ministries might assist the working party members, but the discussions are led by the officials posted to the permanent representations.

For the within-sector comparison of Council decision-making in the Environment policy field, I chose two Directives. The Ambient Air Directive aims to decrease air pollution through the establishment of monitoring mechanisms and the setting of common quality standards. The Batteries Directive regulates the contents of batteries and their recycling. After an early agreement with the EP, the Council

Environment 131

directly adopted the Ambient Air Directive in its first reading. In contrast, the Batteries Directive was only adopted in third reading after the Council reached a compromise with the EP in the conciliation committee. Thus, in the case of the Batteries Directive, the study focuses on the adoption of the Council's common position. Both cases allowed for an adoption of the Council decision by qualified majority voting. De facto, Coreper I reached the agreement on the Ambient Air Directive. In contrast, only ministers were able to agree on a compromise in the case of the common position for the Batteries Directive.

Ambient Air Directive

Background and proposal content

The Ambient Air Directive was the fourth daughter Directive of the Air Quality Framework Directive.[1] Each of the four daughter Directives deals with certain types of pollutants in ambient air. The Directive investigated in this study regulates the concentration and measurement of heavy metals and polycyclic aromatic hydrocarbons (PAHs) in ambient air.[2] The regulated heavy metals include arsenic, cadmium, mercury and nickel. The main justification for the introduction of this proposal was health concerns. According to the Commission proposal, all of the regulated pollutants are known to have adverse effects on human health and expo- sure to them should therefore be as low as possible.[3] In contrast to the suggestions in the Framework Directive and the provisions in earlier daughter Directives, the proposal for the fourth daughter Directive did not suggest binding limit values for heavy metal concentrations. Instead, the proposal only suggested non-binding target values for the concentration of PAHs. According to the official position of the Commission, cost-effective means to attain concentration levels that would not have negative effects on human health did simply not exist.[4] Although the proposal did not contain any binding air quality standards for the regulated pollutants, the Commission proposed relatively extensive monitoring and reporting requirements. Overall, the Commission proposal contained the following innovations:[5]

---

1 Council Directive 96/62/EC of 27 September 1996 on ambient air quality assessment and manage- ment. 21 November 1996, OJ L296, pp. 55–63.
2 PAHs are organic pollutants primarily formed by incomplete burning of carbon-containing materi- als like wood, coal, diesel, fat or tobacco (further information can be found online, for example at: http://dhfs.wisconsin.gov/eh/ChemFS/fs/PAH.htm [accessed 22 August 2011]).
3 Commission (2003): Proposal for a Directive of the European Parliament and of the Council relating to arsenic, cadmium, mercury, nickel and polycyclic aromatic hydrocarbons in ambient air. 16 July 2003, COM/2003/423, p. 3.
4 Commission (2003): Proposal for a Directive of the European Parliament and of the Council relating to arsenic, cadmium, mercury, nickel and polycyclic aromatic hydrocarbons in ambient air. 16 July 2003, COM/2003/423, p. 21.
5 Commission (2003): Proposal for a Directive of the European Parliament and of the Council relating to arsenic, cadmium, mercury, nickel and polycyclic aromatic hydrocarbons in ambient air. 16 July 2003, COM/2003/423.

132   *Part III: Qualitative analysis*

- The introduction of target values for the air concentration of PAHs.
- The introduction of a requirement for Member States to monitor the air concentration levels of all regulated pollutants as well as the deposition rates of all regulated pollutants except nickel.
- The introduction of mandatory monitoring of all regulated pollutants except mercury at fixed sites if concentration levels are above certain assessment thresholds. This provision also determined the minimum number of sampling points according to the population size of the agglomeration.
- The introduction of background monitoring of the air concentration levels of all regulated pollutants at a limited number of sites even where the assessment thresholds are not exceeded. This requirement included the requirement to monitor the deposition rates of all regulated pollutants except nickel. The provision also determined the minimum number of sampling points per square kilometre of Member State territory.
- The requirement for Member States to inform the Commission about any violations of assessment thresholds or a target value and about the measures undertaken to reduce the concentration of the pollutant.
- The requirement for Member States to regularly inform the public as well as environmental and consumer organisations about ambient air concentrations and deposition rates of the regulated pollutants.
- The requirement for the Commission to report on the implementation of the Directive by 2008 at the latest and to propose amendments if further improvements regarding the concentration levels seem feasible.

Of course, most aspects of the proposal were questioned during Council negotiations by one or the other delegation, but many delegations concurred that the modest goals set out to actually prevent and reduce the regulated air pollutants did not justify the extensive monitoring and reporting requirements contained in the proposal.

Negotiation process

The Council adopted the Ambient Air Directive relatively swiftly, about 16 months after the introduction of the proposal by the Commission. More remarkably, the actual negotiation process took less than four months (see Table 10.1). The bulk of the negotiations within the Council and even between the Council and the EP were conducted at working party level (see Figure 10.1). The Working Party on the Environment met seven times to discuss the dossier. Coreper I got involved only towards the end of the negotiation process to solve the last outstanding issues and to ratify the final agreement with the Parliament. The ministerial level was not involved in negotiations at all. The ministers adopted the Directive only formally several months later, after the compromise text had been screened and corrected by the Council's legal-linguistic experts.

The Commission adopted the proposal on 16 June 2003 and transmitted it to the Parliament and the Council a day later. The Environment committee of the EP

Environment 133

Table 10.1 Ambient Air Directive: main decision-making events

Date	Collective actor	Event
16-07-2003	Commission	Adoption of proposal
17-07-2003	Commission	Transmission to Council and EP
09-09-2003	EP committee	Appointment of rapporteur
26-11-2003	EP committee	Discussion of draft report
17/18-12-2003	WP	First reading of proposal
13-01-2004	WP	Discussion of WP report and Presidency proposal
21-01-2004	EP committee	Adoption of report
03-02-2004	WP	Discussion of WP report
16-02-2004	WP	Discussion of WP report and Presidency proposal
04-03-2004	WP	Discussion of WP report
09-03-2004	EP plenary	Policy debate
11-03-2004	Trilogue	Negotiations with EP and Commission
11-03-2004	WP	Discussion of WP report and trilogue report
15-03-2004	Trilogue	Negotiations with EP and Commission
19-03-2004	Coreper I (II-item)	Discussion of WP report and trilogue report
22-03-2004	WP	Discussion of Commission proposal for recitals
31-03-2004	Coreper I (I-item)	De facto adoption of Directive
20-04-2004	EP	Adoption of opinion
20-04-2004	Commission	Agreement on EP amendments
10-11-2004	Coreper I (I-item)	Inclusion of Directive in A-item list
15-11-2004	Education, Youth, and Culture Council (A-item)	Formal adoption of Directive

Notes: EP = European Parliament, Coreper = Committee of Permanent Representatives, WP = Working party.

appointed the Austrian Johan Kronberger, an independent, as its rapporteur soon after the summer break. In contrast, the Italian Presidency of the Council did not put the proposal on the agenda of the Environment working party until the end of its term in December. Thus, the rapporteur presented his draft report in the EP committee on 26 November, about three weeks before negotiations in the Council eventually started. The rapporteur suggested far-reaching modifications of the Commission proposal. In particular, the draft report suggested the introduction of limit values for all pollutants except mercury.

The Working Party on Environment had a thorough first reading of the Commission proposal during a one-and-a-half day meeting on 17 and 18 December. Although the Italians insisted on chairing the meeting, the Irish delegation was already directing the discussions behind the scenes. Ireland was to take over the Presidency from Italy at the beginning of 2004. Already, before the first working party meeting, the Irish delegation had discussed the proposal with most delegations in bilateral talks. Thus, the incoming Presidency was very well

134 *Part III: Qualitative analysis*

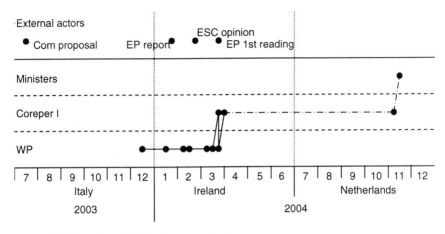

Figure 10.1 Ambient Air Directive: negotiation process.

Source: Data based on an analysis of Council documents.

Note: Coreper = Committee of Permanent Representatives, WP = Working Party.

informed about the problems and positions of the other Member States. The Irish official also had had early contacts with the EP's rapporteur. Given that these consultations did not indicate any insurmountable obstacles for reaching a timely agreement, the Irish delegation decided already at this stage to aim at a first-reading agreement with the Parliament.[6] During the first working party meeting, many delegations questioned the usefulness of heavy monitoring requirements in the absence of explicit obligations to assure high air quality. At the same time, several delegations considered binding limit values as proposed in the EP rapporteur's draft report as too stringent.[7] As a compromise solution, the Irish delegation suggested to introduce non-binding target values not only for PAHs, but also for arsenic, cadmium and nickel.

The working party discussed the compromise proposal during its next meeting on 13 January 2004. Ireland now formally chaired the meeting. The working party members accepted the inclusion of the provision for target values. The working party also agreed to the Dutch suggestion to distinguish lower and upper assessment thresholds. For concentration levels below the lower assessment threshold, modelling and estimation techniques are sufficient for the assessment of air quality. For concentration levels between the lower and upper assessment threshold, a combination of measurement and modelling techniques may be used. The working party agreed to use the original assessment thresholds as values for the new target values. Thus, the new upper assessment thresholds for the different types of heavy metals were 30–50 per cent lower than the original thresholds.

---

6 Interview D.

7 Council (2004): Report of the meeting on 17 and 18 December 2003 of the Working Party on Environment. 22 December 2003, 16290/03, p. 1.

Environment 135

The result of the reduction of the assessment threshold was that more areas qualified for the mandatory measurement at fixed sites. However, other changes to the proposal reduced the monitoring requirements. The working party agreed to lower the number of sampling points required for the fixed measurement of heavy metals. The requirements for rural background monitoring were also reduced from one measurement station per 50,000 km^2 to one measurement station per 75,000 km^2.

The EP committee adopted the report of its rapporteur with some minor amendments on 21 January. The EP committee supported the introduction of limit values, but only by a very small majority of two votes. Some Member States in the Council also favoured stricter standards. At the working party meeting on 3 February, Denmark reiterated its demand for binding limit instead of non-binding target values. For certain types of heavy metals, Austria, Germany and Sweden supported this demand. Other delegations still regarded the measurement requirements as too demanding. Spain, Portugal and Finland complained that the required number of measurement points for rural background monitoring was too high. Several delegations (ES, DK, EL, FR, IT, PT) also demanded a lower minimum requirement for the number of sampling points for fixed measurement.

After the meeting, the Presidency distributed a new draft provision. This new proposal further reduced the sampling points required when the upper assessment threshold for arsenic, cadmium and nickel concentrations was exceeded.[8] The chair of the working party also invited delegations to submit written contributions with text suggestions that would meet their most pressing concerns. At the same time, the Presidency announced that it was 'exploring the possibilities of working towards a first-reading agreement with the EP' and urged delegations to scrutinise the current draft of the proposal carefully with a view to quickly concluding the negotiations.[9]

As a result of the discussions during the meeting on 16 February, the Presidency provided an overall compromise package.[10] This package confirmed the approach based on target rather than limit values. The draft also included another reduction of the sampling points required for the measurement of heavy metals above the assessment threshold as suggested by the Presidency's earlier draft. In addition, the text further lowered the number of sampling points for background measurement to one site per 100,000 km^2 and introduced the possibility of joint measurement by Member States. The Presidency also proposed to limit the measurement of deposition rates to background sampling only. The Presidency declared that it intended to reach an agreement on the dossier in the half-day meeting on 4 March and to devote the meeting on 22 March to consider the EP's first-reading amendments. At this time, the plenary vote on the committee report of the EP was scheduled for 9 March.

---

8 Council (2004): Meeting document: Presidency proposal. 12 February 2004, DS 81/04.

9 Council (2004): Report of the meeting on 3 February 2004 of the Working Party on Environment. 6 February 2004, 6016/04, p. 2.

10 Council (2004): Report of the meeting on 16 February 2004 of the Working Party on Environment. 21 February 2004, 6549/04.

136 *Part III: Qualitative analysis*

Indeed, the delegations accepted large parts of the Presidency compromise proposal in the meeting on 4 March.[11] However, the Member States accepted the monitoring provision only after the requirements for the fixed measurement of PAHs were even further reduced. The proposal prescribed the number of required measurement sampling points according to the size of the population in an agglomeration zone. The larger the population in a certain area, the more measurement points would have to be installed. To reduce the measurement requirements, the working party agreed to merge two of the original eight population size categories and to apply the sampling point number originally required of the category with the lower population size to the newly merged category. This reduction was a compromise, given that several delegations (DE, ES, FI, PT, UK) had demanded to reduce the number of population size categories by half.

The EP discussed the Commission proposal and the committee report on 9 March. On the request of the rapporteur, the EP decided to postpone its vote on the dossier to its last plenary session in the legislative term in order to allow for a possible first-reading agreement with the Council. The different party groups in the EP mainly differed on the introduction of limit values. The rapporteur as well as representatives of the green and socialist party groups defended the call for limit values, but a speaker of the conservative party group argued against it. The conservative speaker agreed with the position of the Commission that limit values would impose disproportional costs on industry. The sincerity of the position of the socialist party group seems also questionable. The socialist shadow rapporteur stressed that the committee's position was, among other things, a negotiation position and that he aimed for target values as the final result of negotiations with the Council.

The Presidency and the Commission met with the EP rapporteur and his shadow rapporteurs for the first time in the morning of 11 March, although the Council had not agreed on a position on several points yet. The working party meeting on 4 March had left several issues unresolved, although they were of rather minor significance. The Presidency appealed to delegations to 'make as much effort as possible to lift scrutiny reservations and resolve other outstanding issues with a review to agreeing to a Council position that can be fully supported by all delegations'.[12] In the trilogue meeting on 11 March, the rapporteur signalled that the EP could accept a solution based on target values. However, the rapporteur insisted that the date for attaining the target values should be set to 2010 and that the Commission would be required to consider the introduction of limit values in its implementation review at that time. The Council had agreed to 2014 as the date for attaining the target values. The rapporteur also demanded the inclusion of two further EP amendments, a provision to cease the deposition of mercury within 20 years and a provision to measure the emissions of gaseous mercury in ambient air and mercury deposition.

---

11 Council (2004): Report of the meeting on 4 March 2004 of the Working Party on Environment. 8 March 2004, 7087/04.

12 Council (2004): Report of the meeting on 4 March 2004 of the Working Party on Environment. 8 March 2004, 7087/04, p. 2.

The Presidency informed the working party about the trilogue meeting in a meeting in the afternoon of the same day.[13] As a response to the EP's demands, the working party agreed to make specific references to both the possibility of introducing limit values and 'to further action in relation to mercury' in the report and review requirements of the Commission. The delegations also agreed to introduce additional recitals on the dangers of mercury and on the planned Commission strategy to protect human health and the environment from the effects of mercury. As a compromise, the working party accepted the Presidency's proposal to lower the date for achieving the target values to 2012. This date was halfway between the Council's and the EP's position. Even at a time when agreement with the EP seemed close, several points in the proposal were still under discussion within the Council itself. Several Member States still had objections. Thus, the Presidency urged delegations again to try to accept the compromise proposal. France, Italy and Finland were still demanding an even lower number of background sampling points. The Italian delegation was also not satisfied with the wording calling on Member States to take all necessary measures to ensure that concentration levels do not exceed the target values. The Council text qualified this statement by referring to measures 'not entailing disproportionate costs'. However, the Italian delegation preferred the formulation 'save where not achievable through proportionate measures'.[14]

At the second trilogue meeting just four days later on 15 March, the rapporteur made clear that the new suggestions by the working party were not completely acceptable to the EP. In a written response, the EP indicated that the date for attaining the target values of 2012 was agreeable.[15] As part of an overall compromise agreement, the EP was also willing to accept the Council's text revisions concerning mercury. However, the EP demanded a stronger reference to a possible introduction of limit values after the Commission review as part of such a deal. In order to possibly lift the remaining reservations of Member States on the Council's text and to give the Presidency a new mandate for continued negotiations with the EP, the chair of the working party decided to refer the dossier to Coreper I. The Presidency stressed that this meeting would be a final attempt to find an acceptable solution for a first-reading agreement. The Presidency also asked Coreper to instruct the working party to finalise the recitals in the light of agreement on the articles.

In the meeting on 19 March, Coreper members lifted all footnotes in the Council text without major changes to the dossier. In response to the EP demands, the deputy permanent representatives slightly modified the references to considering the introduction of limit values after the Commission review. Although a final agreement

---

13 Council (2004): Report of the meeting on 11 March 2004 of the Working Party on Environment and the trilogue meeting on 15 March 2004. 16 March 2004, 7398/04.

14 Italy wanted to ensure that the commitment imposed by target values was as weak as possible, but the insistence on this formulation rather than the formulation in the Council text is most likely due to a mistranslation by non-native English speakers (Interview D).

15 Council (2004): Addendum to the report of the meeting on 11 March 2004 of the Working Party on Environment and the trilogue meeting on 15 March 2004. 17 March 2004, 7398/04 ADD 1.

138   *Part III: Qualitative analysis*

with the EP had not been reached yet, the working party already examined the recitals of the Directive in its meeting on 22 March. Without a further trilogue meeting, the EP subsequently agreed to the new Council proposal. Coreper adopted the agreement on 31 March without discussion and mandated the Presidency to inform the Parliament that the Council would be in a position to accept the proposal as amended by the EP if the EP's amendments included the provisions agreed between the two institutions. The EP plenary adopted the compromise amendments supported by the rapporteur as well as the socialist, liberal and conservative party groups in its meeting on 20 April. On 11 November, Coreper decided without discussion to include the item on the agenda of the Education, Youth and Culture Council meeting, in which the Directive was formally adopted as an A-item on 15 November.

Batteries Directive

Background and proposal content

The Commission proposal for a Directive on batteries had two major goals.[16] The first goal was to further reduce the pollution of the environment by introducing collection and recycling rates for all batteries put on the EU market. Additional risk management measures for batteries containing hazardous substances accompanied these general provisions. The second goal was to improve the functioning of the internal market by harmonising product requirements. The Directive repealed an earlier, far less ambitious Directive which was confined to the treatment of batteries containing substantial amounts of hazardous substances, such as mercury, cadmium and lead.[17] The previous Directive prohibited the marketing of batteries containing mercury from 1 January 2000, required that the batteries covered by the Directive should be collected separately and that Member States should develop four-yearly programmes aimed at reducing the heavy metal content of batteries and the share of heavy metal in the waste stream. A later amendment of the original Directive also required that the label of these batteries should indicate their separate collection and their heavy metal content.[18]

The Commission argued that the measures in force were not sufficient to ensure high collection and recycling rates, because the original Directive did not

---

16 Commission (2003): Proposal for a Directive of the European Parliament and of the Council on batteries and accumulators and spent batteries and accumulators. 21 November 2003, COM/2003/723.

17 Council Directive 91/157/EEC on batteries and accumulators containing certain dangerous substances. 26 March 1991, OJ L78, pp. 38–41; as amended by Commission Directive 93/86/EEC adapting to technical progress Council Directive 91/157/EEC on batteries and accumulators containing certain dangerous substance. 23 October 1993, OJ L264, pp. 51–52; and by Commission Directive 98/101/EC adapting to technical progress Council Directive 91/157/EEC on batteries and accumulators containing certain dangerous substance. 5 January 1999, OJ L1, pp. 1–2.

18 Commission Directive 93/86/EEC adapting to technical progress Council Directive 91/157/EEC on batteries and accumulators containing certain dangerous substance. 23 October 1993, OJ L264, pp. 51–52.

prescribe 'measurable and verifiable instruments' to control the disposal of batteries.[19] Furthermore, the Directive did not apply to all battery types, but covered only batteries containing a certain amount of dangerous substances. The Sixth Community Environment Action Programme described the prevention and recycling of waste as one of the primary environmental objectives for the years 2002 to 2012. In line with these objectives, the Commission proposed to introduce the following measures:

- a requirement for Member States to set up efficient collection schemes covering all portable batteries, not only those including dangerous substances;
- a uniform minimum collection target for portable batteries calculated on the basis of grams per inhabitant;
- an additional collection target of 80 per cent of the quantity spent annually for portable nickel–cadmium (NiCad) batteries;
- a monitoring and reporting requirement for Member States regarding the quantities of NiCad batteries in the municipal solid waste stream;
- a legal obligation for producers of industrial and automotive batteries to take these batteries back after their use;
- the prohibition of the land-filling and incineration of industrial and automotive batteries;
- a general recycling requirement for all collected batteries to create a closed-loop system;
- a requirement to set up recycling facilities offering the best available recycling techniques;
- harmonised minimum recycling efficiency levels for different types of batteries;
- provisions requiring Member States to support research and development in new recycling technologies for batteries;
- provisions establishing the responsibility of producers for financing the collection and recycling of spent batteries, including historic waste generated before the entry into force of the new Directive;
- a requirement for Member States to inform consumers about the dangers of the substances used in batteries, the collection and recycling schemes as well as their role in those schemes;
- a requirement for Member States to send an implementation report to the Commission every three years;
- a requirement for the Commission to review and report on the implementation of the Directive after receiving the Member State reports and to possibly suggest amendments;
- a requirement for Member States to lay down penalties for the infringement of the Directive and to inform the Commission about these measures.

---

19 Commission (2003): Proposal for a Directive of the European Parliament and of the Council on batteries and accumulators and spent batteries and accumulators. 21 November 2003, COM/2003/723, p. 6.

140   *Part III: Qualitative analysis*

According to the Commission, extending the scope of the Directive to all batteries promoted not only environmental goals but also benefited the proper functioning of the internal market. So far, national collection and recycling schemes had differed in their scope, some covering all batteries and others only those covered by the earlier Directive. Requiring all Member States to adopt schemes to cover all kinds of batteries would establish a level playing field. Setting common product requirements, such as marketing restrictions or labelling obligations would also reduce barriers to trade. Thus, the proposal was based on a dual legal basis. The proposal suggested to harmonise product requirements based on the 'Internal Market' legal basis of Article 95 TEC and to harmonise measures designed to reduce the generation and to increase the recycling of batteries based on the 'Environment' legal basis of Article 175 TEC. The Commission proposal did not include bans of any types of batteries, although bans of batteries with adverse effects on the environment were clearly an option. As in the case of the Ambient Air Directive, the proposal suggested relatively modest policy change in this respect. Indeed, the issue of introducing a ban on NiCad batteries turned out to be the major division during negotiations in the Council and the Parliament.

Negotiation process

The Council made no attempts to reach an agreement on the Batteries Directive with Parliament in the first reading. The adoption of the first Council decision took about four months longer than in the case of the Ambient Air Directive (see Table 10.2). The actual negotiations on the Batteries Directive took about seven months. This time period is also considerably longer than the four months of negotiations on the Ambient Air Directive. In the case of the Batteries Directive, the Working Party on the Environment discussed the proposal 11 times (see Figure 10.2). Coreper I was strongly involved in the negotiation process, too. The deputy permanent representatives discussed parts of the dossier during four meetings. Interestingly, Coreper I referred the dossier back to the working party several times for further discussions before it forwarded the dossier to ministers. But eventually, Environment ministers had to resolve the last outstanding issues and come to a final agreement.

Negotiations in the Council started seven months after the adoption and transmission of the Commission proposal on 24 November 2003. The Irish Presidency had apparently set other priorities during the first half of 2004. Thus, the first consideration of the dossier by the working party took place only at the end of the Irish Presidency on 8 June 2004. This initial discussion took place on request of the Dutch delegation. The Netherlands were the successor in the Presidency chair and had asked the Irish delegation for a deliberation on the proposal. As in the case of the Ambient Air Directive, proceedings in the Parliament had been quicker than in the Council. In fact, the EP had already adopted its first-reading amendments on 20 April. The Commission had accepted several of these amendments completely or in parts.

Environment 141

Table 10.2 Batteries Directive: main decision-making events

Date	Collective actor	Event
24-11-2003	Commission	Adoption of proposal
24-11-2003	Commission	Transmission to Council and EP
27-11-2003	EP committee	Rapporteur appointment
16-02-2004	EP committee	Discussion of draft report
06-04-2004	EP committee	Adoption of report
20-04-2004	EP plenary	Adoption of opinion
20-04-2004	Commission	Partial agreement with EP amendments
08-06-2004	WP	First reading of proposal
02-07-2004	WP	Discussion of WP report
05/08-09-2004	WP	Visit of Dutch battery recycling facilities
07-10-2004	WP	Discussion of WP report and draft impact assessment
21-10-2004	WP	Discussion of WP report, draft impact assessment, and Presidency proposal
10-11-2004	WP	Discussion of WP report and draft impact assessment
18-11-2004	WP	Discussion of WP report, draft impact assessment, and Presidency proposal
24-11-2004	Coreper I (II-item)	Discussion of WP report and draft impact assessment
25-11-2004	WP	Discussion of WP report
01-12-2004	Coreper I (II-item)	Discussion of WP report
03-12-2004	WP	Discussion of WP report and Presidency proposal
07-12-2004	WP	Discussion of WP report and Presidency proposal
08-12-2004	Coreper I (II-item)	Discussion of WP report and Presidency proposal
09-12-2004	WP	Discussion of WP report and Presidency proposal
13-12-2004	Coreper I (II-item)	Discussion of WP report and Presidency proposal
20-12-2004	Environment Council (B-item)	Political agreement on common position
13-01-2005	WP	Discussion of Presidency proposal on recitals
15-07-2005	Coreper I (I-item)	Inclusion of common position in A-item list
18-07-2005	Agriculture and Fisheries Council (A-item)	Formal adoption of common position

Notes: EP = European Parliament, Coreper = Committee of Permanent Representatives, WP = Working party.

Two major changes proposed by the EP concerned a total ban of batteries including more than a certain amount of lead and cadmium, and a change of the measurement of the collection targets from grams per inhabitant to proportions of annual sales. Especially the ban on NiCad batteries was a highly salient issue and prompted one of the largest lobbying efforts the Parliament had seen in recent years. The battery-producing industry went so far as to produce a comic-strip that painted a very bleak picture of the world after a ban on NiCad batteries. The lobbyists distributed the comic strip at the entrance points to the plenary room just

142 *Part III: Qualitative analysis*

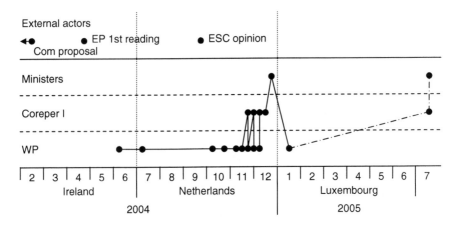

Figure 10.2 Batteries Directive: negotiation process.
Source: Data based on an analysis of Council documents.
Note: Coreper = Committee of Permanent Representatives, WP = Working Party.

before the EP voted on the amendments to the Batteries Directive. In the view of one observer, many Members of the EP regarded the comic-strip as an unrealistic and almost ridiculous exaggeration of the negative consequences of a ban on NiCad batteries. As a result, the comic strip had apparently a rather counter-productive effect on the voting behaviour in Parliament.[20] In the end, the cadmium ban amendment was adopted with the support of the socialist, liberal and green party groups. The conservative party groups opposed a ban. In any case, the Commission rejected both the amendment calling for a NiCad ban and the amendment calling for the measurement of collection targets as a proportion of annual sales.

In the working party meeting on 8 June, delegations considered the original proposal as well as the amendments suggested by Parliament. In the only meeting chaired by the outgoing Irish Presidency, Member States gave their initial comments on the dossier. Four contested issues became apparent during the discussions: the dual legal basis, the size of collection targets, restrictions on the use of cadmium and, related to the last point, the requirements for the monitoring of NiCad batteries in the municipal waste stream.[21] After this meeting, the Council Secretariat drafted a new text, which incorporated the EP amendments accepted by the Commission. This text formed the basis for subsequent discussions in the Council under the chairmanship of the Dutch Presidency. The Dutch had made the Directive a priority and aimed for an informal agreement on the Council's

20 Interview H.
21 Council (2004): Report of the meeting on 8 June 2004 of the Working Party on Environment. 22 June 2004, 10743/04, p. 1.

Environment 143

common position at the meeting of Environment ministers at the end of their Presidency on 20 December.[22]

The second meeting of the working party took place on 2 July. The Dutch Presidency was initially concerned that Member States with little or no experience in the recycling of batteries, particularly the newly acceded Member States, would oppose the proposal simply because they feared that building up the necessary collection and recycling infrastructure would be too complicated and too costly.[23] Thus, rather than starting with a detailed discussion of the proposal paragraph by paragraph, the Dutch Presidency prepared discussion papers on the methods for monitoring the collection targets and on the restriction of cadmium in batteries.[24] In the papers, the Presidency outlined the pros and cons of several policy options regarding the two issues and asked for a detailed discussion by Member States. As part of this discussion, several Member States presented their national systems for measuring collection rates. Many delegations (AT, BE, DE, FI, SE, LT, LV) sided with the view of the EP and spoke in favour of measuring targets in terms of percentages of annual battery sales, but several other delegations (CZ, IE, UK) agreed with the Commission to set up targets in terms of grams per inhabitant. Regarding the restrictions on the use of cadmium, many delegations were in favour of an eventual phase-out of cadmium (AT, BE, CZ, DE, DK, ES, FI, IT, NL, PT, SE), although not necessarily in the way proposed by the EP. Other delegations opposed a ban (FR, IE, PL, UK) and sided with the Commission, which had suggested a closed-loop system for NiCad batteries.[25] As part of the Presidency's effort to reassure inexperienced Member States regarding their 'fear' of the presumably difficult and costly task of establishing collection and recycling schemes, the Dutch delegation invited the working party members for a study trip to the Netherlands. During this four-day trip from 5 to 8 September, the working party members visited several Dutch battery recycling facilities.

Parallel to the debates on the Batteries Directive in the Working Party on Environment, the Working Party on Competitiveness and Growth discussed the use of impact assessments to evaluate the substantive effects of Council amendments. The Competitiveness Council of 17 and 18 May 2004 had called for the development of such impact assessments as part of inter-institutional efforts to improve EU law-making.[26] Based on a recommendation of the Competitiveness Working Party in its high-level composition, Coreper decided on 23 June to ask the Presidency

---

22 Council (2004): Dutch Presidency: Provisional agendas for Council meetings prepared by Coreper (Part 1). 30 June 2004, 11014/04, p. 25.

23 Interview G.

24 Council (2004): Report of the meeting on 2 July 2004 of the Working Party on Environment. 24 September 2004, 12728/04, pp. 2–3.

25 Council (2004): Report of the meeting on 2 July 2004 of the Working Party on Environment. 24 September 2004, 12728/04, pp. 2–3; and Council (2004): Report of the meetings on 7 and 21 October 2004 of the Working Party on Environment. 4 November 2004, 14228/04, p. 8.

26 Council (2004): Outcome of proceedings of the Competitiveness Council on 17 and 18 May 2004: Council conclusions. 10 June 2004, 9995/04, pp. 6–8.

144   *Part III: Qualitative analysis*

to suggest a pilot project for such an assessment. The Presidency selected the proposal for the Batteries Directive for the pilot project.[27] The Competitiveness Working Party approved this choice at its meeting on 16 July and Coreper confirmed it on 20 July. The Coreper decision charged the Working Party on Environment to identify one or more amendments to be subjected to an impact assessment and to carry out the assessment.[28]

Based on the discussions during the first two meetings, the chair of the Working Party on Environment decided to suggest a change in the measurement of the collection targets to percentage of annual sales rather than grams per inhabitant. The Presidency also proposed a partial cadmium ban, limited to portable batteries and allowing a transition period for cordless power tools. This change implied the abolishment of the requirements to monitor NiCad batteries in the municipal waste stream, which many delegations had regarded as too burdensome. The Presidency recommended the amendments related to the partial cadmium ban as suitable candidates for the impact assessment and prepared a draft impact assessment for discussion by the working party at its first meeting after the summer break on 7 October. The Presidency took the position that the amendments would have a positive environmental impact and that the very small negative economic effects on industry and consumers would be far outweighed by savings in terms of collection and monitoring costs.[29] The working party agreed with the selection of the proposed amendments for the impact assessment and had an initial exchange of views on the draft impact assessment on 7 October.

During the meetings of 7 and 21 October, the working party examined the proposal in more detail. By the time of the first meeting, many delegations had prepared detailed written comments on individual articles and paragraphs. Regarding the collection rate, the Dutch Presidency had originally proposed a target for portable batteries of 30 per cent by weight of annual sales. This target was to be achieved within four years. An unspecified but higher target was supposed to be realised after another six years. As a response to discussions at the meeting on 7 October, the Presidency proposed a modified compromise. The chairman suggested a rate of 60 per cent to be achieved after 12 years. But to take account of differences in the collection capacity of existing systems in Member States, the compromise suggested setting linearly increasing targets for each year to reach that collection rate. This compromise was supposed to alleviate concerns about the achievability of the four-year target voiced by Member States whose current collection rates were very low.

27 Council (2004): Presidency note: Pilot project for impact assessments of Council amendments. 16 July 2004, 11464/04.
28 Council (2004): Report of the meeting on 2 July 2004 of the Working Party on Environment. 24 September 2004, 12728/04, p. 3.
29 Council (2004): Presidency note: Discussion paper for impact assessment of Council amendments. 24 September 2004, 12731/04.

Environment   145

During the meetings on 10 and 18 November, the Presidency proposed some new compromise provisions.[30] The first substantial change suggested by the chairman concerned the definition of a producer. Several delegations (AT, BE, ES, LU) had requested a clarification of the original provision. In their view, the Commission's definition did not allow for a clear identification of a producer at all stages of the supply chain, which was necessary to implement the principle of producer responsibility. The Presidency's amendment catered to this demand. At the meeting on 18 November, the working party also considered a revised version of the draft impact assessment produced by the Presidency. Several delegations (BE, DK, DE, ES, AT, SE) could accept the assessment that the partial cadmium ban would have positive environmental and net-economic effects without any larger negative social consequences. In contrast, other Member States (CZ, EL, FR, IE, IT, LV, PT, UK) had doubts about the extent of the positive environmental impact of the partial cadmium ban and stressed the need to have a closer look at the social and economic impact. Despite these contradicting views about the result of the impact assessment, no delegation objected to forwarding the draft impact assessment to Coreper for further discussions.

In the light of ongoing disagreement among Member States about possible restrictions on the use of cadmium and on the assessment of the impacts of a partial ban, the Presidency decided to ask Coreper for further directions on the issue. The Presidency outlined four possible options: the first option concerned a partial ban as suggested by the Presidency and supported by a number of delegations (BE, DK, ES, CY, NL, AT, SI, FI, SE). The second option proposed also a partial ban, but with a longer transition period for cordless power tools. The third option suggested a partial ban with a review requirement for the exclusion of cordless power tools after four years. Several delegations (CZ, DE, IE, IT, PT, SK) were in favour of either option two or three. However, Denmark, Finland and Sweden indicated that option three was unacceptable to them. France, Poland and the UK opposed any cadmium ban on the grounds that the environmental benefits did not clearly outweigh the social and economic costs. At this time, several delegations (CY, LV, LT, MT, HU) were still undecided. The fourth option referred to the original proposal text of a closed-loop system for NiCad batteries. Only the Commission still favoured this option.

Coreper I discussed the possibility of a partial cadmium ban at its meeting on 24 November. At the beginning, the discussion revolved around the impact assessment of the ban. Soon, the impossibility of reaching a consensus on this issue became apparent. After about ten minutes of fruitless debate, the chair of Coreper decided to put the impact assessment aside and to continue the discussions in the standard mode of Coreper negotiations.[31] Several delegations

---

30 Council (2004): Meeting document for the meeting on 18 November 2004 of the Working Party on Environment: Presidency suggestions for amendments. 16 November 2004, DS 765/04.

31 Interviews F and G.

146　*Part III: Qualitative analysis*

changed their positions during the meeting. Only France kept supporting the original Commission proposal for a closed-loop system for NiCad batteries. Thus, the original provision in the Commission proposal was not a viable option anymore. However, no agreement could be reached on the precise form the partial cadmium ban should take.

The delegations were also not able to resolve several other obstacles in the next meeting of the working party on 25 November. Thus, the Presidency decided to ask Coreper for guidance on the remaining issues as well. Disagreement continued on the definition of industrial and portable batteries. The precise definition of those terms was of considerable importance, as they affected the scope of the partial cadmium ban, the collection regimes, the prohibition on land-filling batteries, and the rules on producer responsibility. The Presidency suggested including a recital with examples to aid the legal interpretation of the definitions. A new Presidency draft suggested a collection target of 20 per cent after six years, 35 per cent after nine years and 60 per cent after 12 years. The size of the collection rates were at this moment only acceptable to a small number of delegations (BE, EE, NL, SK, SE). Some delegations (CY, CZ, EL, LV, MT, PL) requested a transitional period for Member States with specific national difficulties. Rather than allowing for extended transition periods, the UK suggested to adopt collection targets that could actually be met by all Member States in good time. Finally, regarding the recycling of waste batteries, some Member States (EL, IT, PT, UK) rejected the 100 per cent recycling target for industrial and automotive batteries. A number of delegations (EL, IT, LV, SK, UK) also doubted the practicality and proportionality of the recycling rates suggested for other battery types. The Commission replied that higher collection and recycling standards belonged to the fundamental goals motivating the proposal.

The next meeting of the working party took place two days later on 3 December. In this meeting, the working party followed up on the discussions in Coreper on 24 November and 1 December. With regard to the partial cadmium ban, the chair of Coreper had concluded that the working party should identify a 'bridge' between option 1, a partial ban with a four-year transition period for cordless power tools as proposed by the Presidency, and option 3, a partial ban with an exemption for cordless power tools to be reviewed by the Commission after four years.[32] The chair of the Working Party provided six alternative provisions that could constitute such a bridge, three providing for the initial inclusion of cordless power tools in the ban and three providing for their initial exclusion. Within these two groups, alternatives varied according to the procedure through which a decision on the future status of cordless power tools after the initial four years would be made. These options included the Comitology, consultation and co-decision procedure. With regard to the definitions of battery types, the Presidency provided several new draft recitals

---

32 Council (2004): Meeting document for the meeting on 3 December 2004 of the Working Party on Environment: Presidency discussion document. 30 November 2004, DS 811/04.

Environment 147

explaining the distinction between portable batteries on the one hand, and automotive and industrial batteries on the other. The new recitals also included substantive examples for the different types.[33]

As a result of the deliberations during the working party meeting, the Presidency suggested a global compromise package. This package was discussed by the working party on 7 December and by Coreper a day later on 8 December. The Presidency pointed out that the goal was to reach an agreement on the proposal at the meeting of Environment ministers on 20 December.[34] With regard to the partial cadmium ban, the compromise package included an exemption for cordless power tools that would only end after four years if the EU institution made an explicit amendment towards this end through the co-decision procedure. This compromise proposal was a far-reaching concession by the Dutch Presidency. The Presidency accommodated proponents of a moderate restriction on cadmium batteries because it anticipated that subsequent negotiations with the Parliament would move the final policy outcome closer towards a stricter cadmium ban again.[35] However, many delegations (AT, BE, DK, ES, FI, HU, LT, PL, SE, SI) regarded this form of the cadmium ban as too modest; and proponents of lax restrictions (DE, EL, FR, LV, UK) still considered it to be too far-reaching. Germany opposed the inclusion of a review clause, and France still rejected any form of a cadmium ban, largely as a result of the severe lobbying of a large French battery-producing company.[36]

Regarding the collection targets, the Presidency now proposed goals of 20 per cent to be reached after six years and 40 per cent to be reached after nine years. This proposal was also a relatively large concession to the more reluctant Member States, as many delegations (AT, BE, DE, DK, EE, ES, FR, IE, NL, SE, SK) had signalled that they could accept the earlier suggested collection target of 60 per cent after 12 years, too. However, particularly the new Member States (CZ, CY, EL, LT, MT, PL) requested transitional arrangements. The United Kingdom, Hungary, and Latvia requested that targets should be set at such a low level that all Member States would actually be able to meet them. The transposition deadline was also of relevance in this respect. Many delegations (CY, CZ, FR, IE, IT, LV, MT, PL, SI, UK) requested 30 months to transpose the Directive, rather than 18 months as suggested in the Commission proposal. The Presidency's compromise solution included a 24-month transposition period. The collection target of 40 per cent of last year's sales was approximately equivalent to the target of 160 grams per inhabitant of the original Commission proposal. As the Presidency pointed out, this target would have to be achieved after five-and-a-half years according to the Commission proposal. In contrast, the Presidency's compromise solution provided Member States with an additional three-and-a-half years to reach the target.

---

33 Council (2004): Meeting document for the meeting on 3 December 2004 of the Working Party on Environment: Presidency suggestions for new recitals. 30 November 2004, DS 813/04.
34 Council (2004): Presidency note. 6 December 2004, 15537/04.
35 Interview G.
36 Interview H.

148   *Part III: Qualitative analysis*

Besides these main points, a number of other issues were still open at this point. In fact, the Presidency note to the working party and Coreper outlining the compromise solution lists 12 'other issues' not included in the compromise.[37] The Member States only found agreement on one important issue: the definition of different battery types. The delegations accepted the Presidency proposal to define portable batteries as the default category and to list examples of the different types of batteries in the recitals. The working party discussed the dossier again on 9 December. As a result of the discussions in Coreper, the Presidency suggested to reduce the second collection target from 40 to 35 per cent. But in order to accommodate the supporters of high collection rates, the Presidency also suggested setting a third target of 50 per cent to be achieved after 12 years. Besides this main issue, the working party also dealt again with many minor points. Overall, eight of the 12 'other issues' could be resolved during the working party and Coreper meetings on 7, 8 and 9 December. However, with the exception of the definitions of battery types, all the major issues remained contested.

In the last Coreper meeting on 13 December, the deputy permanent representatives resolved most outstanding minor issues.[38] Notably, delegations accepted the suggested compromise to set the transposition deadline after 24 months. With regard to the three main issues, the positions of Member States consolidated around different options. One group of Member States (AT, BE, DK, EE, ES, FI, LT, SE, SI, SK) clearly favoured a ban including cordless power tools with a transition period that could be extended by the Commission through the Comitology procedure. Another group of Member States (CY, CZ, DE, EL, FR, HU, IE, IT, LV, MT, PL, PT, UK) demanded the exclusion of cordless power tools, but could accept a review of the exception after a certain time period by the Commission. This Commission review could then be followed by a new co-decision proposal to include cordless power tools in the ban. Regarding the collection targets, all delegations accepted the 20 per cent target to be achieved after six years. With respect to the second collection target to be achieved after nine years, some delegations (CY, CZ, DE, FR, LV, MT, PL, SK) favoured a 40 per cent target. Another group (EL, HU, IT, LT, PT, SI, UK) could not accept more than 35 per cent. Regarding the final target after 12 years, several delegations (AT, BE, DK, EE, ES, FI, FR, NL, SE, SK) preferred a target of 60 per cent, while a number of delegations (DE, HU, IE, LT, PL) supported a target of 50 per cent. The remaining delegations did not support a third target at all. Finally, the positions on the recycling targets remained virtually the same. Several delegations (EL, ES, HU, IT, LV, PT, UK) were still opposed to the general recycling target of 55 per cent.

The Environment ministers discussed these issues on 20 December. The discussions on the proposal were quite time-consuming. The partial cadmium ban

---

37 Council (2004): Presidency note. 6 December 2004, 15537/04, pp. 7–8.
38 Council (2004): Presidency note. 14 December 2004, 15995/04.

proved to be the most contentious issue. A compromise proposal by the German Environment minister Jürgen Trittin finally bridged the division between the two camps in the Council.[39] After lengthy negotiations, Trittin suggested that the exclusion of cordless power tools might be acceptable to the proponents of an extensive ban if the provision on the Commission review included a statement that the review should be conducted 'with a view to the prohibition of cadmium in batteries and accumulators'.[40] Most Member States could indeed agree to this proposal. Only Ireland was unhappy about the 'closed' nature of the Commission review and abstained from the vote. In contrast, several other delegations (AT, DK, EE, ES, FI, LT, SE, SL) were unhappy about the common position because the ban on cadmium did not go far enough in their views. In a joint statement, they called on the Commission to promptly review the Directive with a view to prohibit the use of cadmium in batteries.[41] Belgium even abstained from the vote because it was not satisfied with the low level of environmental ambition defined in the Council's common position.

Some delegations were discontent with the Council's common position for other reasons. Italy and Greece abstained as well, but mainly because they considered the collection and recycling targets as unrealistically high. The collection targets had eventually been set to 25 per cent after six years and 45 per cent after ten years. The final target values were thus located between the most preferred target values of the two main groups of Member States. With respect to the recycling target for non-heavy-metal batteries, the final outcome was a target of 50 per cent, slightly lower than the 55 per cent originally proposed by the Commission and sustained by the Presidency.

Although ministers had reached a political agreement, the working party had to discuss the dossier once more to finalise the recitals. This meeting took place on 13 January 2005, under the chairmanship of the new Luxembourgian Presidency. The Council formally adopted the common position more than half a year later at the beginning of the UK Presidency. Without discussion, Coreper decided on 15 July to include the common position as an A-item on the agenda of the Agriculture and Fisheries Council. The Agriculture ministers adopted the common position without deliberation on 18 July. The final version of the Batteries Directive was eventually signed by the Presidents of the Parliament and the Council on 6 September 2006, after extensive negotiations between the two institutions in second and third reading of the co-decision procedure had taken place. Interestingly, the EP demands did not alter the outcome on the three issues most contentious in Council negotiations. The provisions on the partial cadmium

---

39 Interview F.

40 Council (2005): Draft minutes of the 2632nd meeting of the Council of the European Union (Environment), held in Brussels on 20 December 2004. 25 February 2005, 16275/04 Rev. 1.

41 Council (2005): Draft minutes of the 2632nd meeting of the Council of the European Union (Environment), held in Brussels on 20 December 2004. 25 February 2005, 16275/04 Rev. 1, p. 16.

150   *Part III: Qualitative analysis*

ban and on the targets for the collection and the recycling of batteries remained the same as in the Council's common position. Due to a change in the position of the liberal party group, the EP did not reintroduce its amendment regarding a total cadmium ban in the second reading.

Comparative analysis

Negotiation process

The two decision-making processes show several commonalities. The Commission proposal suggested rather moderate changes in both instances, at least with regard to provisions that imposed costs on European industries. In the case of the Ambient Air Directive, the Commission proposal did not include any air quality goals at all. The Council soon amended the proposal to include at least non-binding target values for the concentration of all air pollutants. The Parliament even promoted the introduction of binding limit values. Similarly, the original Commission proposal for the Batteries Directive did not include a ban on cadmium in batteries. In contrast, the Parliament suggested a total ban on NiCad batteries. The Council could not agree on a total ban, although such a ban was favoured by a large number of Member States. In any case, the Council's common position of a partial ban on cadmium in batteries was still going further than what the Commission had originally proposed.

According to EU officials, the relatively moderate Commission proposals are a result of a constant tension between the views of different directorates general (DG) within the Commission.[42] The goals of DG Environment, which was primarily responsible for drafting the dossiers, to promote stricter regulation protecting the environment are often opposed by the industry-friendly DGs Internal Market and Enterprise and Industry. These DGs regard the protection of the interests of European industries as their primary objectives. However, DG Environment is usually also aware of the prevailing preferences in the other institutions. Thus, DG Environment has less incentive to resist the watering-down of its draft proposal during the Commission's internal decision-making process if it expects that the Parliament and the Council will 'correct' the changes imposed by the demands of the other DGs. This finding also illustrates the importance of committees in the Council and the EP for counter-acting the agenda setting power potentially conferred on to the Commission by its exclusive right to initiate Community legislation. The committee system equips the Council with the capacity to make informed changes to Commission proposals that are not in the common interest of Council members (König and Proksch 2006a).

Noteworthy also is that discussions in the Council started only several months after the introduction of the proposals. The Commission transmitted the

42 Interviews H and C.

Environment 151

proposal for the Ambient Air Directive during the first month of the Italian Presidency in July 2003, but the first discussion did not take place until the middle of December. The incoming Irish Presidency de facto already led these discussions. The Commission transmitted the proposal for the Batteries Directive at the end of November 2003, also during the Italian Presidency. However, neither the Italian nor the subsequent Irish Presidency put the dossier on the agenda. On request of the incoming Dutch Presidency, the working party discussed the proposal only once during the last month of the Irish Presidency. Both the lack of discussion during certain Presidencies and the requests by incoming Presidencies to discuss a dossier already during one of the last working party meetings under the current Presidency point to the latitude Presidencies have to decide about the start of negotiations on a dossier and about how much attention a dossier receives. While the Ambient Air Directive was clearly a priority for the Irish Presidency, the Batteries Directive was not.[43] The latter was only taken up by the Dutch Presidency, which already envisaged a political agreement on the Batteries Directive for the end of its term before the term had even started.[44]

The decision-making processes also showed similarities in the timing of meetings of different Council bodies. In both instances, the Council body to first deal with the dossier was the working party. In contrast to the procedure in the Agriculture formation, where the SCA decides first about how a dossier is dealt with, Coreper does not concern itself with such matters. The Presidency decides when and by which working party a dossier is discussed. The initial deliberation process was also quite similar. The working party first discussed each dossier a number of times. In contrast to the area of Agriculture, the Presidency did not move the dossiers up to higher Council levels relatively early in the process to give general guidance on some particularly contested issues. The Presidency referred the dossiers to Coreper only towards the end of the negotiation process to reach an actual agreement on specific topics. The difference in the timing of moving the proposal up to Coreper as shown in Figure 10.3 is largely due to the summer break at the beginning of the Dutch Presidency. From mid July to mid September, months 2–4 in the figure, only few meetings take place in Brussels.

However, Figure 10.3 also indicates that the remaining process differed quite remarkably. The deputy permanent representatives essentially reached an agreement on the Ambient Air Directive already during the first Coreper meeting. The subsequent working party meeting dealt with the finalisation of the recitals

---

43 The indicative agendas of Council meetings under the Irish Presidency forecasted a political agreement on the Ambient Air Directive by the end of the Presidency at the latest; the provisional agendas do not mention the Batteries Directive. See Council (2003): Irish Presidency: Provisional agendas for Council meetings prepared by Coreper (Part 1). 16 December 2003, 16175/03.
44 Council (2004): Dutch Presidency: Provisional agendas for Council meetings prepared by Coreper (Part 1). 30 June 2004, 11014/04, p. 25.

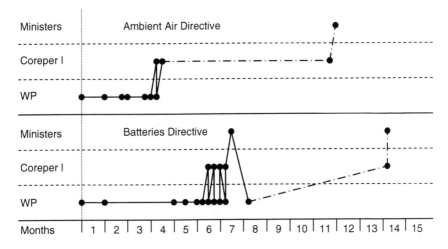

Figure 10.3 Environment: comparison of negotiation processes.

Source: Data based on an analysis of Council documents.

Note: Coreper = Committee of Permanent Representatives, WP = Working Party.

and the second Coreper meeting ratified the agreement with the European Parliament. In contrast, Coreper was more actively involved in the decision-making process on the Batteries Directive. The deputy permanent representatives discussed the proposal on four occasions. After the first three meetings, Coreper sent the dossier back to the working party for further discussions. Only the fourth and final Coreper meeting before the Environment Council succeeded in reducing the number of open issues to a manageable level. Once again, the working party fixed the recitals after the actual agreement had been reached, but this time the agreement was only reached by ministers themselves.

Decision-making levels

Table 10.3 shows the types of negotiation outcomes against the decision-making level in the Council for the two cases. Two facts are interesting. First, no clear pattern regarding the division of labour among the different committee levels can be discerned. As in the Agriculture cases, the metaphor of the Council structure as a 'filtering system' is only partly reflected in the data. In the case of the Ambient Air Directive, the number of issues decided by Coreper I is not that much smaller than the number of issues decided in the working party. In the case of the Batteries Directive, Coreper I decided even more issues than the working party. Although ministers decided indeed a smaller number of issues than either Coreper or the working party, the proportion of ministerial decisions still amounts

Environment 153

Table 10.3 Environment: types of negotiation outcomes by Council levels

Type of Outcome	Ambient Air Directive				Batteries Directive			
	WP	Coreper I	Ministers	Total	WP	Coreper I	Ministers	Total
Proposal	5	4	0	9	6	12	2	20
Amendment	6	1	0	7	6	5	1	12
Compromise	4	5	0	9	4	6	6	16
Total	15	10	0	25	16	23	9	48

Source: Data based on an analysis of Council documents. See the appendix to this chapter for more detailed information on the individual issues.

Notes: Coreper = Committee of Permanent Representatives, WP = Working Party.

to almost 20 per cent of the total number. Thus, in terms of the proportion of issues decided at a certain level, the Council hierarchy did not work very effectively as a filter in these two cases.

Practitioners often argue that the working party deals only with the technical details of a dossier, whereas Coreper and particularly the ministers decide the important issues. This argument leads to the consideration of issue salience as the first potential explanatory factor. The case studies indicate that the salience of an issue plays an important role in explaining Council decision-making, but it only provides a partial explanation. In the case of the Batteries Directive, ministers discussed only very salient issues that imposed substantial adjustment costs on either battery producers or national administrations. Of course, the introduction of binding limit values for air concentration in the case of the Ambient Air Directive would have had very costly consequences on certain industries as well. But the Member States that favoured this option came nowhere near to a qualified majority or even a blocking minority. In fact, Denmark was the only Member State that consistently favoured limit values for all regulated pollutants. Thus, although the nature of the thresholds set for the monitoring of air pollutants strongly affected certain types of industries, it did not make it on the ministers' agenda because there was a near-consensus on the larger benefits of non-binding target values. A similar reasoning applies to most other issues in the Ambient Air Directive. Individual or groups of Member States demanded adjustments of the Commission proposal, but because most of these demands were in one way or another just aimed to reduce the burden on particular national administrations, other Member States had no reason to oppose them.

In contrast, a strong division existed in the Council between a large group of Member States favouring an extensive or even a total ban of NiCad batteries and an equally large group of Member States opposing such a ban. A similar division was apparent on the issues of collection and recycling targets. Mainly Member States with experience in battery recycling pleaded for a more extensive ban on

154 *Part III: Qualitative analysis*

cadmium in batteries and higher collection and recycling targets. The strong lobbying of the battery-producing industry resulted in some Member States opposing a cadmium ban, even if they generally favoured a more ambitious collection and recycling system. The position of Germany is one such example. Taken individually, the salience of an issue is unlikely to be sufficient for an issue to be discussed by ministers. If Member States agree on a certain course of action, no reason exists to discuss an issue at higher levels of the Council, even if the issue is very salient. Thus, the Environment case studies support the earlier finding that issue salience affects committee decision-making only if Member States disagree on the most preferable policy option.

The Environment cases also exhibit some weak evidence corroborating the hypothesised effect of qualified majority voting. If qualified majority voting is allowed, the positions of Member States that are not backed by a blocking minority can simply be ignored. In the case of the Batteries Directive, ministers discussed only issues that were contested by a large number of Member States. Similarly, in the case of the Ambient Air Directive, Coreper discussed mostly issues that involved several Member States demanding changes. Only the Battery Directive issues discussed by Coreper also included a number of demands raised by individual or a couple of Member States.

The involvement of the EP did not seem to have a major effect on the Council level at which a decision was taken. In the case of the Batteries Directive, the text on which the Council based its negotiations already included the EP amendments accepted by the Commission. In addition, several players in the Council who favoured a cadmium ban and high collection and recycling targets counted on the environmentally friendly attitudes of the EP to move the final outcome closer to their positions in later rounds of the co-decision procedure. Therefore, the EP opinion might have had an indirect influence on the content of the Council decision, but an impact on the Council level at which the decision has been taken is not apparent. In the case of the Ambient Air Directive, the Irish Presidency exploited the fact that the Parliament had its last plenary meeting of the legislative term in April 2004 to induce 'a sense of urgency' into Council negotiations.[45] In order to reach an early agreement with the Parliament, Council negotiations had to proceed swiftly. Under normal circumstances, attempts to reach an early agreement with the EP are likely to protract Council negotiations. In the case of the Ambient Air Directive, the existence of a deadline for such an agreement might have actually helped to speed-up negotiations in the Council. The deadline might have also increased the chances that an issue was decided at lower levels in the Council, but there is no direct evidence for such an effect.

What role did uncertainty about the consequences of legal provisions play? Interestingly, some indications exist that the effect of uncertainty operates in fact contrary to expectations. The cadmium ban in the Batteries Directive exemplifies this point. The Council chose the amendment for a partial ban on NiCad batteries

45 Interview D.

as a pilot study for impact assessments exactly because the environmental and economic consequences of such a ban were highly uncertain. However, lacking an agreed methodology and relevant data, the working party could not agree on a consensual evaluation of the cost and benefits of a ban. In fact, the impact assessment concluded that

> since it is impossible to quantify the impacts of the various options with more precision, let alone to put a monetary value on it, the final decision on whether the environmental benefits of any particular option justify the economic and social costs must remain a political decision.[46]

Thus, uncertainty was actually a major reason why ministers discussed the cadmium ban, although political conflict and salience acted probably in concert with uncertainty in this instance.

Yet, other evidence also exists that support the original hypothesis. Certain points were simply too complex to be discussed by ministers. The issue of the precise definition of battery types is an example. The distinction between industrial and portable batteries crucially determined the scope of several provisions in the proposal, including the scope of the cadmium ban. Thus, the distinction between portable and industrial batteries was arguably just as important as the inclusion of cordless power tools in the ban. However, while ministers eventually needed to decide the issue of a ban of cordless power tools, the deputy permanent representative immediately resolved the disagreement about the definitions of battery types in the first meeting in which they discussed the issue.

A crucial difference between these two instances of decision-making was the existence of an information asymmetry between the members of different Council levels. However, the information asymmetry did not concern the practical consequences of the legal text, but rather the legal consequences of the wording in the text. In contrast to practical consequences, which cover remote environmental, social and economic developments caused by a piece of legislation, legal consequences refer to the types of situations covered by a provision and the rules prescribed to such generic situations. The legal consequences of individual provisions can be known with relative certainty if one is familiar with the content and structure of a proposal. Thus, after a brief by their working party experts, the deputy permanent representatives had a good idea about the legal consequences of changes to provisions like the definitions of battery types. The working party experts also sat directly beside their bosses in Coreper meetings and could give direct advice when needed. Although working party experts usually attend ministerial meetings as well, they sit at the back of the room without direct access to their superiors. In addition, the time of ministers is generally more limited than the time of Coreper members. Any briefs for ministers have to be even shorter than those for the members of Coreper. Thus, although Coreper members were just as uncertain about the practical consequences of

---

46 Council (2004): Draft impact assessment. 22 November 2004, 14943/04 ADD 1.

156 *Part III: Qualitative analysis*

changes to the definitions of battery types as the ministers, Coreper members were more aware of their legal consequences. In instances where committee members have an informational advantage, making a decision in Coreper is less risky than leaving the decision up to ministers. In the end, the deputy permanent representative would be blamed for an uninformed decision by his or her minister, at least when the minister's bad decision was just a result of ignorance about the legal details of the dossier.

The case descriptions also point to the priorities of the Presidency as an important variable for explaining the decision-making level in the Council. In the case of the Ambient Air Directive, the effect of the EP involvement and the effect of the Presidency priority are hard to disentangle, basically because the Presidency used the prospect of an early agreement with the EP as an incentive for Member States to reach a timely decision. Nevertheless, the Presidency priority seems to be the main causal factor. The negotiations with the EP might have introduced additional points of conflict which could only be decided at Coreper level. However, the decision to engage in negotiations with the EP in the first place is a result of the ambitions of the Irish Presidency to conclude the dossier during the first reading. Coreper discussed only those internal Council issues that were of rather minor significance and hardly conflictual. Thus, in the absence of Presidency impatience, the working party might have reached a decision on the dossier, albeit later in time and then in the form of a common position. The priorities of the Dutch Presidency also played a major role in the adoption of the common position on the Batteries Directive. In the month before the last meeting of Environment ministers during the Dutch Presidency, the Presidency used every weekly Coreper meeting to discuss the dossier. In addition, the working party discussed the file on four occasions. The impatience of the Presidency also explains the relatively large number of issues decided at Coreper level in the case of the Batteries Directive.

Considering the cases as a whole, Presidency priority seems to be the main factor explaining the involvement of Coreper in the case of the Ambient Air Directive, although this factor worked through the first-reading negotiations with the Parliament. Quite a number of contested points were raised by Member States, but these points did not result in fundamental divisions between larger groups of Member States. Thus, the absence of preference divergence also played a role. The possibility of qualified majority voting might have helped to keep the level of conflict low as well, but the Ambient Air Directive case showed no clear evidence in favour of or against this hypothesis. In the case of the Batteries Directive, the strong involvement of Coreper is probably also due to the priorities of the Dutch Presidency. However, the involvement of ministers was a result of issue salience in combination with preference divergence between larger groups of Member States. The pattern that ministers discussed only issues contested by groups of Member States large enough to be able to block a decision is consistent with the voting rule hypothesis. The absence of uncertainty about the legal consequences of provisions was also a precondition for ministerial discussions.

Environment 157

Appendix: development of individual negotiation issues

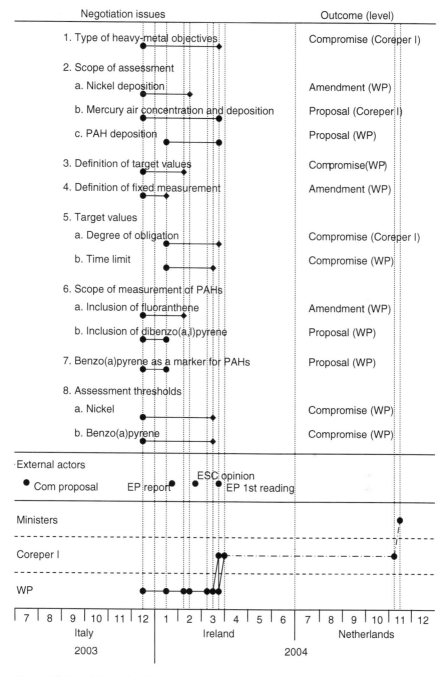

Figure 10.4 Ambient Air Directive: negotiation issues (continued over page).

Note: See footnote 39 on page 124 for further information on this figure and its data sources.

158 *Part III: Qualitative analysis*

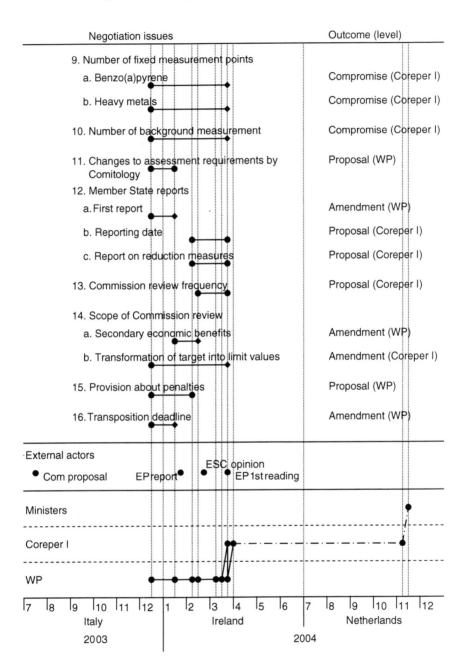

Figure 10.4 Continued.

Environment 159

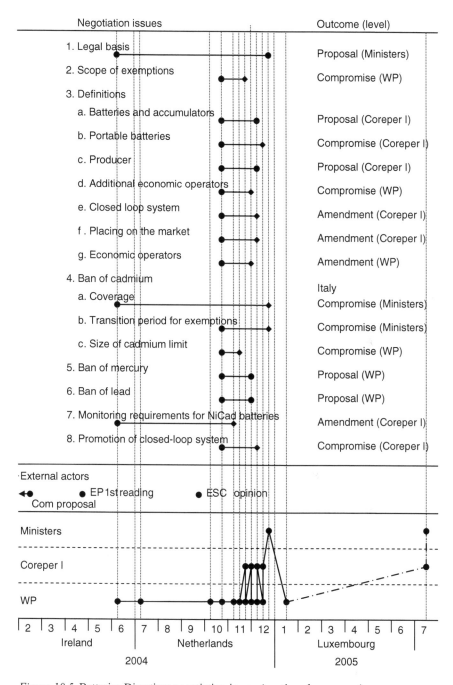

Figure 10.5 Batteries Directive: negotiation issues (continued over page).

Note: See footnote 39 on page 124 for further information on this figure and its data sources.

160 *Part III: Qualitative analysis*

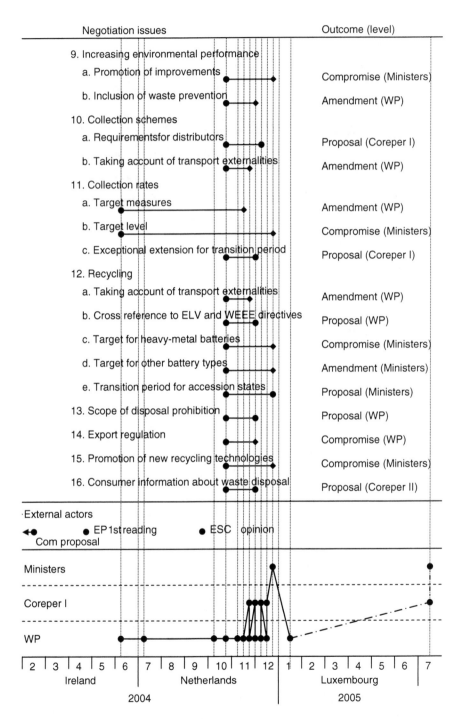

Figure 10.5 Continued.

Environment 161

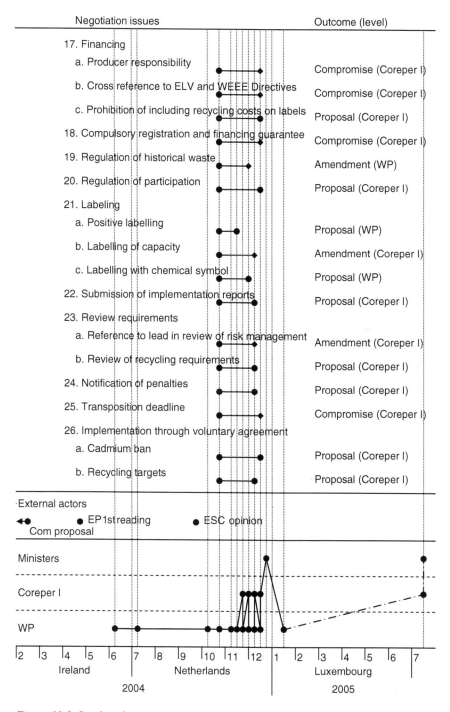

Figure 10.5 Continued.

11 Economic and Financial Affairs

In contrast to Environment and Agriculture, the Economic and Financial Affairs area does not constitute a cohesive policy field. Many observers distinguish between at least two major sub-fields: measures related to the European Monetary Union and measures related to the Budget.[1] The two sub-fields are characterised by different actors, institutions and mechanisms involved in policy-making.[2] The same is true for the less prominent, smaller sub-fields of Financial Services and Taxation. The Community method of policy-making is most prevalent in these sub-areas. The Commission introduces proposals and the Council together with the Parliament decide on binding legislation. In the case of Financial Services, a qualified majority is sufficient to make a decision in the Council and legislative decision-making occurs through the co-decision procedure. In the case of Taxation, the consultation procedure applies and the Council can adopt acts only by unanimity. The latter feature makes the field of Taxation a good comparison case for an examination of the effect of the voting rule on committee decision-making.

Compared with the Agriculture and Environment fields, the EU institutions passed little legislation in the area of Taxation. Although the original Treaty of Rome already contained an article authorising the harmonisation of indirect taxation, the integration of tax regimes made little progress over the years. The view provisions adopted by the Council concentrated mainly on the harmonisation of value-added tax and, to some extent, excise duties. In contrast to indirect taxation, direct taxation does generally not affect the free movement of goods and the freedom to provide services. Therefore, direct taxation remains in principle the sole responsibility of Member States. However, Member States adopted a number of measures to prevent tax avoidance and double taxation in 1990.[3]

---

1 For example, see the distinct treatments of these policy sub-fields in Hix (2005) and Wallace (2005).
2 For an overview and discussion of distinct policy-making modes in the Economic and Financial Affairs Council formation, see Korkman (2004).
3 See the 'Summaries of EU legislation: Taxation' at http://europa.eu/legislation_summaries/taxation/index_en.htm (accessed 22 August 2011).

Economic and Financial Affairs 163

Among these measures were the Parent-Subsidiary Directive and the Mergers Directive.[4] The proposals for these Directives had been pending in the Council since the late 1960s. To alleviate alleged shortcomings, the Commission proposed amendments to the Directives already in 1993, only three years after their adoption. These proposals also met a stalemate in the Council. New impetus for legislative activity in the field of Taxation came only in 2001, after the publication of a Commission Communication outlining the strategic priorities 'for the years ahead'.[5] The Commission introduced several new legislative proposals on direct as well as indirect taxation during the following years. The Commission made also new attempts to amend the Parent-Subsidiary Directive and the Mergers Directive. The Commission transmitted revised proposals for amending these Directives in 2003. The following case studies describe and analyse the process leading to the adoption of these proposals. The goal of the Parent-Subsidiary Directive was to eliminate tax obstacles to the distribution of profits among associated companies located in different EU Member States. The Mergers Directive introduced the deferral of the taxation of capital gains accrued through restructuring companies in the form of mergers, divisions, transfer of assets and exchanges of shares across Member States' borders until the date the acquired assets were actually sold. The proposed amendments to the original Directives extended and updated the existing provisions.

The Working Party on Tax Questions (Direct Taxation) discussed both the proposal amending the Parent-Subsidiary Directive and the proposal amending the Mergers Directive. Similar to the working parties in the Agriculture formation, the Direct Taxation working party consisted mainly of experts from national ministries, who travel to Brussels just to attend the working party meetings. Counsellors specialised in tax questions from the permanent representations might also attend meetings, but in contrast to practices in the Environment working party, the experts from the national ministries usually take the lead in negotiations. Due to the legal complexity of the matter, the working party members are mostly lawyers specialised in international tax questions. The working party reports to Coreper II, the senior formation of Coreper composed of the permanent representatives themselves. The Economic and Financial Affairs ministers constitute the top of the hierarchy. Similar to Agriculture ministers, Economic and Financial Affairs ministers meet almost on a monthly basis. At least the agenda of these meetings almost always included tax questions during the study period.

---

4 Council Directive 90/435/EEC of 23 July 1990 on the common system of taxation applicable in the case of parent companies and subsidiaries of different Member States. 22 September 1990, OJ L225, pp. 6–9. Council Directive (90/434/EEC) of 23 July 1990 on the common system of taxation applicable to mergers, divisions, transfers of assets and exchanges of shares concerning companies of different Member States. OJ L225, 20 August 1990, pp. 1–5.

5 Commission (2001): Tax policy in the European Union: Priorities for the years ahead. 10 October 2001, COM/2001/260.

164   *Part III: Qualitative analysis*

Parent-Subsidiary Directive

Background and proposal content

The Council adopted the Parent-Subsidiary Directive originally in 1990. The proposal amending the Directive replaced an earlier initiative of the Commission, which had been blocked in the Council since 1993.[6] However, rather than lowering the ambitions set out in the proposal of 1993, the Commission extended the set of issues to be modified in the new proposal. Based on a mandate of the Council, the Commission had conducted a study in 2001 on company tax provisions and their impacts on the functioning of the internal market and the competitiveness of European companies.[7] The goal of this study was to examine possible tax obstacles to cross-border economic activities and to identify remedies. A Commission Communication set out the conclusions from this study. Among other things, the Communication recommended extending the scope of the Parent-Subsidiary Directive, both in terms of the types of companies and the types of transactions covered.[8] The Economic and Financial Affairs Council had concluded already in November 2000 that the scope of the Directive should be enlarged. The ministers had declared that the updating of the list of companies to which the Directive applies was a priority.[9] In 2002, the Commission convened several meetings of the responsible Commission expert group with delegates from the Member States to discuss possible changes to the existing legislation. After these consultations, the Commission transmitted a proposal for changes to the Parent-Subsidiary Directive to the Council in July 2003. The Commission considered a common consolidated tax base throughout the EU to be the only viable way to eliminate all tax obstacles to the proper functioning of the internal market.[10] However, given the fierce resistance of some Member States to a common tax base, the Commission decided to limit the proposal to measures that would improve the most pressing tax problems covered but not addressed by the existing legislation. In the case of the Parent-Subsidiary Directive, the following changes were proposed to remedy problems of the original Directive:

---

6 Commission (1993): Proposal for a Council Directive amending Directive 90/435/EEC of 23 July 1990 on the common system of taxation applicable in the case of parent companies and subsidiaries of different Member States. 26 July 1993, COM/1993/293.

7 Commission (2001): Commission staff working paper: Company taxation in the Internal Market. 23 October 2001, SEC/2001/1681.

8 Commission (2001): Towards an Internal Market without tax obstacles: A strategy for providing companies with a consolidated corporate tax base for their EU-wide activities. 21 October 2001, COM/2001/582, p. 12.

9 Council (2000): Press release of the 2312th Council meeting (Economics and Finance), held on 26 and 27 November 2000 in Brussels. N. d., 13861/00, p. 27.

10 Commission (2003): Proposal for a Council Directive amending Directive 90/435/EEC on the common system of taxation applicable in the case of parent companies and subsidiaries of different Member States. 29 July 2003, COM/2003/462, pp. 3–4.

Economic and Financial Affairs 165

- An extension of the list of types of companies covered by the Directive. Among other company types, the extension included companies operating under the newly created European company (SE) statute.
- An extension of the applicability of the Directive to residents of a Member State that have an interest in a company that is located and taxed in another Member State but treated as transparent by the former State. This provision was supposed to prevent double taxation of the resident.
- A reduction of the conditions to qualify as a parent company by lowering the minimum holding threshold in another company from 25 to 10 per cent. This change extended the exemption of withholding tax charged on distributed profits considerably.
- An extension of the Directive to situations where permanent establishments of companies receive profits from related entities.
- A provision allowing companies to prove that their real management costs of holding a subsidiary are lower than the flat rate of up to 5 per cent of profits set by the Member State. If a company can prove that the real costs are below the flat rate set by the Member State, only the real management costs are excluded from tax deduction.

Despite the long preparation and extensive consultation prior to the adoption of the proposal, Member States indicated diverging views on all of these provisions when negotiations eventually started in the Council's preparatory bodies.

Negotiation process

The Commission adopted and transmitted the proposal to amend the Parent-Subsidiary Directive to the Council on 29 July 2003. The Italian Presidency took up the proposal directly after the summer break. The Presidency intended to reach a decision on the dossier by the end of the year.[11] Indeed, not only an informal agreement was reached by the end of the Italian Presidency, but the Directive was also formally adopted by that time (see Table 11.1). The actual negotiation process in the Council took less than three months. The Working Party on Tax Questions (Direct Taxation) discussed the dossier during six meetings. After the first three working party meetings, the chair of the working party decided to refer the proposal to Coreper II and the Economic and Financial Affairs ministers for further guidance. After three more working party meetings, the Permanent Representatives reached an informal agreement on the dossier, which was confirmed by ministers as an A-point and later also formally adopted as a legislative act (see Figure 11.1).

11 Council (2002): Draft operational programme for the Council for 2003 submitted by the Greek and Italian Presidencies. 3 December 2002, 14944/02.

166   *Part III: Qualitative analysis*

Table 11.1 Parent-Subsidiary Directive: main decision-making events

Date	Collective actor	Event
29-07-2003	Commission	Adoption of proposal
29-07-2003	Commission	Transmission of proposal to Council and EP
08-09-2003	WP	First reading of proposal
18-09-2003	WP	Discussion of WP report
24-09-2003	WP	Discussion of WP report
30-09-2003	Coreper II (II-item)	Discussion of WP report
01-10-2003	WP	Discussion of WP report
07-10-2003	Economic and Financial Affairs Council (B-item)	Policy debate
13-10-2003	WP	Discussion of WP report and Presidency proposal
24-10-2003	WP	Discussion of WP report
31-10-2003	WP	Discussion of WP report
05-11-2003	Coreper II (II-item)	Discussion of WP report
13-11-2003	Coreper II (II-item)	Discussion of Coreper report, de facto political agreement on Directive
25-11-2003	Economic and Financial Affairs Council (A-item)	Formal political agreement on Directive
16-12-2003	EP plenary	Adoption of opinion
16-12-2003	Commission	Refusal of EP amendments
18-12-2003	Coreper II (I-item)	Inclusion of Directive in A-item list
22-12-2003	Environment Council (A-item)	Formal adoption of Directive

Notes: EP = European Parliament, Coreper = Committee of Permanent Representatives, WP = Working party.

The working party discussed the dossier for the first time on 8 September.[12] Some disagreements of Member States about the proposed changes became already apparent at this stage. Several current (BE, EL, ES, DE, DK, PT) and future Member States (PL, CZ) voiced disconcert about the suggested reduction of the minimum holding requirement. Germany and France objected to the new provision allowing parent companies to prove that their actual management costs were lower than the flat rate for non-deductible costs. The flat rate could be fixed by Member States and constituted a valuable source of tax revenue. The working party members also discussed several other issues. The extension of the Directive to cover permanent establishments of parent companies was a particularly complex matter. Parent companies, subsidiaries and permanent establishments of parent companies in other countries could form a number of different triangular relationships in terms of shareholdings and profit distributions. These triangular relationships could be distinguished according to the configurations of the countries of residence of the different entities. The discussions centred on what types of triangular relationships were already covered by the existing

12 Council (2003): Report of the meeting on 8 September 2003 of the Working Party on Tax Questions (Direct Taxation). 16 September 2003, 12552/03.

Economic and Financial Affairs 167

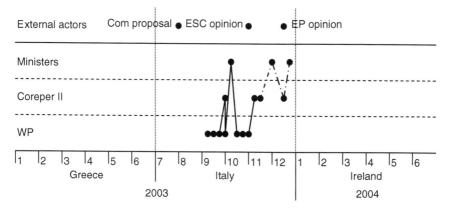

Figure 11.1 Parent-Subsidiary Directive: negotiation process.

Source: Data based on an analysis of Council documents.

Note: Coreper = Committee of Permanent Representatives, WP = Working Party.

and what types would be covered by the new provisions of the Directive. Similarly, a number of questions arose regarding the practical implications of the new provisions related to companies considered fiscally transparent. Several delegations (DE, ES, FI, FR, NL, SE) asked for explanations on this issue.

The next working party meeting took place ten days later on 18 September. During this meeting, the working party members considered all provisions of the dossier except the annex, the transposition date and the remaining purely formal provisions.[13] The working party based its discussions on written contributions of several Member States (ES, FR, NL, SE) about the somewhat unclear provisions regarding the extensions of the Directive to permanent establishments and fiscally transparent companies. The Commission produced a note to clarify the provision on the extension to permanent establishments. The note outlined different triangular relationships between parent companies, subsidiaries and permanent establishments and indicated whether the existing or the newly proposed provisions covered any of these different configurations. The discussion of the configurations yielded different results. In one configuration, the parent company and the subsidiary resided in the same Member State, but the permanent establishment was located in another Member State (case III). The permanent establishment received dividend payments from the subsidiary located in the other Member State. In this instance, the working party members concluded that the neither the original Directive nor the new provisions included this configuration, but agreed that an additional provision should be introduced to cover such a situation.

---

13 Council (2003): Report of the meeting on 18 September 2003 of the Working Party on Tax Questions (Direct Taxation). 22 September 2003, 12740/03.

168   *Part III: Qualitative analysis*

In two other instances, disagreement about the implications of the existing legislation became apparent. In one configuration, the parent company was located in one Member State and the subsidiary and the permanent establishment together in another Member State (case II). Again, the permanent establishment received payments from the subsidiary, but this time the two companies were both located in the same Member States. The Commission and the Irish delegation argued that the original Directive already covered cases where permanent establishments received payments from subsidiaries located in the same Member State. However, several other Member States (AT, BE, DE, ES, FR, PT) questioned this interpretation and demanded that changes should be made to the Commission proposal to make sure that the Directive applied only to cross-border payments. In yet another configuration, the parent company and its subsidiary were located in two different Member States and the permanent establishment was located in a non-EU country. Again, the Commission and the Irish delegation maintained that the existing rules already covered cases in which the parent company and the subsidiary were in different Member States and the parent company attained the minimum holding requirement of the subsidiary only indirectly through its connection with a permanent establishment located in a third country (case IV). Belgium, Germany and Spain did not share this interpretation. The Commission pointed out that its new proposal did not refer to this case, but that it was willing to formulate an amendment to explicitly include this scenario.

The problems related to the extension of the provisions to transparent companies could not be resolved in this meeting. Germany objected to the inclusion of this provision in its current form and the Czech Republic indicated problems based on incompatibilities of the provision with its internal legislation. Germany especially was concerned that the provisions on fiscally transparent companies might permit tax evasion. The Presidency suggested changing the provisions to clarify that the suggested new rules on the tax treatment of transparent companies were optional and did not constitute any obligations for Member States.

The working party met for the third time on 24 September. The discussions focused again on triangular relationships between companies. The Presidency added new provisions to the proposal to explicitly cover the case in which the parent company and the subsidiary, both located in the same Member State, satisfy the minimum holding requirement only through the connections with a permanent establishment resident in another Member State (case III). For the moment, all delegations except Germany accepted the new text. However, the coverage of another configuration met more resistance. Several Member States (BE, DE, FI, FR, ES, PT) maintained that the configuration where both the permanent establishment and the subsidiary are located in the same Member State, and the former receives dividend payments from the latter (case II), was a matter for domestic legislation. During this meeting, Belgium also joined the French and German request to drop the provision allowing companies to prove their real management costs.

Economic and Financial Affairs   169

At this stage, the Presidency decided to consult the ministers on the questions identified to be of a rather political nature. These questions included the minimum shareholding requirement and the possibility for companies to provide evidence for the actual non-deductible management costs. The working party invited ministers to 'give an orientation' on these points and to 'confirm the importance and the appropriateness of the objectives of the proposal'.[14] But before discussions by ministers, the proposal first had to be considered by the permanent representatives. Coreper examined the dossier on 30 September as part of its efforts to prepare the meeting of Economic and Financial Affairs ministers on 7 October. The discussion in Coreper was of a more procedural nature, the permanent representatives made no attempts to actually solve some of the outstanding substantial issues. However, the permanent representatives decided to reformulate the questions posed to ministers. Rather than to give guidance on the specific issues of the minimum shareholding requirement and the possibility for companies to prove their real management costs, the permanent representatives decided to ask the Council to 'verify that there are no major political difficulties for the adoption of the Directive'.[15]

The working party did not await the discussions by ministers but continued the negotiations on 1 October.[16] Regarding the extension of the provisions of the Directive to permanent establishments, France withdrew its reservation on the inclusion of the case where the permanent establishment receives payments from a subsidiary located in the same Member State (case II). However, other delegations (BE, DE, FI, PT, ES) still objected to the inclusion of this case. In addition, a number of delegations (FI, NL, PT) joined Germany and also entered scrutiny reservations on the new provision to cover the case were the parent company and the subsidiary are located in the same Member State and the permanent establishment is located in a different Member State (case III). The positions on all other issues did not change. As a result of the orientation debate by ministers on 7 October, the Presidency and the Commission encouraged delegations to resolve the remaining issues in view of a speedy adoption of the dossier. At this stage, the working party members had largely clarified the implications of the different provisions, had incorporated consensual improvements in the dossier and had clearly stated the positions of their governments.

At the working party meeting on 13 October, the Presidency presented a compromise proposal.[17] Regarding the extension of the provisions of the Directive to permanent establishments, the Presidency suggested to explicitly exclude case II from the scope of the Directive. This exclusion had been demanded by Belgium, Germany, Finland, Portugal and Spain. Regarding case III, the Presidency also

---

14 Council (2003): Presidency note. 26 September 2003, 12949/03.
15 Council (2003): Presidency note. 2 October 2003, 12949/1/03.
16 Council (2003): Report of the meeting on 1 October 2003 of the Working Party on Tax Questions (Direct Taxation). 2 October 2003, 13187/03.
17 Council (2003): Presidency note. 13 October 2003, 13510/03.

170 *Part III: Qualitative analysis*

proposed changes to make sure that the respective amendment referred to this case only. Germany and Belgium still reserved their positions, but the latter country indicated that the revised wording went in the right direction. The remaining delegations (BE, ES, FI, NL, PT), which had objected to one or both of those provisions, entered scrutiny reservations. Some other delegations (IE, LU, UK) indicated that they could accept the new changes, although they feared that the exclusion of case II could be challenged before the European Court of Justice (ECJ).

Most delegations had signalled in the previous working party meeting that they could agree to a gradual reduction of the minimum holding requirement. Thus, the Presidency suggested a two-step approach. First, the threshold would be reduced from 25 to 20 per cent of the shares as soon as the Directive entered into force. A year later, the threshold would be further reduced to 10 per cent of the shares. While all delegations accepted the mechanism of a gradual and simultaneous reduction, some delegations (BE, DK, EL, PT) could not agree to the proposed timing and extent of the reductions. The Presidency also suggested dropping the provision allowing companies to provide evidence for their real non-deductible management costs. The deletion of this provision had been demanded by Belgium, France and Germany.

All delegations eventually agreed to the amended provisions on the extension of the Directive to permanent establishments with regard to cases II and III. The working party also decided to delete the possibility for companies to prove their real non-deductible management costs. Thus, the subsequent working party meeting on 24 October focused on the remaining issues. With respect to the minimum holding requirement, the Danish delegation agreed now to the proposed mechanism for its reduction. However, Belgium, Greece and Portugal were still dissatisfied. The German delegation suggested that a provision should be added that explicitly stated that profits distributed from a subsidiary to its parent company through a permanent establishment in a non-EU country could, but would not have to be, exempt from withholding tax. The German proposal aimed at excluding case IV from the scope of the provision. All other delegations opposed this demand. Germany also objected to the inclusion of additional company types of other Member States as fiscally transparent in the annex of the Directive. The Presidency had included these company types on requests by Belgium, France, Spain and Portugal.

The last discussion of the dossier in the working party took place on 31 October. Delegations could resolve most issues during the meeting. The working party members found a compromise solution for the reduction mechanism of the minimum holding requirement. The working party agreed to a reduction to 20 per cent in 2005 when the Directive entered into force, followed by further reductions to 15 per cent in 2007 and 10 per cent in 2009. The working party also accepted a change in the provision regulating the treatment of fiscally transparent companies. Excluding the option that Member States could exempt profits distributed by fiscally transparent companies from taxation allowed Germany to accept the provision.

At the end of the meeting, only two issues remained open. Germany still insisted that the Directive should allow Member States to apply a withholding tax to profits that a parent company situated in a Member State received from a subsidiary also situated in a Member State through a permanent establishment located in a third country (case IV). The Commission retained that the original Directive already excluded this possibility and that the inclusion of such a provision would constitute an 'unacceptable step backwards'.[18] Rather than retain its objection to the inclusion of company types of other Member States in the annex, Germany now demanded the inclusion of a reference to all 'other entities constituted under German law subject to German tax'.[19] Including this reference would have meant allowing a number of semi-public organisations especially common in Germany to benefit from the provisions of the Directive. Several delegations (AT, EL, ES, FI, IE, PT, UK) rejected this demand on the grounds that the provision does not ensure that these entities were companies according to the requirements set out in the Directive. At this stage, the Presidency concluded that the working party had completed the 'technical discussion' and invited the permanent representatives to reach an agreement on the outstanding issues.[20]

Coreper discussed the two remaining issues on 5 November. Regarding the inclusion in the annex of a general clause regarding German companies, delegates reached a solution. The working party agreed to add an additional sentence, but this sentence referred not to 'entities', as originally proposed by the German delegation, but to 'companies'. Previously, the working group had already accepted the addition of similar clauses to the list of companies of a number of other Member States (BE, EL, ES, FR, LU). Thus, Germany did not yield any real concessions on this point. Subsequently, Austria and the Netherlands also requested the inclusion of such a statement in the lists of their company types.

In order to decide on the application of the Directive to cases where the parent company in a Member State received profits from a subsidiary in a Member State through a permanent establishment located in non-EU country (case IV), Coreper heard the opinion of the legal service. The Council's legal service concurred with the Commission that the original Directive already covered such situations. However, the legal service also stressed that the interpretation of EU legislation is the prerogative of the ECJ. The legal service argued that, if there was any ambiguity in the original Directive about its applicability to case IV, the amendments in the current draft proposal would not affect this ambiguity. Thus, the new proposal would not in any way change the legal status quo. Yet, the changes proposed by the German delegation would most likely reduce the scope of the Directive.[21] The German delegation first entered a scrutiny reservation to examine this argument but lifted the reservation at the following meeting of Coreper on

18 Council (2003): Presidency note. 4 November 2003, 14237/03 Rev. 1, p. 2.
19 Council (2003): Presidency note. 4 November 2003, 14237/03 Rev. 1, p. 10.
20 Council (2003): Presidency note. 4 November 2003, 14237/03 Rev. 1, p. 1.
21 Council (2003): Opinion of the Legal Service. 11 November 2003, 14619/03.

172   *Part III: Qualitative analysis*

13 November. The political agreement reached by the ambassadors was then endorsed as an A-point by the Economic and Financial Affairs ministers at their meeting on 25 November. After the EP had given its opinion on 16 December and the legal-linguistic experts had finalised the text, Coreper decided on 18 December to have the Directive formally adopted as an A-point by Environment ministers on 22 December.

Mergers Directive

Background and proposal content

The Mergers Directive has essentially the same policy background as the Parent-Subsidiary Directive. The Council first adopted both Directives in 1990, after they had been blocked in the Council for more than 20 years. As in the case of the Parent-Subsidiary Directive, the Commission had already transmitted a first proposal to amend the Mergers Directive in 1993. However, the Member States were not able to accept these amendments. Following several studies and Commission Communications underlining the importance of harmonising taxes in certain areas and particularly in the area of corporate tax, the Commission submitted a revised proposal to the Council in October 2003. The Commission transmitted the new proposal to amend the Mergers Directive less than three months after the transmission of the new proposal to amend the Parent-Subsidiary Directive. Like the revised proposal for the Parent-Subsidiary Directive, the revised proposal amending the Mergers Directive dealt with matters similar to those in the failed previous proposal but also added provisions dealing with new issues. The main goal of the new proposal was to extend the scope of the Directive and to improve the methods provided for the deferral of the taxation of capital gains.[22] In particular, the Commission proposed the following changes:

- An extension of the scope of the Directive to partial divisions. Partial divisions refer to split-offs where a company transfers only parts of its assets and liabilities to another company. In contrast to a division, the transferring company continues to exist.
- An extension of the scope of the Directive to cover the conversion of a branch of a company into a subsidiary of that company if the company and the branch are located in different Member States.
- An extension of the types of companies covered by the Directive as listed in the Directive's annex, including the recently established legal types of 'European Company'(SE) and 'European Cooperative Society' (SCE).
- An extension of the scope of the Directive to cover exchanges of shares in which the shares are acquired from a shareholder not resident in the EU.

---

22 Commission (2003): Proposal for a Council Directive amending Directive 90/434/EEC of 23 July 1990 on the common system of taxation applicable to mergers, divisions, transfers of assets and exchanges of shares concerning companies of different Member States. 17 October 2003, COM/2003/613.

Economic and Financial Affairs   173

- Provisions to eliminate double taxation in the case of a transfer of assets or exchanges of shares.
- Provisions on the tax treatment of fiscally transparent entities to ensure that one Member State does not tax an entity directly, while another Member State considers the entity as transparent and therefore attributes the entity's profits to its residents who have an interest in the entity.
- An adjustment of the criterion and the size of the minimum holding requirement set as a threshold for the exemption from taxation of capital gains derived from a holding in the transferring company.
- Provisions on the tax treatment of the transfer of registered office of the SE or SCE from one Member State to another.

Before the introduction of the proposal, the Commission had consulted Member States through the relevant Commission expert group. Nevertheless, all of the changes suggested in the proposal were contested in the Council.

Negotiation process

The Council received the new Commission proposal to amend the Mergers Directive on 17 October 2003. In contrast to the swift adoption of the proposal amending the Parent-Subsidiary Directive, the Council reached a formal decision on the proposal amending the Mergers Directive only 16 months after the transmission of the proposal. The actual negotiation process in the Council lasted just over a year (see Table 11.2). Interestingly, the Working Party on Tax Questions (Direct Taxation) discussed the dossier on 18 occasions during that period. Eventually, the working party members also reached the final agreement. Coreper II or the Economic and Financial Affairs ministers did not get involved in the negotiations on the dossier (see Figure 11.2).

The Italian Presidency took up the proposal soon after its submission by the Commission. The Direct Taxation working party examined the dossier on 14 November for the first time. After this initial exchange of views, the Presidency concluded that most delegations welcomed the dossier.[23] The Presidency classified the issues identified during the meeting under five headings and proposed to organise negotiations accordingly. Thus, the next session of the working party on 21 November dealt mainly with provisions related to the scope of the Directive: the application to partial divisions, the application to the conversion of branches into subsidiaries and the application to the exchange of shares when not all shareholders resided in a Member State. In addition, the working party discussed the threshold for tax exemptions for capital gains derived from the holding in the transferring company. The Commission prepared and circulated papers explaining the implications of the different provisions at the beginning of the meeting.[24]

---

23 Council (2003): Presidency note. 19 November 2003, 14972/03.
24 Council (2003): Report of the meeting on 21 November 2003 of the Working Party on Tax Questions (Direct Taxation). 15 December 2003, 16114/03.

174   *Part III: Qualitative analysis*

Table 11.2 Mergers Directive: main decision-making events

Date	Collective actor	Event
17-10-2003	Commission	Adoption of proposal
17-10-2003	Commission	Transmission
14-11-2003	WP	First reading of proposal
21-11-2003	WP	Discussion of Commission proposal
18-12-2003	WP	Discussion of WP report
13-01-2004	WP	Discussion of WP report
05-02-2004	WP	Discussion of WP report
10-03-2004	EP plenary	Adoption of opinion
10-03-2004	Commission	Refusal of EP amendments
15-03-2004	WP	Discussion of WP report and Presidency proposal
30-03-2004	WP	Discussion of WP report
27-04-2004	WP	Discussion of WP report
05-05-2004	WP	Discussion of WP report
25-05-2004	WP	Discussion of WP report
24-06-2004	WP	Discussion of WP report
07-07-2004	WP	Discussion of WP report
16-09-2004	WP	Discussion of WP report
30-09-2004	WP	Discussion of WP report
12-10-2004	WP	Discussion of WP report
29-10-2004	WP	Discussion of WP report
18-11-2004	WP	Discussion of WP report
25-11-2004	WP	Discussion of WP report, de facto political agreement on Directive
01-12-2004	Coreper II (I-item)	Inclusion of political agreement on Directive in A-item list
07-12-2004	Economic and Financial Affairs Council (A-item)	Formal political agreement on Directive
09-02-2005	Coreper II (I-item)	Inclusion of Directive in A-item list
17-02-2005	Economic and Financial Affairs Council (A-item)	Formal adoption of Directive

Notes: EP = European Parliament, Coreper = Committee of Permanent Representatives, WP = Working party.

The United Kingdom and Germany opposed the application of the Directive to partial divisions and entered scrutiny reservations. The working party did not agree to any substantial changes with respect to the application to conversions of branches into subsidiaries. Spain and Austria had problems with a provision allowing the granting of tax relief provided for by the Directive also to shareholders of third countries. The two countries feared that the provision could be interpreted as an obligation for Member States rather than an option.[25] The working party modified the threshold for the exemption from the tax due on capital gains to

25 Council (2003): Room document no. 3: Note from Spain on specific aspects of the proposal for a Directive amending Directive 90/434/EEC. 18 December 2003.

Economic and Financial Affairs 175

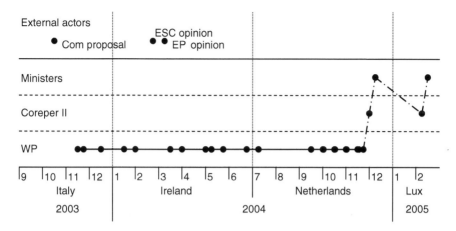

Figure 11.2 Mergers Directive: negotiation process.

Source: Data based on an analysis of Council documents.

Note: Coreper = Committee of Permanent Representatives, WP = Working Party.

correspond with the new threshold established in the Parent-Subsidiary Directive. Austria and Sweden also requested additional entities to be included in the list of company types covered by the Directive. For the time being, the Presidency included the new types of companies in the list in the Directive's annex without a discussion in the group.

The delegations devoted the following meeting on 18 December mainly to the provisions aimed at relieving double taxation and regulating the tax treatment of transparent companies.[26] Again, the Commission provided written contributions to explain the consequences of the proposed amendments. The allegedly technical provisions on the treatment of transparent companies turned out to be controversial.[27] Several delegations (DE, DK, FI, FR, PT, SE) entered scrutiny reservations and the UK reserved its position. In a written contribution, Denmark explained its concerns that the proposed provisions on transparent companies would introduce loopholes that would prevent Denmark to tax capital gains and gains from the exchange of securities.[28] Poland also voiced concerns.

With regard to the proposed rules to avoid double taxation related to the exchange of shares, the group could only agree that such a problem exists and that further discussions were needed. Germany entered a scrutiny reservation, Austria and Spain suggested that the Directive should allow Member States to employ

26 Council (2003): Report of the meeting on 18 December 2003 of the Working Party on Tax Questions (Direct Taxation). 22 December 2004, 16353/03.
27 Council (2003): Report of the meeting on 14 November 2003 of the Working Party on Tax Questions (Direct Taxation). 19 November 2004, 14972/03.
28 Council (2003): Room document no. 2: Note from Denmark on the extension of the Mergers Directive to transparent entities. 18 December 2003.

176   *Part III: Qualitative analysis*

alternative national solutions to the double taxation problem with effects equivalent to those of the mechanism suggested in the proposal.[29] The working party members also accepted that a double taxation problem existed with respect to the transfer of assets, but could not agree on a suitable solution. A number of delegations (DK, IE, LU, PT, SE) feared that shares could be rapidly resold by shareholders of companies transferring assets. To avoid such an abuse of the provisions, these Member States requested the inclusion of a minimum holding period. Austria and Spain requested to allow Member States to set up their own, but equivalent solutions to the double taxation problem also in the case of transfer of assets. With respect to the list of companies in the annex, Belgium, France and Luxembourg requested the inclusion of additional types and Germany and Spain reserved their position on possible modifications.

At the working party meeting on 13 January 2004, delegations focused on one new issue: the provisions relating to the transfer of registered office for SE and SCE.[30] Again, the Commission provided written explanations. Several delegations thought that the linkage between the transfer of registered office and the change in tax residence in relation to tax charge was unclear. The Commission and the Presidency agreed to reconsider the wording of the provisions in the proposal. At the request of Italy, Portugal and Spain, the Presidency altered the definition of exchange of shares to clarify that the Directive did not only apply to shares acquired to obtain the majority of voting rights, but also to further shares acquired by a shareholder already holding such a majority. With regard to the applicability of the Directive to shareholders resident in third countries, all delegations agreed that EU residents should not lose the benefits of the Directive in the case where they acquired shares from both EU and non-EU residents. However, Spain was still concerned that the provision could be interpreted as forcing Member States to apply the Directive completely to third-country residents. Finally, the Netherlands requested the addition of a general clause in the annex stipulating that the Directive covered all companies constituted under Dutch law and subject to Dutch corporate tax.

In the meetings on 5 February and 15 March, the working party discussed again the extension of the Directive to partial divisions, the provision related to the further acquisition of shares by a majority shareholder, the double taxation problem, and the treatment of fiscally transparent companies. Most delegations favoured an extension of the benefits of the Directive to partial divisions. However, the UK retained a scrutiny reservation. Germany proposed a change of the text. The proposed change included a restriction of partial divisions to situations where at least one branch of activity was retained in the transferring company.

---

29 Council (2003): Room document no. 1: Note from Austria on the Austrian system for avoiding economic double taxation. 18 December 2003; and Council (2003): Room document no. 3: Note from Spain on specific aspects of the proposal for a Directive amending Directive 90/434/EEC. 18 December 2003.

30 Council (2004): Report of the meeting on 13 January 2004 of the Working Party on Tax Questions (Direct Taxation). 22 January 2004, 5476/04.

Economic and Financial Affairs   177

Germany wanted to make sure that the rest of the transferring company did not turn out to be an empty shell.[31] Regarding the acquisition of further shares by a majority shareholder, most delegations could agree to extend the definition of exchange of shares to explicitly include such transactions. However, Spain objected and several other delegations (FI, FR, IT, PT) entered a scrutiny reservation on the amended definition.

At the meeting on 5 February, Spain presented detailed examples of its national method to avoid double taxation. These examples were supposed to illustrate that the effect of the Spanish method was equivalent to that of the measures proposed in the Commission proposal. Germany, supported by Austria and Spain, agreed that the Directive should include an obligation to eliminate double taxation, but suggested that the mechanism for doing so should be left to the domestic legislation of Member States. The Presidency requested that all delegations would have positions on the question of the elimination of double taxation at the next meeting on 30 March. Other delegations (FI, NL, UK) distributed written comments on the consequences of the proposed rules for the treatment of transparent entities. These notes did not contain the positions of the delegations or written amendments, but questions and requests for clarification.[32] In response, the Presidency circulated a note for the meeting on 15 March, illustrating the practical implications of the proposed provisions through general examples. The Presidency produced the note to aid the identification of issues that were of concern to Member States.

During the remaining six meetings under the Irish Presidency, the working party screened possible solutions to different problems of Member States. The chair of the working party provided several compromise proposals to accommodate the concerns of Member States. The discussions focused mainly on the transfer of registered office of the SE and SCE, the tax treatment of transparent entities and the mechanisms to eliminate double taxation. However, proposals that satisfied one Member State immediately raised concerns by others. Due to the complex matter of the proposal, finding solutions that were acceptable to all Member States was rather difficult. In the end, the working party had considered several different drafts for all the provisions without reaching a real breakthrough. Regarding the change in the definition of exchange of shares, France lifted its scrutiny reservations. However, Portugal joined Spain in opposing the proposed change and Finland retained its scrutiny reservation. Italy demanded a reference to the change in the recitals.

The working party only reached agreements on two minor points. Delegations accepted the German suggestion to limit the definition for partial divisions to splits retaining at least one branch of activity in the transferring company. As also suggested by Germany, the provision allowing explicitly for the possibility

---

31 Interview M.

32 Council (2004): Room document no. 2: Note from Finland on the tax treatment of transparent entities. 5 February 2004; Council (2004): Room document no. 4: Note from the Netherlands on the tax treatment of transparent entities. 5 February 2004; Council (2004): Room document no. 2: Note from the UK on the tax treatment of transparent entities. 5 February 2004.

178   *Part III: Qualitative analysis*

of applying the Directive to cases where EU shareholders acquired holdings from third country shareholders was deleted by the working party. However, the Member States agreed to adopt a statement for the Council minutes clarifying that shareholders should also benefit from the Directive in cases where the shares originated from both EU and non-EU country residents. Following the accession of the new Member States, the Presidency included the types of companies established in these countries and to be covered by the Directive in the annex of the proposal.

The first meeting under the Dutch Presidency took place on 7 July and was still mainly occupied with considering different drafting suggestions for the provisions on the transfer of registered office of SCE and SE. At this stage, the working party had held twelve meetings and had considered numerous draft texts on the conflictual issues. Still, no agreement was in sight. Thus, the Dutch Presidency decided to pursue a different approach. Given the complex nature of the issues, the Dutch started comprehensive bilateral talks with Member States to sound out their positions and their specific problems, rather than to continue to present compromise proposals that would satisfy one Member State but cause objections by others.[33] As a result of these bilateral talks and the working party meetings on 16 and 30 September, the Presidency presented new draft provisions and possible solutions in a room document for the working party meeting on 12 October. The Presidency also announced that it was prepared to move the proposal 'up to the political level of Coreper and the EcoFin Council' if the next two meetings proved that some issues could not be solved by the working party.[34]

Regarding the measures to avoid double taxation, the working party had not made any progress during the two meetings in September. The Presidency identified a consensus on the principle to avoid double taxation, but not on the method to implement this principle. Thus, the Presidency suggested including a general provision obliging Member States to provide domestic laws to avoid double taxation. Although a general method would still be recommended in the Directive, Member States would be free to choose a different method with equivalent effects. The working party achieved some moderate progress on the provisions with regard to the transfer of registered office of an SE or SCE. Some changes in the text partly resolved the concerns of the UK and Italy about the tax residency of a registered office after its transfer. The UK also indicated willingness to compromise on the issue excluding a dual resident SE or SCE from the scope of the Directive. With regard to the provisions regulating the case where the SE or SCE has a permanent establishment in another Member State, Sweden joined Poland and entered a scrutiny reservation. Germany and the UK still opposed the current wording of the provision. In response, the Presidency presented a new draft provision.

---

33 Interview M.

34 EcoFin stands for Economic and Financial Affairs. Council (2004): Room document no. 1 of the meeting on 12 October 2004 of the Working Party on Tax Questions (Direct Taxation). 12 October 2004, p. 1.

Economic and Financial Affairs   179

In the meeting on 30 September, the Commission pointed out that there was no question whether the treatment of transparent entities should be regulated, because the enlargement had already brought company types into the scope of the Directive that could be considered transparent. The question centred rather on how this issue should be regulated. Nevertheless, the opposing delegations (DE, FI, FR, PL, PT, SE, UK) retained their scrutiny reservations. The UK suggested a number of principles which such a provision should satisfy in order to be acceptable to the UK and other sceptical delegations. After the meeting on 12 October, the Presidency suggested specific compromise proposals for the measures on the avoidance of double taxation as well as for the treatment of transparent companies.[35] The compromise regarding the avoidance of double taxation included two possible formulations for an opt-out from the application of the mechanism provided for in the proposal. The compromise regarding the treatment of fiscally transparent companies aimed at respecting the principles suggested by the UK.

In the meeting on 29 October, the working party accepted the Presidency compromise suggestion on the treatment of fiscally transparent companies. The compromise proposal satisfied the demands of the UK and several other delegations (DE, FI, FR, PL, PT, SE). However, some delegations still could not agree to any provision regulating the mechanisms to prevent double taxation. Thus, the Presidency decided to drop any reference to a specific mechanism. Germany especially had been a staunch opponent of any mechanism prescribed at the European level. However, Austria, Spain and France had also supported Germany's demands. Regarding the definition of exchange of shares, Spain dropped its reservation against the extension of the definition to include further acquisitions of shares by a shareholder already in possession of a majority of the shares. However, Portugal still opposed the change of the definition. The Italian and UK delegations were now satisfied with the provision on the transfer of registered office of SE and SCE.

At this stage, the Commission official in charge of the proposal seriously contemplated to withdraw it. The Member States had agreed to completely remove the provisions regarding the prevention of double taxation from the proposal and had watered down the provisions on the treatment of transparent companies considerably. However, the political level in the Commission decided against a withdrawal of the proposal. The amendments still improved on the status quo and the Commission would have risked considerable political damage by withdrawing the proposal against the collective will of the Member States.[36]

At the meeting of 18 November, the working party almost finalised the proposal. Portugal lifted its reservation on the extension of the definition of exchange of shares to include also exchanges in which the shareholder was

---

35 Council (2004): Room document no. 1 for the meeting on 29 October 2004 of the Working Party on Tax Questions (Direct Taxation). 29 October 2004.

36 Interview M.

180   *Part III: Qualitative analysis*

already holding a majority of the shares. Only the UK still retained scrutiny reservations on the provisions regarding transparent companies and the transfer of registered office of SCE and SE. However, Spain demanded now a provision to explicitly exclude entities from the scope of the Directive that profited from low-tax regimes. This demand was targeted against the inclusion of companies located in Gibraltar, which benefited from a special tax regime. Earlier, the UK had attempted to explicitly cover these companies by including a reference in the annex of the Directive to companies 'under the laws of a European territory for whose external affairs a Member State is responsible'.[37] The working party agreed on a step-wise entry into force of the Directive. The provisions related to the SE and the SCE would enter into force on 1 January 2006 and the remaining provisions on 1 January 2007. Again, the UK maintained a scrutiny reservation on the early entry into force of the provisions concerning the SE and SCE.

At the last meeting on 29 November, the UK lifted its remaining scrutiny reservation and also Spain withdrew its demand to exclude companies from the scope of the Directive which benefit from harmful tax regimes.[38] Thus, the working party reached agreement on the proposal without any involvement of Coreper or ministers. Coreper decided on 1 December without discussion to include the dossier in the A-item list of Economic and Financial Affairs ministers. The Economic and Financial Affairs ministers confirmed the informal agreement on 7 December. After the finalisation of the text by legal-linguistic experts of the Council, the permanent representatives decided on 9 February 2005, again without discussion, to have the Directive adopted by Economic and Financial Affairs ministers as an A-item. The ministers adopted the dossier without deliberation on 17 February.

Comparative analysis

Negotiation process

One important commonality of the two cases concerns their historical background. Decision-making in the field of Taxation had always been highly contentious. The Council adopted the original Directives only several decades after their introduction by the Commission. Shortly after their adoption in 1990, the Commission already saw a need to propose amendments. However, Member States could not agree on these amendments and they were eventually replaced in 2003 by the revised proposals. The lengthy and at times unsuccessful decision-making processes in the field of Taxation are a direct result of the requirement to reach Council decisions by unanimous consent combined with

37 Council (2004): Report of the meeting on 7 July 2004 of the Working Party on Tax Questions (Direct Taxation). 6 August 2004, 11873/04.
38 Council (2004): Report of the meeting on 29 November 2004 of the Working Party on Tax Questions (Direct Taxation). 29 November 2004, 15341/04.

Economic and Financial Affairs 181

the very divergent views about tax policy in the different Member States. In a long-term perspective, the unanimity requirement is itself a consequence of the divergent preferences of Member States. Taxes are not only an essential source of revenue for Member State administrations, but also an important instrument of economic policy. Given the very different economic policy traditions, Member States are very reluctant to pool sovereignty in this field at the European level. The Commission is aware of the resistance of Member States to harmonise their tax systems. The Commission introduced relatively few proposals in this area with relatively limited ambitions. In the case of corporate taxation, the Commission actually favoured the introduction of a common consolidated tax base to eliminate all tax obstacles to the functioning of the internal market. In this respect, the two proposals discussed in this study were only second-best solutions to 'address the most pressing practical tax problems of internationally active companies'.[39] Therefore, the unanimity requirement already restrained the extent of the changes suggested in the initial Commission proposals. Further below, I discuss in how far the unanimity requirement also affected the subsequent negotiations in the Council committees directly.

Similar to the Agriculture and unlike the Environment cases, the working party started negotiations soon after the Commission had introduced their proposals. In fact, the Italian Presidency originally planned to have the two proposals adopted by the end of its term.[40] The Italian Presidency succeeded in this goal with respect to the Parent-Subsidiary Directive, but not with respect to the Mergers Directive. Two factors can account for the discrepancy. First, the Commission transmitted the proposal amending the Mergers Directive later than anticipated. The Presidency expected to receive the proposal during the first half of its term, but the Commission introduced it only in the middle of October. In contrast, the Council received the Parent-Subsidiary Directive in the first month of the Italian Presidency. Second, and more importantly, the proposal amending the Mergers Directive contained more far-reaching amendments than the proposal amending the Parent-Subsidiary Directive. The proposal amending the Parent-Subsidiary Directive aimed mostly at extending, updating and changing existing provisions of the Directive. In contrast, the proposal amending the Mergers Directive suggested several provisions to regulate new issues, such as the transfer of registered office of the SE and SCE as well as the measures to prevent double taxation in the case of a transfer of assets or an exchange of shares. The proposal amending the Mergers Directive did not only extend the approach of the existing legislation, but also introduced genuinely new provisions.[41]

---

39 Commission (1993): Proposal for a Council Directive amending Directive 90/435/EEC of 23 July 1990 on the common system of taxation applicable in the case of parent companies and subsidiaries of different Member States. 26 July 1993, COM/1993/293, p. 4.

40 Council (2002): Draft operational programme for the Council for 2003 submitted by the Greek and Italian Presidencies. 3 December 2002, 14944/02, p. 14.

41 Interview L.

182 Part III: Qualitative analysis

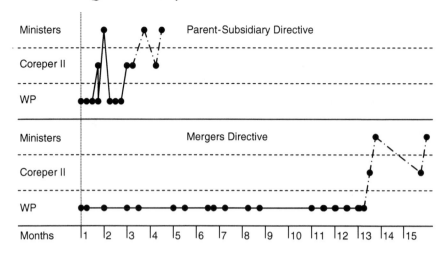

Figure 11.3 Taxation: comparison of negotiation processes.

Source: Data based on an analysis of Council documents.

Note: Coreper = Committee of Permanent Representatives, WP = Working Party.

As illustrated in Figure 11.3, the two decision-making processes show marked differences. In the case of the Mergers Directive, the working party exclusively discussed the proposal. In contrast, the Italian Presidency had already asked Coreper II and the Economic and Financial Affairs ministers for guidance on some political questions of the Parent-Subsidiary Directive after the third meeting of the working party. However, the ministers did not make any concrete decisions during this meeting. As a result of the orientation debate, the Presidency and the Commission urged the delegations to lift their remaining reservations to allow for a speedy adoption of the dossier.[42] In this respect, decision-making on the Parent-Subsidiary Directive resembled the negotiation process in the Agriculture cases. After a further four meetings, the working party had almost reached an agreement. The only remaining contested point was the demand of Germany to explicitly exclude the configuration from the coverage of the Directive, in which a parent company received profits from a subsidiary through a permanent establishment not located in a Member State. The German delegation feared that covering such a situation would allow tax evasion. However, the Commission argued that the existing Directive already covered this case and opposed any change that would result in a step backwards. The Council's legal service supported the Commission's interpretation and pointed out that the absence of any further amendments in this respect would not impair the legal status quo. Thus, the new proposal would not negatively affect the

42 Council (2004): Draft minutes of the 2530th meeting of the Council of the European Union (Economic and Financial Affairs), held in Luxembourg on 7 October 2003. 6 November 2003, 13379/03.

German position. This assertion eroded any justification for further opposition to the proposal by the German delegation. Overall, the working party also reached a far-reaching agreement on the substance of the Parent-Subsidiary Directive. The Coreper discussions only served the purpose to convince the German delegation to drop its last objection to the proposal.

The working party discussions on the proposal amending the Mergers Directive started directly after the discussions on the Parent-Subsidiary Directive had ended. In contrast to discussions on the Parent-Subsidiary Directive, which had been taking place in short sequence on an almost weekly basis, the intervals between the meetings on the Mergers Directive were usually longer. At least to some extent, the longer intervals are explained by the higher complexity of the issues involved. The delegations needed time for detailed internal discussions and analyses of the proposals and counter-proposals in order to identify their different effects. Although the Dutch Presidency early during its term raised the possibility of referring the proposal to ministers, the working party reached complete agreement on the dossier. Interestingly, the informal agreement reached at the committee levels in the Council were in both cases confirmed by an informal political agreement of ministers adopted through the A-item procedure. Besides ensuring that Member States did not re-open the agreement, the informal adoption also allowed the respective Presidencies to present the successful adoption of a dossier, just in case the work of the legal-linguistic experts did not finish in time to allow for the formal adoption of the proposal during the term of the Presidency. Indeed, the Council formally adopted the amendments to the Mergers Directive only during the subsequent term of the Luxembourgian Presidency.

Decision-making levels

Although the two proposals show very different negotiation processes, the types of decisions made at different Council levels show a very similar pattern (see Table 11.3). First, the working party decided most issues, even in the case of the Parent-Subsidiary Directive, in which both the Council and Coreper II were directly involved. Second, the working party resolved most of the contested points through a partial or complete acceptance of the wishes of its members. This result confirms the impression from the qualitative case descriptions that the final outcomes were solutions on the lowest common denominator. In the case of the Parent-Subsidiary Directive, the negotiations went relatively smoothly as the proposal did not contain any strongly controversial points. In the case of the Mergers Directive, the proposal required substantial adjustments to meet the consent of all Member States. These changes to the proposal were so far-reaching that the Commission seriously contemplated withdrawing the proposal.

The case descriptions present strong evidence for the impact of the voting rule on the outcome of Council decision-making. However, the impact of the voting rule on the level of Council decision-making is less clear-cut. If the Commission introduces mostly modest proposals in areas where the unanimity rule applies,

184　*Part III: Qualitative analysis*

Table 11.3 Taxation: types of negotiation outcomes by Council levels

Type of outcome	Parent-Subsidiary Directive				Mergers Directive			
	WP	Coreper II	Ministers	Total	WP	Coreper II	Ministers	Total
Proposal	1	1	0	2	2	0	0	6
Amendment	5	0	0	5	6	0	0	2
Compromise	4	1	0	5	3	0	0	3
Total	10	2	0	12	11	0	0	11

Source: Data based on an analysis of Council documents. See the appendix to this chapter for more detailed information on the individual issues.

Notes: Coreper = Committee of Permanent Representatives, WP = Working Party.

Member States should reach agreements easier and therefore more decisions should actually be made at the committee level. A dependence on the voting rule of the Commission's choice of introducing a proposal and of what to include in it reverses the expectation regarding the empirically observable implications of the effect of the voting threshold. As outlined in Chapter 3, previous empirical studies expected a positive effect of the possibility of qualified majority voting on indicators of decision-making efficiency. The endogeneity of the Commission decision to introduce a proposal in the first place might explain the weakness or even absence of any negative effect of the unanimity rule on committee decision-making. If the Commission introduces no or only uncontroversial proposals in policy areas where the unanimity rule applies, we would expect to see those proposals adopted without much delay. The observable result would be a positive rather than a negative relationship between the unanimity rule and committee decision-making.

Unfortunately, the current cases do not give much indication about the effect of the voting rule on the level of decision-making in the Council. In the case of the Parent-Subsidiary Directive, the chair of the working party suggested referring two issues to ministers for discussion: the size of the minimum shareholding threshold and the possibility for companies to prove the real amount of their non-deductible management costs. More Member States than would have been needed to constitute a blocking minority under the qualified majority voting rule opposed both suggestions in the Commission proposal. Thus, the Presidency might have referred the two issues to ministers even if voting would have been allowed. However, the Coreper discussion of the idiosyncratic German demand to exclude configurations where a parent company receives profits from a subsidiary through a permanent establishment outside the EU from the scope of the Directive might not have been necessary under a different decision rule. Germany was completely isolated and missed a compelling justification for its request. In the Agriculture and Environment cases, Member States often dropped such idiosyncratic demands if they were unable to rally the support of other delegations.

Preference divergence did not play a major role in explaining the involvement of higher levels in the adoption process of the proposal amending the Parent-Subsidiary Directive. Differences of opinion among Member States were at least as strong on some other issues contained in the proposal amending the Parent-Subsidiary Directive or in the proposal amending the Mergers Directive. If at all, preference divergence among Member States was rather stronger in the case of the Mergers Directive. Certainly, the issues discussed by Coreper and ministers were controversial, but preference divergence by itself was not the decisive factor for having discussions at higher levels. The salience of the issues goes some way to explaining the involvement of higher Council levels. At least the two issues discussed by ministers during the negotiations on the Parent-Subsidiary Directive had direct and significant implications for both the tax revenue of Member States and the tax burden of internationally operating companies. However, many other issues had important consequences in this respect as well and higher Council levels did not discuss them. Thus, salience might be a precondition for an issue to be discussed by Coreper or ministers. But just like preference divergence, salience is not a sufficient condition for the involvement of higher Council levels.

In the Taxation cases, information asymmetry was the most important factor for explaining the level of decision-making. Coreper and ministers could not discuss many of the issues simply because they were too complex. Like in the Environment formation, the information asymmetry did not concern the practical consequences of the Directives, but the legal consequences of the texts. The precise effects of the provisions in terms of tax revenue or cross-border economic activity of European companies were in principle just as uncertain to the international tax lawyers in the working party as to the permanent representatives or the ministers. However, the working party members had an advantage in terms of understanding the legal implications of provisions. Of course, legal implications in turn also affect practical implications, but the working party members had an informational advantage only with respect to the former.

In the case of the Parent-Subsidiary Directive, ministers could easily understand the legal implications of the two issues forwarded to them. The ministers could lower the minimum shareholding threshold for companies to benefit from the Directive, as proposed by the Commission, retain it at the high level prescribed in the original Directive, or change it to an intermediate value as a compromise. Similarly, Member States could allow companies to prove their real management costs as suggested by the Commission or keep the original provision that allowed Member States to apply a flat rate of up to 5 per cent. Only the German request discussed by Coreper at the end of negotiations on the Mergers Directive was related to a considerably more complex matter. However, this issue was basically the sole issue the permanent representatives discussed on this occasion and the working party had narrowed down the question to a decision about whether or not the demand of the German delegation should be met.

186   *Part III: Qualitative analysis*

In both cases, the working party devoted a number of meetings to discuss which circumstances were already covered by provisions of the existing legislation and which circumstances should or should not be covered by the new amendments. In the case of the Parent-Subsidiary Directive, the discussions in the working party focused on different triangular relationships between parent companies, their subsidiaries and their permanent establishments in different countries. In the case of the Mergers Directive, the discussions concentrated on several provisions: the treatment of transparent entities, the prevention of double taxation, and the transfer of registered office of the SE and the SCE. In all these instances, minor changes in wording could result in serious changes of the legal implications. Legal complexity prevented many issues from being discussed at higher levels of the Council. However, the absence of legal complexity did not guarantee that an issue was decided at higher levels of the Council.

As in the Environment formation, the cases show some evidence of the influence of the ambitions of the Presidency on the decision-making level in the Council. In order to move negotiations forward more quickly, the Italian Presidency decided to involve ministers early on some straightforward but politically loaded provisions of the proposal amending the Parent-Subsidiary Directive. No evidence indicates that the Irish Presidency ever thought it would finalise the proposal amending the Mergers Directive during its term, although Ireland promised to work on the proposal.[43] In contrast, from the beginning of its term the Dutch Presidency had planned to reach an agreement on the Mergers Directive by the middle of November.[44] While the chair of the working party did not actually move the dossier up to higher levels of the Council, he informed the working party members about his intention to do so in the case of a lack of progress during the meetings in October.

In summary, the most important factor influencing the decision-making processes in the two examined cases was the information asymmetry regarding the legal implications of provisions. The legal complexity of many of the major provisions made sure that the dossiers were largely decided at working party level. The referral of some of the less complex issues to permanent representatives and ministers in the case of the Parent-Subsidiary Directive is mainly a result of the desire of the Italian Presidency to adopt the dossier by the end of its term. Finally, the involvement of Coreper II at the end of negotiations on the Parent-Subsidiary Directive might have been avoided if voting would have been a possibility.

---

43 Irish Presidency (2004): Europeans working together: Programme of the Irish Presidency of the European Union, January – June 2004, p. 15. http://www.eu2004.ie/templates/document_file. asp?id=1499 (accessed 31 August 2007).
44 Council (2004): Dutch Presidency: Provisional agendas for Council meetings prepared by Coreper (Part 2). 30 June 2004, 11015/04, p. 19.

Economic and Financial Affairs 187

Appendix: development of individual negotiation issues

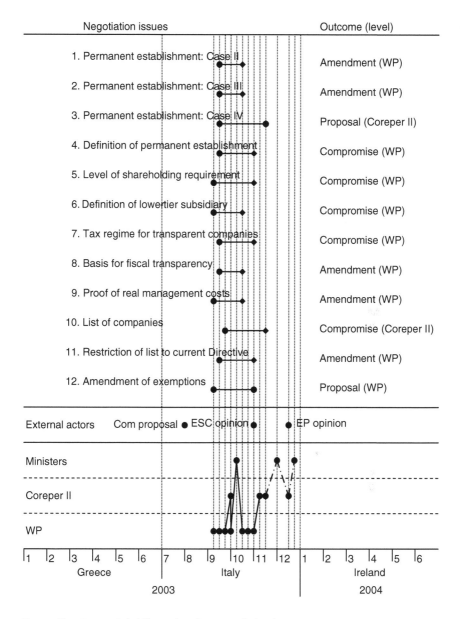

Figure 11.4 Parent-Subsidiary Directive: negotiation issues.

Note: See footnote 39 on page 124 for further information on this figure and its data sources.

188 *Part III: Qualitative analysis*

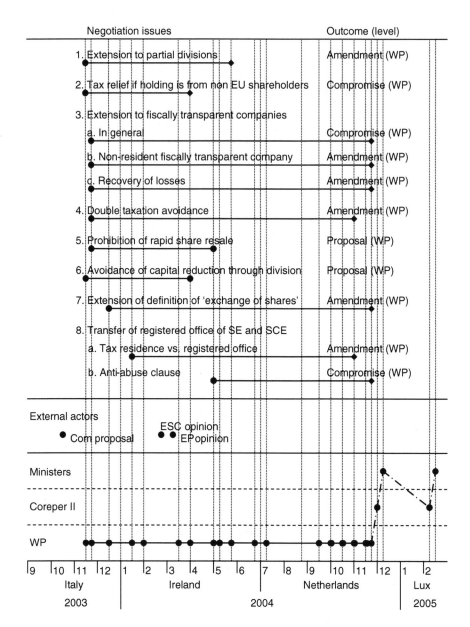

Figure 11.5 Mergers Directive: negotiation issues.

Note: See footnote 39 on page 124 for further information on this figure and its data sources.

12 Summary and between-sector comparison

In the first section of this chapter, I summarise the main results of the case studies in the different Council formations. The focus lies mainly on the discussion of explanatory factors that vary within sectors or even individual cases, but I also mention observations supporting or contradicting hypotheses related to factors constant within sectors when appropriate. I examine the relevance of constant factors in more detail in the cross-sectoral comparison in the second section of the chapter.

Summary of the within-sector comparisons

In the field of Agriculture, I examined decision-making on proposals amending the Leaf Tobacco and Geographical Indications Regulation, respectively. Working parties played a relatively minor role in these cases. The SCA managed the whole process to a large extent. The lack of any larger information asymmetries goes a long way in explaining the high involvement of the senior committee in this sector. In both cases, the SCA asked ministers for an early policy debate. The Spanish Presidency employed the ministerial discussions as an instrument to step up the pace of negotiations. The Spanish Presidency was eager to conclude negotiations on both Regulations during its term. But in the end, the involvement of higher levels in the Council was also due to the divergent views of Member States on highly salient issues.

In the case of the Tobacco Regulation, only ministers were able to agree on the provisions indicating the future direction of the EU tobacco production regime and the related reorientation of the Community Tobacco Fund. Although the direct, practical effects of these amendments were minor, they had the potential to lead the future reform of the tobacco regime in a direction that was strongly opposed by countries with a significant proportion of tobacco-producing farmers. In the case of the Geographical Indications Regulation, most issues decided by the SCA had also strong implications for the interests of specific national industries or individual companies. However, unlike in the Tobacco Regulation case, only one or two Member States contested these provisions for mainly idiosyncratic reasons. The fact that opposing Member States did not

190   *Part III: Qualitative analysis*

constitute a blocking minority might have improved compromise-building. In any case, the influence of the voting rule was illustrated by the adoption of the SCA agreement by a qualified majority of Member States. Denmark especially was strongly opposed to the Geographical Indications Regulation. Without the possibility of voting, ministers might have had to discuss the dossier to make a consensual agreement possible.

In the Environment formation, I studied the adoption of the Ambient Air Directive and the adoption of the Council's common position on the Batteries Directive. In these cases, the relevant working party had a more important role to play. In general, negotiations started in the working party and the Presidency moved them up to higher levels only to reach decisions on specific issues, not to have a general policy debate by ministers as in the Agriculture cases. In the Ambient Air Directive case, some indications exist that the Irish Presidency involved Coreper I towards the end of the negotiations only to reach an early agreement with the EP. An early agreement with the EP allowed the adoption of the Directive before the end of the Irish Presidency term. The Ambient Air Directive involved important issues with potentially strong adverse effects on industry, but the divergence of preferences among Member States was rather moderate. The latter characteristic explains why the involvement of Coreper I was limited.

The Batteries Directive shows a clear impact of the impatience of the Presidency on the involvement of higher Council levels. In addition to a number of working party meetings, the Dutch Presidency had the Batteries Directive discussed in each meeting of Coreper during the last month before the gathering of Environment ministers at the end of the Presidency's term. However, the Batteries Directive was also characterised by a large preference divergence between large groups of Member States. In addition, some of the issues, including all those decided by ministers, were highly salient to Member States, either because the new provisions involved high administrative adjustment costs or because they had negative effects on large battery-producing domestic companies. In both cases, Member States dropped many idiosyncratic demands during early working party meetings. This finding also points to the relevance of the possibility to take decisions by a vote.

The effect of the EP is more difficult to discern. In the case of the Batteries Directive, the involvement of the EP might have had an impact on the content of the Council's common position. The supporters of a stricter ban of cadmium anticipated a similar position of the EP in second reading and were therefore more willing to make concessions on this point. However, an effect on the level of Council decision-making is not identifiable. In the case of the Ambient Air Directive, the attempt to reach a first-reading decision might be partly responsible for the discussion of some of the issues by Coreper. However, this effect was hard to distinguish from the effect of Presidency impatience.

Finally, the Batteries Directive illustrated nicely the impact of uncertainty on committee decision-making. The case exemplifies a conceptual difference between uncertainty about the real-world implications of a proposal and the uncertainty about the legal implications of a proposal. On the one hand, the working party could not reach a consensus on the practical implications of a partial cadmium ban. The working party concluded that, in the absence of reliable assessment methods and data, the introduction of a partial cadmium ban remained a political question. On the other hand, the issue of the definitions of battery types was not moved up to ministers, although the definitions critically affected the scope of several important provisions in the Directive. Only the working party and Coreper I discussed the issue to prevent ministers from brokering a compromise agreement with unintended consequences.

Of course, the practical implications are partly a result of the legal implications. However, the practical implications of a policy in terms of costs and benefits with regard to several desirable goals are usually just as uncertain to committee members as to ministers. In contrast, committee members have an informational advantage with regard to the legal meaning of the wording in the text of the proposal. In other words, committee members have the time and resources to evaluate the abstract consequences of a change in the wording of a certain provision in the context of the other provisions of the proposal and the broader legal system of the EU.

In the field of Taxation, I examined decision-making on the proposals amending the Parent-Subsidiary Directive and the Mergers Directive. The legal uncertainty just discussed was a main characteristic of both cases. The working party members, most of them international tax experts, needed several meetings just to discuss and understand the legal implications of the dossiers. Although several of the provisions had profound impacts on public tax revenues and the tax burden of internationally operative companies, neither Coreper II nor ministers discussed any of these salient issues. Considerable differences in opinions of Member States existed on these issues, too. In the other sectors, the main conflict lines usually ran between larger groups of Member States. However, in the field of Taxation, the major conflict lines ran between the Commission and different Member States. The Presidency and the Commission seriously considered all objections raised by delegations, even if they were raised by individual Member States for very idiosyncratic reasons. This finding also illustrates the effect of the unanimity rule.

In the case of the Parent-Subsidiary Directive, the Italian Presidency sought an early confirmation by ministers that no political obstacles existed to the adoption of the Directive. This request was in line with its goal to adopt the Directive within its Presidency term. At the end of the negotiations, Coreper II discussed a rather complex matter. However, the working party had narrowed down the issue to a yes/no decision. This instance is also an indication that the voting rule matters. The involvement of Coreper was necessary to discuss a demand by a single Member State. If qualified majority voting would have been possible, the issue might not have been on the agenda of the permanent representatives. In the case of the Mergers Directive, neither Coreper II nor ministers were involved in negotiations. However, the Dutch Presidency was prepared to move the proposal to higher Council levels if the working party did not make progress to allow the adoption of the proposal during its Presidency term.

192 *Part III: Qualitative analysis*

Between-sector comparison

The evidence for or against factors that are constant within Council formations can best be examined through a cross-sectoral comparison. These constant factors include the voting rule, the involvement of the EP and the socialisation of committee members. The EP had clearly no effect on committee decision-making in the Agriculture and Taxation cases, where the consultation procedure was applicable. The EP opinion was not even discussed by Council bodies in those cases. In the Environment Council formation, the EP might have influenced the involvement of different Council levels in the case of the Ambient Air Directive. In this case, the Presidency entered into negotiations with the EP to reach a first-reading agreement. As the current legislative term of the EP was soon to end, the referral of the Directive to Coreper might have served the purpose of speeding up the decision-making process. However, the Presidency impatience led to the attempt for an early agreement with the EP in the first place. Thus, the ultimate causal factor for the involvement of Coreper was not the EP involvement as such, but the impatience of the Presidency that led to the attempt to reach a first-reading agreement. The Presidency instrumentalised the end of Parliament's term as a deadline to reach a timely agreement in the Council.

The case studies show some indications of an effect of the voting rule. In Agriculture and Environment, where Member States are allowed to adopt decisions by qualified majority voting, higher Council levels discuss mainly highly salient issues that are characterised by considerable preference polarisation among Member States. In the field of Taxation, where Member States have to make decisions by unanimity, major conflict revolves also around issues raised by individual or a very small number of Member States that would not constitute a blocking minority under qualified majority voting. The evidence for any effects of socialisation is weaker. The Presidency and other Member States sometimes try to reach a compromise with Member States that could theoretically be outvoted. For some reason, the Member States do not redeem the efficiency benefits of voting in those instances. However, the lack of voting is not necessarily a result of socialisation. The lack of voting could just as well be the result of considerations regarding the proper implementation of legislation by the Member States or the long-term character of the interactions in the Council. The Presidency and the Commission might accommodate hesitant Member States to make sure that the adopted act is later implemented correctly. Alternatively, the long-term interaction among Council members could sustain a system of generalised exchange over time.

The effects of socialisation should be most visible in the Environment working party. The members of the Environment working party are usually seconded to the permanent representations in Brussels and meet several days a week. Furthermore, the Environment working party is more insulated than Coreper or the SCA. However, the case studies did not show any signs that the Environment working party was particularly effective in reaching agreements. Like Coreper, the SCA in Agriculture meets every week. Furthermore, the SCA contains some

Summary and between-sector comparison 193

very long-standing members. The potential for socialisation should therefore be large in this committee, too. However, the SCA regularly votes on conflictual issues. The irregularly meeting working parties in Agriculture did indeed not reach many decisions on the issues contained in the examined dossiers, but the lack of decisions is more likely a result of the close tap the SCA keeps on policy-making in Agriculture rather than the lack of socialisation of working party members. Finally, the Direct Taxation working party should also be a good candidate for observing the effects of socialisation. The working party consists of policy experts, meets regularly and is relatively insulated. Indeed, the dominant negotiation mode in this working party is clearly arguing, not bargaining. However, the working party relies so much on arguments and persuasion because of the unanimity rule in the Council. The prospects for compromises are relatively limited if each Member State can veto the proposal.[1] The actual outcome of negotiations showed all signs of a classic solution at the lowest common denominator.

In summary, the qualitative case studies have pointed to five explanatory factors. Most of them were already considered in the quantitative analysis, although some of them are in need of conceptual refinement. The results suggest that the preference divergence, unanimity rule and high salience make agreements at lower levels of the Council hierarchy less likely. The case studies give little indication for any effect of socialisation or EP involvement on the level at which decisions are made in the Council. Uncertainty is a main factor that makes a decision at lower Council levels more likely. However, this concept is better defined as limited knowledge about the legal instead of practical consequences of a dossier. Finally, the case studies pointed to one additional important explanatory factor: the priorities of the Presidency of the Council. A decision is less likely to be reached by a committee if the Presidency aims at a speedy adoption of the dossier. Table 12.1 summarises the intra- and inter-sectoral comparisons. The table indicates the degree of ministerial involvement in each case as well as the values on the different explanatory factors. Low ministerial involvement stands for no ministerial discussion at all, moderate ministerial involvement means that ministers discussed but did not decide the dossier, and high ministerial involvement indicates that ministers made the final decision on the dossier. The table distinguishes between a low and a high value on the explanatory factors.

The table makes clear that firm conclusions about the effects of individual factors cannot be drawn purely based on a comparison of characteristics at the proposal level. Such an analysis would be overdetermined because the number of explanatory factors is larger than the number of cases (see e.g. Häge 2007b). The table gives a useful but only partial picture of the information used in the comparative case study analysis. The conclusions of the analysis are not only based on between-case variation as described in the table, but also on within-case variation over time and across issues. Thus, a few additional explanatory remarks on

---

1 Interview K.

194 *Part III: Qualitative analysis*

Table 12.1 Summary of the within-sector and between-sector comparison

	Agriculture		Environment		Taxation	
	Geographical Indications	Leaf Tobacco	Ambient Air	Batteries	Parent-Subsidiary	Mergers
Ministerial involvement	Moderate	High	Low	High	Moderate	Low
Preference divergence	High	High	Low	High	High	High
Salience	High	High	High	High	High	High
Presidency priority	High	High	High	High	High	High
Legal uncertainty	Low	Low	Low	Low	High	High
Voting threshold	Low	Low	Low	Low	High	High
EP involvement	Low	Low	High	High	Low	Low
Socialisation	High	High	High	High	Low	Low

Notes: Ministerial involvement indicates whether ministers were not involved at all (low), discussed (moderate) or decided (high) the dossier. Preference divergence indicates whether Member States disagreed substantially. Salience indicates whether the policy would impose significant costs on large domestic groups or organisations. Presidency priority indicates whether the Council Presidency planned to finalise negotiations on the dossier during its term. Legal uncertainty refers to uncertainty about the legal consequences of textual changes in the dossier. The voting threshold indicates whether the qualified majority (low) or unanimity (high) voting rule applied. EP involvement indicates whether the EP could only give a non-binding opinion (low) or had veto power (high). Socialisation indicates whether the members of the most involved committee were based in Brussels and met on a regular basis (high) or were based in national ministries and only met for discussing a specific dossier (low).

each of the cases in the table are in order. As established already above, the involvement of the EP and the socialisation of committee members did not affect decision-making in any of the cases considered. Therefore, I will not discuss these factors again in the following remarks.

In the case of the Geographical Indications Regulation, ministers discussed the dossier mainly because the Spanish Presidency at the time wanted to speed-up negotiations. Despite high salience, preference divergence and the absence of legal uncertainty, the SCA made the final decision. The possibility to outvote a few reluctant delegations made a difference here. The situation was very similar in the case of the Leaf Tobacco Regulation. Again, the Presidency first referred the proposal to the ministers for a discussion to accelerate the negotiation process. But in contrast to the Geographical Indications Regulation, the ministers did not only discuss but also make the final decision on the Leaf Tobacco Regulation. In the Leaf Tobacco case, each of the opposing groups of Member States formed a blocking minority. Thus, making a decision by vote in the SCA was not an option. Given the absence of legal uncertainty and the high salience of the dossier, it was up to the ministers to reach a compromise.

In the case of the Ambient Air Directive, the proposal included many salient issues, but Member States did not disagree much about the right course of action. Without the pressure by the Irish Presidency to finalise the dossier before the end of the EP's term, the adoption of the dossier might not even have required the involvement of Coreper. In the case of the Batteries Directive, large opposing camps of Member States, high salience and the absence of legal uncertainty made the final decision by ministers both necessary and possible. The lack of any earlier discussion by ministers was somewhat surprising, given that the Dutch Presidency attributed a high priority to the adoption of this dossier. The Dutch Presidency seemed to have preferred to rely on Coreper rather than ministers to advance the negotiations.[2]

Finally, the two Taxation cases exhibited all features usually associated with ministerial involvement. In the face of the unanimity rule, any Member State could block the adoption of the dossier and Member States indicated enough points of disagreement with the proposal text to have incentives to do so. Both cases also concerned rather salient issues. Thus, the main factor keeping the ministerial involvement low in these cases was the high level of legal uncertainty. The ministerial discussion of a few issues in the case of the Parent-Subsidiary Directive is somewhat of an exception. Still, exactly these issues had very straightforward legal implications. In contrast to the Mergers Directive case, the Italian Presidency was eager to finalise the negotiations on the Parent-Subsidiary Directive during its term. Thus, the Presidency referred the most comprehensible issues to ministers for a discussion in order to move the negotiations forward. The legal consequences of the remaining issues were too obscure to be discussed at higher Council levels.

Up to now, the discussion has focused purely on the results of the comparative case study analysis. In the next chapter, I discuss in how far these results can be reconciled with the results of the quantitative analysis reported in Chapter 7.

---

2 The stronger reliance on Coreper might simply be due to the fact that Environment ministers meet only twice during a Presidency period. In contrast, Agriculture and Economic and Financial Affairs ministers meet almost every month.

Part IV
Synthesis and conclusion

13 Discussion of research results and theory building

Most observers of Council decision-making agree that committees of national experts and diplomats play a crucial role in the operation of the Council. Given that national officials are not directly controlled or accountable to their domestic parliaments, the involvement of bureaucrats in legislative decision-making of the Council raises important questions about the democratic legitimacy of Council decisions. Given that much of the negotiations in the Council occur in its committees, studying the role and influence of these committees is also important for our scientific understanding of how decisions are reached in the Council, as well as for explaining the speed and the outcome of Council decision-making. Despite the vital role of committees in ensuring the functioning of the Council, the extent to which these committees actually dominate Council decision-making has so far received scant attention in the literature. The goal of this study was to shed more light on the important but so far largely neglected topic of committee decision-making in the Council.

The study focused on legislative decision-making in the Community pillar of the EU and aimed at answering two related questions about the involvement of Council committees. The first question asked about the extent to which Council committees make legislative decisions, and the second question asked why certain legislative decisions are made by committees and others by ministers. To answer these questions, I relied on both a quantitative, large sample analysis as well as a more detailed, qualitative comparison of individual decision-making cases. The quantitative study was based on a sample of 439 legislative decision-making cases for which the Commission introduced a proposal between 1 July 2000 and 1 January 2004. The sample covered all internal policy areas subject to legislation under the EU's first pillar. I used the sample both to describe the extent to which legislative proposals were exclusively handled by committees as well as to statistically analyse which factors influence the probability that a legislative proposal is only discussed by committee members.

In line with the exploratory nature of this study, only the most robust findings from the statistical analysis formed part of the selection criteria for the qualitative comparison. For the qualitative analysis, I selected six decision-making cases from three different policy sectors: two in the field of Agriculture, two in the field of Environment, and two in the field of Taxation. While the quantitative analysis

200   *Part IV: Synthesis and conclusion*

focused exclusively on proposal-level characteristics, the qualitative analysis also allowed an investigation of individual issues within proposals. Furthermore, I used the qualitative analysis to examine the plausibility of causal mechanisms advanced by extant theories, to gauge the adequacy of existing theoretical concepts, and to discover additional explanatory factors not considered in the quantitative analysis.

In this chapter, I first summarise the main findings of the empirical analyses and consider whether and in how far the quantitative and qualitative results can be reconciled. I also spell out some shortcomings of the current study. Based on the discussion of the relevance of individual explanatory factors, I then outline how the different factors combine and interact to produce a decision at a certain Council level. This second section of the chapter constitutes a first step towards a procedural theory of Council decision-making.

Synthesis of the quantitative and qualitative research findings

Regarding the extent of committee decision-making, the quantitative study indicated that the ministers are much more involved in legislative decision-making of the Council as often suggested. Rather than 10–15 per cent, the ministers are actively involved in more than 60 per cent of all legislative decision-making cases. This finding is a clear correction of the received wisdom. However, the qualitative findings qualify this finding to some extent. In the cases in which ministers actually decided or discussed concrete issues, they usually focused on two to three major points of contestation within a proposal. Thus, ministers have an input on a considerable proportion of proposals, but this input is usually limited to a very small number of issues within those proposals. Still, these few issues are usually among the most conflictual ones. The quantitative analysis also showed that the extent of minister involvement varies enormously between different policy areas. The subsequent explanatory analyses aimed at accounting for this variation.

A major constituent of many if not most explanations of political decision-making are policy preferences of actors. The qualitative case studies also identified preference divergence as major factor explaining committee decision-making. However, the quantitative study did not find any evidence of the influence of preference divergence on the level of decision-making in the Council. Several reasons might account for this discrepancy. First, the qualitative study pointed out that preference divergence is not a sufficient, but only a necessary condition for the involvement of higher Council levels. Linear additive regression models, such as the one used in the quantitative study, assume that independent variables stand in a 'necessary and sufficient'-like relationship with the dependent variable. Thus, the discrepancy between the findings could be due to a misspecification of the statistical model.

However, a more likely reason seems to be the low validity of the preference indicator. I constructed the preference indicator from expert estimates of party positions on different EU policies. In this respect, the indicator is a marked improvement on earlier quantitative studies of EU decision-making, which either omit Member State preferences completely (Golub 1999; Schulz and König 2000) or rely on data originally developed to measure the salience of policies to political parties (Franchino 2007; König 2007). In contrast to the expert data used in this study, the salience data is based on party manifestoes published for national elections and therefore also not focused directly on policies at the European level. Despite these advantages of the measure, the case studies clearly show the limitations of using general indicators of policy preferences in statistical analyses modelling Council decision-making. The policy preference indicators refer to general policy attitudes of parties. Yet, literally all case studies indicate that Member States' preferences are related to specific provisions of individual dossiers. Furthermore, the Member States usually promote policies that favour domestic industries and even individual companies rather than policies that implement more general party ideological stances.

For example, in the case of the Geographical Indications Regulation, much conflict resulted from Member States' desire to protect their regional producers or their domestic companies who labelled their products with a foreign geographical name, respectively. In the case of the Tobacco Leaf Regulation, countries with a significant number of raw tobacco producers opposed countries that did not have tobacco farmers receiving subsidies from the Community's tobacco regime. Fearing large implementation costs for national industries, Member States almost unanimously opposed the demand of the EP to introduce binding limit values rather than non-binding target values to restrict air pollution in the case of the Ambient Air Directive. The Batteries Directive case showed a similar constellation; the EP's call for a ban on NiCad batteries was mainly opposed by Member States with a sizable battery-producing industry at home. Finally, in the Taxation cases, several Member States opposed provisions in the Commission's proposal aimed at regulating incompatibilities between national tax systems. Even in this sector, the case studies showed that Member States opposed different provisions for very different reasons. Member States with high tax rates feared the creation of loopholes that would allow tax evasion, while Member States with a large financial sector feared that European regulation in this area would reduce the competitiveness of their companies. Arguably, Member States were not in principle opposed to European legislation in this area, but preferred no European legislation to European legislation that would not reflect their national interests.

With the possible exception of the Taxation cases, the actual preferences of Member States can hardly be reduced to a single scale indicating how far a Member State supported or opposed EU policy in a certain sector. Indeed, the preference indicator is problematic both in terms of the level of aggregation as well as the policy content it measures. In light of the shortcomings of the quantitative indicator and the numerous theoretical arguments expecting an effect of preference divergence, the results of the qualitative case studies seem to be more trustworthy. The qualitative case studies indicate that preference divergence is a necessary condition for the involvement of higher Council levels in decision-making.

202   *Part IV: Synthesis and conclusion*

Still, the case studies also indicate that what constitutes preference divergence depends critically on the formal decision-making rule. If qualified majority voting is a possibility, the issues discussed at higher Council levels are usually contested by a number of Member States. In particular, ministers discuss mostly issues characterised by a considerable degree of preference polarisation. Thus, under qualified majority, preference divergence is most consequential if it involves strong groups of Member States opposing each other. In contrast, if the unanimity rule applies, one objecting Member State is sufficient to obstruct negotiations. The quantitative study also indicates an effect of the voting rule, but the effect is not very robust. The weakness of the observable effect is possibly due to the influence of the voting rule on the Commission decision to introduce a proposal in the first place. The case studies showed that the Commission does not introduce a proposal when it expects that the proposal will fail. This empirical finding is in line with earlier theoretical accounts of EU decision-making (Steunenberg 1994) that hypothesised that the Commission will anticipate the reaction of the other legislative institutions when deciding about introducing a legislative proposal. A rejection of the proposal is much more likely under the unanimity than under the qualified majority rule. Even if the Commission introduces a proposal in a much contested policy field, the proposal is usually not very ambitious in order to be acceptable to all Member States. Thus, the relatively weak effect of the voting rule could be due to a selection effect. The proposals introduced by the Commission and observed by the researcher under the unanimity rule are generally less controversial and less far-reaching than the proposals introduced under the qualified majority rule. Proposals that meet the consensus of Member States do not have to be discussed at higher levels of the Council. In the light of this problem, the weak observable effect in the quantitative analysis is not surprising. Given the additional support gained through the qualitative analysis, the hypothesis that the voting rule matters for committee decision-making cannot be rejected.

Although the possibility of voting clearly affects the dynamics and outcomes of negotiations, the actual act of voting is still a last resort in the Council. The absence of voting is sometimes interpreted as supporting the notion that Council decision-making is governed by informal supranational norms and values, the so-called 'culture of consensus' (Heisenberg 2005). However, the absence of voting does not necessarily support the socialisation hypothesis. In fact, the comparative perspective taken in this study shows that the evidence usually cited for the existence of a socialisation effect is highly selective. Certainly, decision-making in Coreper shows some signs of self-restraint among delegations and of efforts to include delegations in compromise solutions even if they could be outvoted (Lewis 2005). However, the SCA is very similar to Coreper in many aspects which are supposed to foster socialisation: the SCA meets every week, the deliberations are rather insulated, and many SCA officials are members of the committee for a long time. Nevertheless, the SCA regularly votes. Similarly, the Environment working party should be one of the most socialised committees in the Council. The working party meets even more often than Coreper or the SCA,

Discussion of research results and theory building 203

is more insulated than the senior committees and, in contrast to many other working parties, its members are mostly seconded to the permanent representations in Brussels. However, the committee decision rate in the field of Environment is one of the lowest in the Council (see Table 6.1).

The lack of any socialisation effect is also strongly supported by the quantitative explanatory analysis. According to theory, socialisation depends crucially on the degree of exposure to an international institutional environment. The number of committee meetings used as an indicator for socialisation captures the exposure of officials to international norms and values rather well. Of course, officials might be influenced by international norms and values in other settings as well, but this kind of socialisation is specific to individual committee members. Norms of reciprocity and self-restraint are unlikely to be sustained in a heterogeneously socialised committee in which the less socialised members continuously take advantage of the accommodating behaviour of the more socialised ones. Regular and contentious interaction is necessary for group norms to develop, to be sustained, and to be transferred to new members. If norms and values of groups are supposed to affect decision-making, the socialisation of a group and not of its individual members is the appropriate focus of measurement. Thus, neither the quantitative nor the qualitative analysis points to any effect of committee socialisation.

The case for the effect of EP involvement is somewhat more ambiguous. The quantitative analysis showed a clear and stable negative effect of EP amendments under the co-decision procedure on the likelihood that a decision is made at the committee level. The case studies clearly showed that the EP does not have any impact on Council decision-making in the case of the consultation procedure. In the consultation cases, the EP opinions were not even discussed during Council meetings. In the co-decision cases, the EP involvement had an effect on the outcome of Council decision-making, but not necessarily on the level at which the decision had been taken. In the case of the Batteries Directive, the resulting common position was relatively moderate in terms of environmental protection, as many pro-environment actors in the Council, including the Presidency, made concessions to more reluctant Member States in the expectation that the EP would 'correct' this outcome in later rounds of negotiations. In the case of the Ambient Air Directive, the Council decision was in fact a compromise solution with the EP in order to adopt the Directive in the first reading.

Thus, the case studies show a clear effect of EP involvement on the content of the final Council decision, but they are less clear-cut about whether the EP involvement influenced the determination of the Council level at which this decision was made. Attempts to reach a first-reading agreement are likely to result in compromises with the EP which often have to be approved at higher Council levels. However, the Ambient Air Directive case showed that the occurrence of such attempts might depend on the priorities of the Presidency. The Presidency decides on whether or not to engage in such negotiations with the EP. The Batteries Directive case did not give any indication that EP involvement affected the Council decision-making level. The EP had adopted its opinion several

204 *Part IV: Synthesis and conclusion*

months before the start of Council deliberations and the negotiations between the institutions started only after the adoption of the Council's common position. Thus, the negative relationship between EP involvement and committee decision-making was not supported by the case study findings. The statistical correlation might be a result of a different theoretical factor. If the correlation is driven by first-reading agreements, Presidency priorities might be the actual, more distant cause. However, this interpretation of the quantitative finding is just informed speculation based on the qualitative analysis of a single case. Other factors that did not play a role in the Environment case studies could be responsible for the correlation as well. For example, the involvement of the EP could result in more publicity, which forces Member States to defend their positions more visibly. In general, the EP involvement correlation is very stable, but the case study results put some doubt on whether the correlation really represents the direct effect of EP involvement or some more indirect causal mechanism.

The quantitative study identified the salience of a dossier as the most important determinant of committee decision-making. Ministers only get involved in Council negotiations on highly salient dossiers. The case studies confirmed this finding. The case studies also pointed to two factors that make a dossier salient. The most salient issues were those with direct, costly consequences on domestic industries and individual companies. For example, in the case of the Batteries Directive, France was the strongest opponent of any kind of ban of NiCad batteries because of domestic pressure by a large French battery manufacturer. The introduction of binding limit values through the Ambient Air Directive would have resulted in considerable implementation costs imposed on industrial producers. In many countries, compliance with these limit values would have required installing pollution filters in factories or even shutting down the worst-polluting companies. This expectation led to the somewhat paradoxical situation that countries who were affected most by pollution were also the strongest opponents of stricter rules. In the case of the Geographical Indications Regulation, both Germany and Ireland opposed time-limits for the co-existence of a registered name and an identical geographical name because they expected that their domestic producers of 'Munster cheese' would have to change their product names in favour of a French producer. In the case of the Leaf Tobacco Regulation, Greece was one of the strongest defendants of the status quo. Immediately after the Commission had announced its proposal, Greek tobacco farmers had been on the streets to protest against the suggested legislation.

A second factor was financial considerations, including adjustment costs to comply with the adopted legislation. In the Taxation cases, Germany, Denmark and other countries with high tax rates on companies were worried about tax evasion that would result in a loss of financial revenues. In the Environment cases, many Member States sought to reduce the administrative requirements to monitor the implementation of the Directives. In the case of the Ambient Air Directive, Member States curbed the measurement standards to assess air quality. In the case of the Batteries Directive, Member States opposed the requirements to monitor NiCad batteries in the municipal waste stream. Overall, the case studies indicate that the salience Member States attach to an issue has little to do with ideological factors but is mainly a result of domestic interest group pressures and national financial interests.

In the quantitative study, I identified uncertainty as a factor increasing the likelihood that a decision is made at the committee level. The case studies also supported this view. However, the case studies also resulted in a conceptual refinement. In standard delegation theories, uncertainty is supposed to relate to the practical consequences of a legal act. Yet, the practical consequences of a dossier are often just as uncertain to committee members as to ministers. In contrast, committee members have a real informational advantage when legal complexity is high. As experts on the dossier, committee members are usually better equipped to judge the legal consequences of changing the wording of a provision. The committee members are better able to anticipate the meaning of changes in the context of the entire proposal and the EU legal order as a whole. Furthermore, officials are expected to prevent their superiors from making mistakes based on a lack of understanding of the implications of changes in a legal provision. Thus, in such cases, officials abstain from referring a dossier to higher levels of the Council hierarchy. Overall, the study showed a clear effect of uncertainty, but this uncertainty refers to the legal complexity of the dossier rather than its practical consequences. Indeed, the case of the Batteries Directive showed that uncertainty about the practical consequences of a dossier is a major source of political conflict among Member States.

The case studies pointed to an additional explanatory factor I did not consider in the quantitative analysis. The Presidency plays a major role in scheduling the work of the different Council bodies. The Presidency decides what is discussed, when and by whom. The case studies show that the Presidency uses these prerogatives to speed-up decision-making on dossiers that it prioritises. At the end of its term, each Presidency is evaluated according to its major achievements in terms of Council decisions adopted. Therefore, the Presidency's goal is to conclude negotiations on as many important and favoured dossiers during its term as possible. Early policy debates at the ministerial level are a primary means of accelerating the negotiation process. These policy debates are used to either reach decisions on particularly contested issues that hold up the discussions in committees on other items or to confirm the general commitment of Member States to the adoption of the proposal. However, the Presidency also moves a dossier to the senior committee or ministers to speed-up the final agreement on the dossier. The members of senior committees and the ministers have more leeway to agree to compromises or trade positions than working party members. Thus, to move the dossier to higher levels of the Council promises better chances for a quick adoption. Future quantitative studies of committee decision-making should also take into account the influence of Presidency impatience on the involvement of different Council levels.

Finally, the qualitative study pointed to the conditional nature of the influence of all these factors. The involvement of higher Council levels is a result of a combination of several necessary conditions. Ministers will only get involved in

206 *Part IV: Synthesis and conclusion*

Council decision-making if there is a sufficient degree of preference divergence among Member States, the issues to be discussed are not legally complex, and the issues are either salient or the dossier is a priority of the Presidency. In addition, the voting rule affects what degree of preference divergence is considered to be sufficient. In other words, committees make decisions on non-conflictual, legally complex, low-salient issues that are of no particular interest to the Presidency. Again, the precise meaning of non-conflictual is critically affected by the voting rule. In the next section, I elaborate on the interplay between different theoretical factors and propose a simple explanatory model for committee decision-making.

Towards a procedural theory of Council decision-making

Examining the effects of individual, independent factors on the decision-making level in the Council is a reasonable starting point for studying the topic. Yet, the case studies have also pointed to a number of contingencies between variables. In this section, I describe the interactions between the factors discussed so far using the concepts of necessary and sufficient conditions.

Preference divergence is by itself not a sufficient condition for an issue to be discussed at higher levels of the Council. The case studies showed numerous instances in which Member States disagreed but agreement was still found in the working party or senior committee. Nevertheless, a significant degree of preference divergence is at least a necessary condition for an issue to be moved up the Council hierarchy. For example, the Ambient Air Directive dealt with the relatively straightforward but salient issue of the type of threshold to be introduced to regulate heavy metal air pollution. Binding limit values would have resulted in considerable implementation costs for industrial polluters. With the exception of Denmark, no Member States seriously demanded such limit values. Instead, the Member States agreed on non-binding target values at the working party level. Thus, if a consensus exists among Member States or preference divergence is very limited, an agreement is reached quickly and no need exists to refer the issue to higher levels in the Council.

Another precondition for the involvement of higher Council levels is the lack of legal complexity. The superiors in national governments use the final decision-making outcome to evaluate the performance of officials in working parties and senior committees. In the end, the officials are also held accountable for undesirable decision-making outcomes resulting from compromises accepted by their minister if she or he only accepted the unfavourable agreement because of a lack of knowledge about the precise legal consequences. The officials are expected to prepare their minister sufficiently to avoid any such mistake. If such a preparation is not possible because of the legal complexity of the matter, the officials abstain from moving the issue higher up the hierarchy. As illustrated especially in the Mergers Directive case, legal complexity is likely to trump the combined effects of salience and preference divergence. No matter how much preference divergence a dossier exhibits or how salient the issues are, the Presidency will not refer the proposal to ministers if the committee can make a more informed decision.

The information asymmetry is the main difference between legal and practical uncertainty. In the case of practical uncertainty, the official is just as ignorant as the minister. Therefore, the official cannot be made responsible if the ministerial decision turns out to have adverse unintended consequences. If the informational asymmetry between officials and ministers does not exist, as in the case of uncertainty about the practical implications of a provision, the incentive to decide complex issues at the committee level disappears.

Thus, the presence of preference divergence among Member States and the absence of legal complexity are necessary conditions for a decision to be made at higher levels of the Council. In contrast, the salience of an issue is not a necessary condition. The case studies showed several instances in which Coreper or even ministers discussed relatively unimportant and technical matters. Prime examples are the Tobacco Regulation and the Batteries Directive. In both instances, the impatience of the Presidency resulted in the 'premature' discussion of the proposals at the senior committee and ministerial level. However, in the presence of preference divergence and the absence of legal complexity, salience is a sufficient condition for discussions at higher Council levels. The same can be said about Presidency priorities. Given preference divergence and the absence of legal complexity, discussions at higher levels of the hierarchy were either a result of the high importance of the issues or of the intention of the Presidency to finalise the dossier during its term.

Based on the preceding discussion, the argument can be summarised as follows: ministerial involvement results from the combination of preference divergence, the absence of legal complexity and either highly salient issues or an impatient Presidency. Equivalently, committees make a decision either when little disagreement exists between Member States, when the issues are legally complex or when the issues are both of low salience and the Presidency is in no haste to adopt the proposal. The theoretical argument is formulated in the form of dichotomous conditions. In the real world, cases often do not fit neatly into any of these categories. However, as a first step towards an explanation and a theory of committee decision-making, this simple argument elucidates the conditional relationships among variables. In the next chapter, I discuss possible consequences of the empirical and theoretical findings for the normative debate and the scientific research on Council decision-making.

14 Conclusion

In this concluding chapter, I first discuss the normative implications of the findings of the analysis. Then I turn to the theoretical and methodological contributions of the research project to the study of Council and EU decision-making. The discussion also points to fruitful avenues for future research in this area.

The legitimacy of Council decision-making

The results of the study paint a rather benign picture of committee decision-making in the Council. If committees decide only about dossiers that are of little interest to Member States and of low priority to the Presidency, that are highly complex in legal terms or on which a consensus exists among Member States, committee decision-making might not raise any normative problems. However, some caveats to this rather positive conclusion have to be noted. Most importantly, legislative decision-making by bureaucrats can be opposed as a matter of principle. National officials are neither directly nor indirectly elected by citizens of Member States and therefore do not have a legitimate mandate to make legislative decisions. However, this position implies rather extreme demands for remedying this situation. In practice, Council decision-making without the involvement of bureaucratic committees would require radical organisational if not constitutional changes of the way the Council and the EU works.

But even if the current organisational structure of the Council is taken as a given, the results point to potential legitimacy problems. The first problem relates to the finding of legal complexity as a sufficient condition for committee decision-making. Legal complexity is not the same as a lack of importance of the issue or a lack of differences in opinions among Member States. Thus, political conflict can also revolve around legally complex issues. In such instances, ministers do not discuss these issues only because they lack the expertise and time to make informed decisions. Indeed, the case studies sometimes give the impression that only issues whose legal implications are self-evident or can be explained by officials in a few sentences make it on the agenda of ministers. Thus, the threshold for an issue to be considered too complex in legal terms to be discussed by ministers seems to be rather low.

Conclusion 209

The second problem relates to the finding that the absence of salience is a necessary condition for committee decision-making. What issues Member States find important is likely to be biased in favour of large and well-organised domestic interests. The case studies indicate that issues are salient to Member States mainly because they affect large domestic companies or industries. The involvement of ministers in Council decision-making is related to the lobbying power of the domestic groups affected by the legislation. No reason exists to expect that the concerns of well-organised and well-connected groups are more important than the concerns of less-organised domestic groups. Thus, the fact that ministers discuss more salient issues does not necessarily mean that these issues are 'objectively' more important than the issues discussed exclusively at the committee level.

As pointed out by Olson (1965: 21), small and special interest groups are more likely to organise than large and general interest groups. For each individual member of a large group, such as consumers, tax-payers or the general public, the success of the organisation promoting the common good of the group does not hinge upon his or her contribution. Although each group member would benefit from realising the common good of the group, his or her incentives to contribute to this realisation are therefore minimal. In fact, each individual member benefits most when the group's common interest is achieved without him or her bearing any cost through the contribution of the other members. In summary, the degree of organisation, funding and connectedness of a group with government authorities is not necessarily a result of the generality or importance of its interests, but rather an indication of the degree to which the group is affected by this collective action problem. Such a distortion in the mobilisation of interests has long been recognised at the European level. Indeed, the Commission directly supports social and citizen groups with financial subsidies to reduce this bias in EU policy-making (Mahoney 2004). However, the domestic level of national interest formation is just as affected by this collective action problem as the European level. The definition of Member States' national positions and their importance might be systematically biased towards small, well-organised domestic groups at the expense of the domestic public at large.[1]

Challenges for future research

The general findings of the study as well as the issues just discussed point to several challenges for future research. Methodological challenges include the

---

1 Note that the extent to which the formation of the national negotiation position is captured by special interests is likely to be related to the extent to which domestic policy-making in general is influenced by powerful interest groups in a certain Member State. While the unrepresentative influence of organised groups on the positions taken by Member States in the Council is a problem for the legitimacy of EU policy-making, this problem is by no means restricted to decision-making at the European level. In fact, the outcome of Council decision-making might be less affected by this problem than the outcome of domestic policy-making. In the Council, the need to reach a compromise among a number of governments, which might be influenced by different types of interest groups to a different degree, should limit the influence of any single type of special interest.

210 *Part IV: Synthesis and conclusion*

quantitative measurement of certain concepts. First, the study indicated the limited usefulness of general policy positions of political parties as measures of Member State preferences. The case studies showed that Member States' negotiation positions are mainly driven by economic and financial considerations, not by party political attitudes.[2] In order to facilitate the examination of preference-based explanations of Council decision-making on large-N samples, indicators of economic and financial national interests need to be developed. The increasingly common practice of using broad policy positions of the parties in government as indicators for Member State preferences (Franchino 2007; König 2007) does not allow for reliable tests of preference-based explanations. Party positions are at best only remotely connected to the positions Member State governments actually represent in Council negotiations. Policy-specific economic and financial statistics of Member States might form a better basis for a measure of Member State preferences. The development of national economic interest indicators also promises advancements for the empirical study of Council conflict lines. Such indicators would allow for a reliable test of the hypothesis that the north–south cleavage often found in studies of Council conflict patterns is related to similarities in the economic structures of Member States.

Another methodological problem regards the measurement of legal uncertainty. In case studies, the researcher experiences the level of legal uncertainty first hand. If the researcher has no prior expertise in a certain policy area, a negotiation process is easier to follow and understand the less legally complex the subject of negotiations is. For quantitative studies, measuring uncertainty poses major problems. Future research should more fully explore the possibilities of computerised content analysis software in this respect. The content and structure of Commission proposals are likely to give indications about the level of legal complexity of the dossier. A measure of legal complexity of dossiers should also be useful for studying delegation in other EU contexts, such as delegation from the EP plenary to its standing committees or from the Council to the Commission.

In terms of theory development, the distinction between legal and outcome uncertainty might also prove fruitful for the study of delegation. The two types of uncertainty are likely to result in different responses by principals. Delegation to specialised committees that have more time to scrutinise a proposal is a more effective response to legal uncertainty than to outcome uncertainty. In contrast, including flexible measures to adjust and update the legal act in the light of implementation problems is a more effective response in the case of outcome uncertainty. Ex ante screening mechanisms can reduce legal uncertainty but ex post adjustment measures are more effective in managing the consequences of outcome

---

2 This finding also contradicts theories that assume EU politics is characterised by a general preference configuration on a specific policy issue. For example, Tsebelis and Garrett's (2000) claim that EU politics is about more or less European integration, that the Commission and the EP have similar preferences, and that they are both more integrationist than any of the Member States is clearly not supported by the analysis.

uncertainty. If principals in the real world are aware of this differentiation, we should expect that differences in the type of uncertainty are met with different institutional arrangements to best counter-act each type's negative consequences.

Further work should also examine the effects of EP involvement on Council decision-making. Theoretically, several scenarios can be imagined in which EP involvement might affect internal Council negotiations. Empirically, the current study yielded rather inconclusive results. The quantitative analysis showed a relatively strong and stable correlation of committee decision-making with the absence of EP involvement, but the qualitative analysis yielded no insights that EP involvement resulted in a decision being made at a higher Council level. More exploratory case studies on the interaction of the EP and the Council in early stages of the co-decision procedure should be useful for a further examination of this factor and for judging the plausibility of different causal mechanisms proposed to explain EP influence.

The study showed that committee decision-making is not related to the extent of exposure of national officials to norms in an international environment. Thus, the socialisation hypothesis was clearly rejected. The rejection of this simple hypothesis does not necessarily mean that the general theoretical argument should be discarded. Maybe the relationship between interaction frequency and co-operative negotiation behaviour is conditioned by other factors; or factors other than interaction frequency also lead to socialisation. But if such conditional or substitutive relationships exist, they need to be spelled out clearly in an explicit theory. Otherwise the socialisation argument defies any empirical rejection through ad hoc adjustments of the theory. More conceptual and theoretical work along the lines of Johnston (2001) and Hooghe (2005) is clearly needed in this area.

The effect of the voting rule also needs some further theoretical consideration. The case studies show qualitatively different dynamics of Council decision-making in instances where different decision-rules apply. The Council acts adopted under the unanimity rule are clearly lowest-common-denominator solutions that satisfy even the most reluctant Member State. In contrast, Member States show much more flexible negotiation positions under the qualified majority voting rule. Still, explicit voting seems indeed to be the last resort and the Member States usually adopt Council decisions through an agreement by over-sized coalitions. Therefore, the voting rule clearly matters, but the procedural voting models of Council decision-making developed so far do not really capture the resulting dynamics. In contrast, Hosli and Machover's (2004: 512) characterisation of the Council decision-making process under qualified majority rule as 'a series of unofficial divisions and straw polls' captures several aspects of the interactions in the Council quite well. After the initial discussion of the Commission proposal, the presidency floats compromise proposals that incorporate changes in response to the positions stated by the Member States in earlier meetings. During this more-or-less lengthy trial-and-error process, many aspects in the proposal are effectively, although not formally, voted down by the Member States. In this view, the Council decision-making process can be interpreted as a search process by a boundedly rational presidency for a solution that is acceptable

212 *Part IV: Synthesis and conclusion*

to the required majority. The fact that proposals are often adopted by oversized coalitions might then be due to incomplete information about the real positions of Member States. In contrast to the 'culture of consensus' argument (Heisenberg 2005), the straw-poll picture offers a clear causal mechanism on how Council decisions are reached. However, similar to the 'culture of consensus' argument, the straw-poll thesis in its current form can also not account for the observed variation in the degree of consensual decision-making across different Council formations. Thus, the apparently co-operative negotiation style in the Council, even in areas where voting is possible, remains one of the major puzzles for research on Council decision-making.

The development of national negotiation positions as well as the importance attached to them by governments also needs more empirical as well as theoretical research. The study indicated that Member State positions largely reflect economic and financial interests either of the state itself or of small and well-organised special interest groups. In addition, the study showed that the importance attached to an issue by Member States played a crucial role in determining the level of decision-making in the Council. Future research should study in more detail the process through which national negotiation positions are formed and through which certain issues become salient for governments. If the resources and the degree of organisation of domestic societal groups really determines the degree to which their interests are represented and defended in Brussels, as indicated by some of the results of this study, then the real legitimacy problem of Council decision-making is not located in the decision-making process in Brussels, but in the domestic formation process of national negotiation positions.

In the preceding discussion, I pointed to many interesting aspects of Council decision-making that deserve more attention in future research. The Council is the main legislative institution in EU politics. Despite the Council's important role in the legislative process, decision-making within the Council has received rather little consideration in empirical research. Only recent years have seen a turn away from individual case studies and anecdotal evidence to more systematic and representative studies of Council decision-making. This movement is to be welcomed. Taking full advantage of the new transparency regime of the Council, I aimed to continue and contribute to this trend. The study considered the extent of committee decision-making and the conditions under which ministers get involved in legislative decision-making of the Council. Thus, the study shed light on another part of the black box of Council decision-making, but many dark corners are left to be illuminated by future research.

References

Achen, Christopher H. (2002): Toward a New Political Methodology: Microfoundations and Art. *Annual Review of Political Science* 5: 423–50.

Andersen, Mikael S. and Lise N. Rasmussen (1998): The Making of Environmental Policy in the European Council. *Journal of Common Market Studies* 36(4): 585–97.

Arregui, Javier, Frans Stokman and Robert Thomson (2004): Bargaining in the European Union and Shifts in Actors' Policy Positions. *European Union Politics* 5(1): 47–72.

Arregui, Javier, Frans N. Stokman and Robert Thomson (2006): Compromise, Exchange and Challenge in the European Union. In Robert Thomson, Frans N. Stokman, Christopher H. Achen and Thomas König (eds): *The European Union Decides*. Cambridge: Cambridge University Press, 124–52.

Bendor, Jonathan and Adam Meirowitz (2004a): Spatial Models of Delegation. *American Political Science Review* 98(2): 293–310.

Bendor, Jonathan and Adam Meirowitz (2004b): Supplementary Appendix to 'Spatial Models of Delegation'. http://www.princeton.edu/~ameirowi/appendix_longf.pdf (accessed 11 December 2007).

Bendor, Jonathan, Amihai Glazer and Thomas H. Hammond (2001): Theories of Delegation. *Annual Review of Political Science* 4: 235–69.

Benoit, Kenneth and Michael Laver (2006): *Party Policy in Modern Democracies*. London: Routledge.

Beyers, Jan (1998): How Supranational is Supranationalism? National and European Socialization of Negotiators in the Council of Ministers. *Acta Politica* 33(4): 378–408.

Beyers, Jan (2005): Multiple Embeddedness and Socialization in Europe: The Case of Council Officials. *International Organization* 59(4): 899–936.

Beyers, Jan and Guido Dierickx (1997): Nationality and European Negotiations: The Working Groups of the Council of Ministers. *European Journal of International Relations* 3(4): 435–71.

Beyers, Jan and Guido Dierickx (1998): The Working Groups of the Council of the European Union: Supranational or Intergovernmental Negotiations? *Journal of Common Market Studies* 36(3): 289–317.

Beyers, Jan and Jarle Trondal (2003): How Nation-States Hit Europe: Ambiguity and Representation in the European Union. *West European Politics* 27(5): 919–42.

Bostock, David (2002): Coreper Revisited. *Journal of Common Market Studies* 40(2): 215–34.

Bowler, Shaun and David M. Farrell (1995): The Organizing of the European Parliament: Committees, Specialization and Co-ordination. *British Journal of Political Science* 25(2): 219–43.

214 *References*

Checkel, Jeffrey T. (2003): "Going Native" in Europe? Theorizing Social Interaction in European Institutions. *Comparative Political Studies* 36(1/2): 209–31.

Clarke, Kevin (2005): The Phantom Menace: Omitted Variable Bias in Econometric Research. *Conflict Management and Peace Science* 22(4): 341–52.

Cox, Gary W. (2006): The Organization of Democratic Legislatures. In Barry R. Weingast and Donald A. Wittman (eds): *The Oxford Handbook of Political Economy*. Oxford: Oxford University Press, 141–61.

Cox, Gary W. and Mathew D. McCubbins (2006): *Legislative Leviathan: Party Government in the House*. Cambridge: Cambridge University Press.

Crombez, Christophe (1996): Legislative Procedures in the European Community. *British Journal of Political Science* 26(2): 199–228.

Crombez, Christophe (1997): The Co-decision Procedure in the European Union. *Legislative Studies Quarterly* 22(1): 97–119.

De Zwaan, Jaap W. (1995): *The Permanent Representatives Committee*. Amsterdam: Elsevier.

Egeberg, Morten (1999): Transcending Intergovernmentalism? Identity and Role Perceptions of National Officials in EU Decision-Making. *Journal of European Public Policy* 6(3): 456–74.

Egeberg, Morten, Günther F. Schaefer and Jarle Trondal (2003): The Many Faces of EU Committee Governance. *West European Politics* 26(3): 19–40.

Elgstrom, Ole, Bo Bjurulf, Jonas Johansson and Anders Sannerstedt (2001): Coalitions in European Union Negotiations. *Scandinavian Political Studies* 24(2): 111–28.

Epstein, David and Sharyn O'Halloran (1999): *Delegating Powers: A Transaction Cost Politics Approach to Policy Making under Separate Powers*. Cambridge: Cambridge University Press.

Farrell, Henry and Adrienne Héritier (2003): Formal and Informal Institutions under Codecision: Continuous Constitution-Building in Europe. *Governance* 16(4): 577–600.

Farrell, Henry and Adrienne Héritier (2004): Interorganizational Negotiation and Intraorganizational Power in Shared Decision Making. Early Agreements under Codecision and Their Impact on the European Parliament and Council. *Comparative Political Studies* 37(10): 1184–212.

Farrell, Henry and Adrienne Héritier (2007): Codecision and Institutional Change. *West European Politics* 30(2): 285–300.

Fouilleux, Eve, Jaques de Maillard and Andy Smith (2005): Technical or Political? The Working Groups of the EU Council of Ministers. *Journal of European Public Policy* 12(4): 609–23.

Franchino, Fabio (2000): Control of the Commission's Executive Functions. Uncertainty, Conflict and Decision Rules. *European Union Politics* 1(1): 63–92.

Franchino, Fabio (2004): Delegating Powers in the European Community. *British Journal of Political Science* 34(2): 269–93.

Franchino, Fabio (2007): *The Powers of the Union*. Cambridge: Cambridge University Press.

George, Alexander L. and Andrew Bennett (2005): *Case Studies and Theory Development in the Social Sciences*. Cambridge, MA: MIT Press.

Gerring, John (2001): *Social Science Methodology: A Criterial Framework*. Cambridge: Cambridge University Press.

Golub, Jonathan (1999): In the Shadow of the Vote? Decision Making in the European Community. *International Organization* 53(4): 733–64.

Golub, Jonathan (2007): Survival Analysis and European Union Decision-Making. *European Union Politics* 8(2): 155–79.

References   215

Golub, Jonathan and Bernard Steunenberg (2007): How Time Affects EU Decision-Making. *European Union Politics* 8(4): 555–66.

Gomez, Ricardo and John Peterson (2001): The EU's Impossibly Busy Foreign Ministers: "No One Is in Control". *European Foreign Affairs Review* 6(1): 53–74.

Häge, Frank M. (2007a): Committee Decision-Making in the Council of the European Union. *European Union Politics* 8(3): 299–328.

Häge, Frank M. (2007b): Constructivism, Fuzzy Sets and (Very) Small-N: Revisiting the Conditions for Communicative Action. *Journal of Business Research* 60(5): 512.

Häge, Frank M. (2008): Who Decides in the Council of the European Union? *Journal of Common Market Studies* 46(3): 533–58.

Häge, Frank M. and Michael Kaeding (2007): Reconsidering the European Parliament's Legislative Influence: Formal vs. Informal Procedures. *Journal of European Integration* 29(3): 341–61.

Hagemann, Sara (2007): Applying Ideal Point Estimation Methods to the Council of Ministers. *European Union Politics* 8(2): 279–96.

Hayes-Renshaw, Fiona and Helen Wallace (1997): *The Council of Ministers*. Houndmills/London: Macmillan Press.

Hayes-Renshaw, Fiona and Helen Wallace (2006): *The Council of Ministers*. Basingstoke: Palgrave Macmillan.

Hayes-Renshaw, Fiona, Wim Van Aken and Helen Wallace (2006): When and Why the EU Council of Ministers Votes Explicitly. *Journal of Common Market Studies* 44(1): 161–94.

Heisenberg, Dorothee (2005): The Institution of 'Consensus' in the European Union: Formal Versus Informal Decision-Making in the Council. *European Journal of Political Research* 44: 65–90.

Hertz, Robin and Dirk Leuffen (2011): Too Big to Run? Analysing the Impact of Enlargement on the Speed of EU Decision-Making. *European Union Politics* 12(2): 193–215.

Hix, Simon (2005): *The Political System of the European Union*. Basingstoke: Palgrave Macmillan.

Hooghe, Liesbet (2005): Several Roads Lead to International Norms, but Few via International Socialization: A Case Study of the European Commission. *International Organization* 59(4): 861–98.

Hooghe, Liesbet, Gary Marks, Marco Steenbergen and Milada Vachudova (2005): Chapel Hill Data Set on Positioning of Political Parties on European Integration 2002. University of North Carolina at Chapel Hill. http://www.unc.edu/%7Ehooghe/parties. htm (accessed 2 May 2006).

Hosli, Madeleine O. and Moshe Machover (2004): The Nice Treaty and Voting Rules in the Council: A Reply to Moberg (2002). *Journal of Common Market Studies* 42(3): 497–521.

Hoyland, Bjorn (2006): Allocation of Codecision Reports in the Fifth European Parliament. *European Union Politics* 7(1): 30–50.

Huber, John D. and Charles R. Shipan (2002): *Deliberate Discretion? The Institutional Foundations of Bureaucratic Autonomy*. Cambridge: Cambridge University Press.

Johnston, Alastair I. (2001): Treating International Institutions as Social Environments. *International Studies Quarterly* 45(4): 487–515.

Judge, David and David Earnshaw (2010): 'Relais Actors' and Co-decision First Reading Agreements in the European Parliament: The Case of the Advanced Therapies Regulation. *Journal of European Public Policy* 18(1): 53–71.

216 References

Juncos, Ana E. and Karolina Pomorska (2006): Playing the Brussels Game: Strategic Socialisation in the CFSP Council Working Groups. *European Integration Online Papers* 10(11). http://eiop.or.at/eiop/index.php/eiop/article/view/2006_011a/34

Kaeding, Michael (2004): Rapporteurship Allocation in the European Parliament. *European Union Politics* 5(3): 353–71.

Kaeding, Michael (2005): The World of Committee Reports: Rapporteurship Assignment in the European Parliament. *Journal of Legislative Studies* 11(1): 82–104.

Kaeding, Michael and Torsten J. Selck (2005): Mapping out Political Europe: Coalition Patterns in EU Decision-Making. *International Political Science Review* 26(3): 271–90.

Kardasheva, Raya (2009): The Power to Delay: The European Parliament's Influence in the Consultation Procedure. *Journal of Common Market Studies* 47(2): 385–409.

Kassim, Hussein (2003): Co-ordinating National Action in Brussels. In Hussein Kassim, Anand Menon, B. Guy Peters and Vincent Wright (eds): *The National Co-ordination of EU Policy*. Oxford: Oxford University Press, 1–46.

Klingemann, Hans-Dieter, Andrea Volkens, Judith Bara, Ian Budge and Michael McDonald (2006): *Mapping Policy Preferences II: Estimates for Parties, Electors, and Governments in Eastern Europe, European Union, and OECD 1990–2003*. Oxford: Oxford University Press.

König, Thomas (2007): Divergence or Convergence? From Ever-Growing to Ever-Slowing European Legislative Decision Making. *European Journal of Political Research* 46: 417–44.

König, Thomas and Thomas Bräuninger (2004): Accession and Reform of the European Union: A Game-Theoretical Analysis of Eastern Enlargement and the Constitutional Reform. *European Union Politics* 5: 419–39.

König, Thomas and Sven-Oliver Proksch (2006a): Exchanging and Voting in the Council: Endogenizing the Spatial Model of Legislative Politics. *Journal of European Public Policy* 13(5): 647–69.

König, Thomas and Sven-Oliver Proksch (2006b): A Procedural Exchange Model of EU Legislative Politics. In Robert Thomson, Frans N. Stokman, Christopher H. Achen and Thomas König (eds): *The European Union Decides*. Cambridge: Cambridge University Press, 211–38.

Korkman, Sixten (2004): The Ecofin Council and the Eurogroup. In Martin Westlake and David Galloway (eds): *The Council of the European Union*. London: John Harper.

Larsson, Torbjoern (2003): Precooking the European Union: The World of Expert Groups. *ESO Report 2003:16*. Stockholm: Expert Group on Public Finance.

Lenschow, Andrea (2005): Environmental Policy: Contending Dynamics of Policy Change. In Helen Wallace, William Wallace and Mark A. Pollack (eds): *Policy-Making in the European Union*. Oxford: Oxford University Press, 305–27.

Lewis, Jeffrey (1998): Is the 'Hard Bargaining' Image of the Council Misleading? The Committee of Permanent Representatives and the Local Elections Directive. *Journal of Common Market Studies* 36(4): 479–504.

Lewis, Jeffrey (2000): The Methods of Community in EU Decision-Making and Administrative Rivalry in the Council's Infrastructure. *Journal of European Public Policy* 7(2): 261–89.

Lewis, Jeffrey (2003a): Informal Integration and the Supranational Construction of the Council. *Journal of European Public Policy* 10(6): 996–1019.

Lewis, Jeffrey (2003b): Institutional Environments and Everyday EU Decision Making. Rationalist or Constructivist? *Comparative Political Studies* 36(1/2): 97–124.

References 217

Lewis, Jeffrey (2005): The Janus Face of Brussels: Socialization and Everyday Decision Making in the European Union. *International Organization* 59(4): 937–71.

Lieberman, Evan S. (2005): Nested Analysis as a Mixed-Method Strategy for Comparative Research. *American Political Science Review* 99(3): 435–52.

McElroy, Gail (2006): Committee Representation in the European Parliament. *European Union Politics* 7(1): 5–29.

McElroy, Gail and Kenneth Benoit (2007): Party Groups and Policy Positions in the European Parliament. *Party Politics* 13(1): 5–28.

McElroy, Gail and Kenneth Benoit (2010): Party Policy and Group Affiliation in the European Parliament. *British Journal of Political Science* 40(02): 377–98.

Mahoney, Christine (2004): The Power of Institutions: State and Interest Group Activity in the European Union. *European Union Politics* 5(4): 441–66.

Mattila, Mikko (2004): Contested Decisions: Empirical Analysis of Voting in the European Union Council of Ministers. *European Journal of Political Research* 43: 29–50.

Mattila, Mikko (2009): Roll Call Analysis of Voting in the European Union Council of Ministers after the 2004 Enlargement. *European Journal of Political Research* 48(6): 840–57.

Mattila, Mikko and Jan-Erik Lane (2001): Why Unanimity in the Council? A Roll Call Analysis of Council Voting. *European Union Politics* 2(1): 31–52.

Meyer, Christoph (1999): Political Legitimacy and the Invisibility of Politics: Exploring the European Union's Communication Deficit. *Journal of Common Market Studies* 37(4): 617–39.

Miller, Warren E. (1999): Temporal Order and Causal Inference. *Political Analysis* 8(2): 119–46.

Moravcsik, Andrew (2002): In Defence of the 'Democratic Deficit': Reassessing Legitimacy in the European Union. *Journal of Common Market Studies* 40(4): 603–24.

Naurin, Daniel (2007): Network Capital and Cooperation Patterns in Working Groups of the Council of the EU. *EUI Working Papers RSCAS 2007/14*. Florence: European University Institute.

Naurin, Daniel (2010): Most Common When Least Important: Deliberation in the European Union Council of Ministers. *British Journal of Political Science* 40: 31–50.

Naurin, Daniel and Rutger Lindahl (2010): Out in the Cold? Flexible Integration and the Political Status of Euro Opt-Outs. *European Union Politics* 11(4): 485–509.

Niemann, Arne (2004): Between Communicative Action and Strategic Action: The Article 113 Committee and the Negotiations on the WTO Basic Telecommunications Services Agreement. *Journal of European Public Policy* 11(3): 379–407.

Nugent, Neill (2003): *The Government and Politics of the European Union*. Durham, NC: Duke University Press.

Nugent, Neill (2006): *The Government and Politics of the European Union*. Basingstoke: Palgrave Macmillan.

Olson, Mancur (1965): *The Logic of Collective Action: Public Goods and the Theory of Groups*. Cambridge, MA: Harvard University Press.

Pierce, Roy (1994): Fresh Perspectives on a Developing Institution. In Bruce Bueno de Mesquita and Frans Stokman (eds): *European Community Decision Making: Models, Applications, and Comparisons*. New Haven, CT: Yale University Press, 1–14.

Plechanovová, Běla (2011): The EU Council Enlarged: North-South-East or Core-Periphery? *European Union Politics* 12(1): 87–106.

Quaglia, Lucia, Fabrizio De Francesco and Claudio M. Radaelli (2007): Committee Governance and Socialization in the European Union. *Journal of European Public Policy* 15(1): 155–66.

218 References

Rasmussen, Anne (2008): Party Soldiers in a Non-Partisan Community? Party Linkage in the European Parliament. *Journal of European Public Policy* 15(8): 1164–83.

Reh, Christine (2007): Pre-Cooking the European Constitution? The Role of Government Representatives in EU Reform. *Journal of European Public Policy* 14(8): 1186–207.

Rohlfing, Ingo (2008): What You See and What You Get. *Comparative Political Studies* 41(11): 1492–514.

Schneider, Gerald, Bernard Steunenberg and Mika Widgrén (2006): Evidence with Insight: What Models Contribute to EU Research. In Robert Thomson, Frans N. Stokman, Christopher H. Achen and Thomas König (eds): *The European Union Decides.* Cambridge: Cambridge University Press, 407–30.

Schofield, Norman, Bernard Grofman and Scott L. Feld (1988): The Core and the Stability of Group Choice in Spatial Voting Games. *American Political Science Review* 82(1): 195–211.

Schulz, Heiner and Thomas König (2000): Institutional Reform and Decision-Making Efficiency in the European Union. *American Journal of Political Science* 44(4): 653–66.

Selck, Torsten J. (2004): On the Dimensionality of European Union Legislative Decision-Making. *Journal of Theoretical Politics* 16(2): 203–22.

Settembri, Pierpaolo and Christine Neuhold (2009): Achieving Consensus Through Committees: Does the European Parliament Manage? *Journal of Common Market Studies* 47(1): 127–51.

Steunenberg, Bernard (1994): Decision Making under Different Institutional Arrangements: Legislation by the European Community. *Journal of Institutional and Theoretical Economics* 150(4): 642–69.

Steunenberg, Bernard (2004): Coordinating Sectoral Policymaking: Searching for Countervailing Mechanisms in the EU Legislative Process. In Charles Beat Blankart and Dennis C. Mueller (eds): A Constitution for the European Union. Cambridge, MA: MIT Press, 139–67.

Thomson, Robert (2011): Resolving Controversy in the European Union: Legislative Decision-Making Before and After Enlargement. Cambridge: Cambridge University Press.

Thomson, Robert, Jovanka Boerefijn and Frans Stokman (2004): Actor Alignments in European Union Decision Making. *European Journal of Political Research* 43(2): 237–62.

Thomson, Robert, Frans Stokman, Christopher H. Achen and Thomas König (eds) (2006): *The European Union Decides.* Cambridge: Cambridge University Press.

Trondal, Jarle (2001): Is There Any Social Constructivist-Institutionalist Divide? Unpacking Social Mechanisms Affecting Representational Roles among EU Decision-Makers. *Journal of European Public Policy* 8(1): 1–23.

Trondal, Jarle (2002): Beyond the EU Membership-Non-Membership Dichotomy? Supranational Identities among National EU Decision-Makers. *Journal of European Public Policy* 9(3): 468–87.

Tsebelis, George (1994): The Power of the European Parliament as a Conditional Agenda Setter. *American Political Science Review* 88(1): 128–42.

Tsebelis, George (2002): *Veto Players: How Political Institutions Work.* Princeton, NJ: Princeton University Press.

Tsebelis, George and Geoffrey Garrett (2000): Legislative Politics in the European Union. *European Union Politics* 1(1): 9–36.

Tsebelis, George and Xenophon Yataganas (2002): Veto Players and Decision-Making in the EU after Nice: Policy Stability and Bureaucratic/Judicial Discretion. *Journal of Common Market Studies* 40(2): 283–307.

References   219

Van den Bos, Jan M. M. (1991): *Dutch EC Policy Making. A Model-Guided Approach to Coordination and Negotiation*. Amsterdam: Thesis Publishers.

Van Schendelen, Marinus P. M. C. (1996): "The Council Decides": Does the Council Decide? *Journal of Common Market Studies* 34(4): 531–48.

Wallace, Helen, William Wallace and Mark A. Pollack (eds) (2005): *Policy-Making in the European Union*. Oxford: Oxford University Press.

Westlake, Martin and David Galloway (eds) (2004): *The Council of the European Union*. London: John Harper.

Whitaker, Richard (2005): National Parties in the European Parliament: An Influence in the Committee System? *European Union Politics* 6(1): 5–28.

Yordanova, Nikoleta (2009): The Rationale Behind Committee Assignment in the European Parliament. *European Union Politics* 10(2): 253–80.

Yordanova, Nikoleta (2010): Inter-Institutional Rules and Division of Power in the European Parliament: Allocation of Consultation and Co-decision Reports. *West European Politics* 34(1): 97–121.

Zimmer, Christina, Gerald Schneider and Michael Dobbins (2005: The Contested Council: Conflict Dimensions of an Intergovernmental EU Institution. *Political Studies* 53(2): 403–22.

Index

abstention *see* voting

accountability 4, 30, 72, 199, 206

adjustment costs 153, 190, 204

agenda 15–16, 19, 32–4, 68, 70–1, 98, 103, 133, 138, 149, 151, 153, 163, 191, 208; *see also* A-point; B-point

agenda-setting power 150

Agriculture Council formation 11, 15, 20, 23, 29, 32, 74, 78–9, 84, 91, 95–8, 100, 103–29, 130, 149, 151, 152, 162–3, 181–2, 184, 189–90, 192–5, 199

A-item *see* A-point

Ambient Air Directive 97, 130–38, 140, 150–61, 190, 192, 195, 201, 203–4, 206

Antici Group 20

A-point 16, 18, 34, 70–1, 98, 108, 123, 138, 149, 165, 172, 180, 183; *see also* agenda

arguing 38–9

Article 36 Committee 19, 30

Austria (AT) 109, 111, 116–17, 119, 133, 135, 143, 145, 147–9, 168, 171, 174–7, 179

bargaining 38–9, 193

bargaining models 39

Batteries Directive 97, 130–1, 138–61, 190, 195, 201, 203–5, 207

Belgium (BE) 50, 112, 117–18, 120, 121n36, 124, 149, 168–70, 176

B-item *see* B-point

blockage of proposal *see* gridlock

blocking minority 126, 153–4, 184, 190, 192, 194

B-point 16, 34, 68, 70–1; *see also* agenda

Budget Council formation 4, 65, 69, 103, 118, 162

case selection 9, 11, 91–8; *see also* sample selection

co-decision procedure 5–6, 12–18, 48–9, 60, 68, 71–2, 74, 76, 80, 86, 98, 100, 130, 146–9, 154, 162, 203, 211; *see also* legislative procedure; formal institutions

Comitology 79, 83, 105, 146, 148

Committee for Civilian Aspects of Crisis Management 19

Committee of the Regions (CoR) 13

Common Agricultural Policy (CAP) 15, 79, 104, 112–13; *see also* Agriculture Council formation

Common Foreign and Security Policy (CFSP) 19, 38

communication network 31, 35–6, 41, 100; *see also* cooperation network

competitiveness 15, 23–4, 143

Competitiveness Working Party 143–4

conciliation committee 17–18, 72, 131; *see also* co-decision procedure

confirmatory research 7–9

consensus 5, 41, 92, 145, 153, 155, 169, 178, 190–1, 202, 206, 208, 212; *see also* voting

Conservative party group in the EP 136, 138, 142

consultation procedure 12–18, 49, 68, 71–2, 74, 98, 104, 127, 146, 163–4, 192, 203; *see also* legislative procedure; formal institutions

cooperation network 3, 31, 35–6; *see also* communication network

core 35, 44–9, 51–3, 58–61, 99;
    see also social choice theory
Culture Council formation 15, 74n3, 76,
    83, 138
Cyprus (CY) 145–8
Czech Republic (CZ) 143, 145–8, 166, 168

decision-making: authority 43, 54–9, 61;
    duration 5, 16, 18, 29–30, 40–2, 51,
    106, 122–3, 184, 189, 192
deductive logic of inquiry 6–9
delegation 6, 10, 42–3, 54–9, 61, 205,
    210; *see also* principal-agent theory
delegation set 54–9
Denmark (DK) 105, 109–13, 116, 119–21,
    135, 143, 145, 147–9, 153, 166, 170,
    175–6, 190, 204, 206
Development Council formation 23, 69
directorate general (DG) of the
    Commission 150
discretion *see* delegation

early agreement under co-decision 48,
    60, 71n1, 86, 130, 136–8, 154, 156,
    190, 192
Economic and Financial Affairs Council
    formation 11, 15, 18–19, 23–4, 58,
    74, 83, 91, 95–8, 162–88, 195n2
Economic and Financial Committee
    18–19
Economic and Social Committee (ESC) 13
Economic Policy Committee 19–20
Education Council formation 15, 74n3,
    76, 138
efficiency *see* decision-making, duration
Employment Committee 18–19
Employment, Social policy, Health and
    Consumer Affairs Council formation
    15, 74, 83
Energy Council formation 15, 23, 74, 76
Environment Council formation 11, 15,
    23, 74, 83–4, 91, 95–8, 130–61,
    162–3, 172, 181, 184–6, 190, 192,
    195n2, 199, 202–4
EP involvement 6, 40, 45, 60–1, 76, 80,
    84, 156, 192–3, 203–4, 211; *see also*
    co-decision procedure; veto
Estonia (EE) 146–9
European Court of Justice (ECJ)
    13, 105, 170

exploratory research 6–9, 92–3, 102,
    199, 211
External Relations Council formation 14,
    15, 23–4, 69

false A-point *see* A-point
false B-point *see* B-point
filtering system 124, 152–3
financial services 162
Financial Services Committee 19–20
Finland (FI) 116–17, 119, 121, 135–6,
    137, 143, 145, 147–9, 167–71, 175,
    177, 179
Fisheries Council formation 15, 23, 74,
    113, 149
formal institutions 5–6, 13, 35, 39–40,
    42–4, 49, 59, 67, 76, 99, 202;
    see also voting, rule; legislative
    procedure
formal rules *see* formal institutions
France (FR) 35, 105, 108–13, 116–19,
    125, 135, 137, 143, 145–8, 166–71,
    175–7, 179, 204
Friends of the Presidency Group 20

game theory 10, 39, 53–4; *see also* social
    choice theory; spatial voting model
General Affairs Council formation 15,
    23–4, 69
Geographical Indications Regulation 97,
    104–15, 121–9, 168, 189, 190, 194,
    201, 204
Germany (DE) 35, 108–13, 116, 119–24,
    125, 135, 136, 143, 145, 147–9, 154,
    166–71, 174–9, 182–5, 204
Greece (EL) 105, 109, 112, 116–20, 124,
    135, 145–9, 166, 170–1, 204
Green party group in the EP 136, 142
gridlock 60, 66, 112, 163–4, 172

hierarchical structure of the Council 4, 12,
    14–16, 18, 20, 28–31, 40, 65, 70, 75,
    86, 124, 126, 153, 163, 193, 205–7
High-Level Working Party on
    Environment and Development 23
Hungary (HU) 145, 147–8

ideal point 44, 46–7, 49, 52–3, 55–9, 118,
    121, 201; *see also* preferences
I-item 15; *see also* agenda

222 Index

II-item 15; *see also* agenda
II-point *see* II-item
impact assessment 143–5, 155
indifference curves 52–3, 55
inductive logic of inquiry 6–9
Industry Council formation 74, 76, 83
informal institutions 5, 6, 38, 60, 202;
    see also norms; consensus; early
    agreement under co-decision
informal rules *see* informal institutions
information asymmetry 126, 155–6,
    185–6, 189, 191, 205, 207; *see also*
    policy uncertainty; legal uncertainty
information extraction 67–8, 76
informational advantage *see* information
    asymmetry
initiation of legislative process *see*
    proposal introduction
institutional rules *see* formal institutions
interaction intensity 37–8, 53, 192, 203,
    211; *see also* meeting frequency of
    Council bodies
interaction style *see* negotiation style
interest group 205, 209, 212; *see also*
    lobbying
inter-institutional negotiations 6, 17–18,
    48, 60, 67, 71n1, 86
internal market 76, 130, 138, 140, 164, 181
Internal Market Council formation 74,
    83–4
internalization of norms and values
    38, 41, 50–1, 53, 60; *see also*
    socialisation
I-point *see* I-item
Ireland (IE) 109, 111–13, 119, 133–4,
    140, 142–3, 145, 147–9, 151, 154,
    156, 168, 170–1, 176–7, 186, 190,
    195, 204
Italy (IT) 105, 108–10, 112–13, 116–21,
    124, 133, 135, 137, 143, 145–9, 151,
    165, 173, 176–9, 181–2, 186, 191,
    195

Justice and Home Affairs (JHA) Council
    formation 13n4, 15, 19–20, 23–4,
    29–30, 58, 74, 83–4

Latvia (LV) 143, 146–8
Leaf Tobacco Regulation 97, 104, 113–29,
    189, 194, 204

left–right dimension 35–6, 76;
    see also party ideology
legal complexity *see* legal uncertainty
legal service of the Council 14, 110–12,
    122, 171, 182
legal uncertainty 156, 163, 183, 185–6,
    190–1, 193–5, 205–8, 210–11; *see
    also* policy uncertainty
legislative procedure 5, 13n3, 39, 48, 65,
    67, 74, 76, 95, 98, 104n1; *see also*
    formal institutions; co-decision
    procedure; consultation procedure
legitimacy 4, 30, 32, 72, 87, 199,
    208–9, 212
Liberal party group in the EP 138, 142,
    150
Lithuania (LT) 143, 145, 147–9
lobbying 141, 147, 154, 209; *see also*
    interest group
logic of appropriateness 38, 50, 79
logic of consequences 38
lowest common denominator solution
    183, 193, 211
Luxembourg (LU) 112, 149, 176, 183,
    109, 145, 170–1, 176

Malta (MT) 145–8
meeting frequency of Council bodies 12,
    24–9, 30, 35, 37, 79, 84, 103, 203;
    see also interaction intensity
Mergers Directive 163, 172–88, 191,
    195, 206
Mertens Group 20
Military Committee 19
mixed-method research 8, 92
most preferred position *see* ideal point

national financial interests 205, 212
necessary condition 58, 200–01, 205–7, 209
negotiation deadline 154, 192
negotiation style 6, 31, 38, 41, 51, 53, 86,
    211–12
Netherlands (NL) 33–4, 50, 112, 119–21,
    134, 140, 142–4, 147, 151, 156, 171,
    176, 178, 183, 186, 190–1, 195
norm violation costs 52–3
norms 37–8, 41, 49–53, 60, 79, 203, 211;
    see also supranational norms
north–south cleavage 35, 36, 210
north–south–east cleavage 36

number of committee meetings 37, 79, 203; *see also* meeting frequency of Council bodies

number of working parties 12, 20, 23–4, 29–30, 130

number of working party meetings *see* meeting frequency of Council bodies

outcome uncertainty *see* policy uncertainty

oversized coalition 45n5, 211–12

Parent-Subsidiary Directive 97, 163–73, 175, 180–88, 191, 195

Pareto-set 45

party ideology 58, 61, 201, 205; *see also* left–right dimension

party policy position 76–9, 200, 210; *see also* ideal point; preferences

performance norms 51–3, 60; *see also* norms; informal institutions

Poland (PL) 143, 145–8, 166, 175, 178–9

policy: complexity *see* policy uncertainty; dimension 3, 36, 44–7, 51–2, 55–6, 76 (*see also* left–right dimension; political conflict lines); importance *see* policy salience; position 39, 52–3 (*see also* party policy position); salience 39, 58, 80, 83, 86, 92, 207–9, 212; stability 43–49, 51–3, 60–1 (*see also* gridlock); uncertainty 6, 24, 43, 54–61, 76, 79, 83–6, 126, 154–5, 185, 190–01, 193, 205, 207, 210–11 (*see also* legal uncertainty)

Political and Security Committee (PSC) 19

political conflict 40, 71, 79–80, 155, 156, 201, 205, 208; lines 3, 36, 103, 116, 191, 192, 210 (*see also* north–south cleavage; north–south–east cleavage)

Portugal (PT) 108, 110–13, 116–17, 119–20, 121n36, 125, 135–6, 143, 145–6, 148, 166, 168–71, 175–7, 179

practical uncertainty *see* policy uncertainty

preferences 39, 42, 44, 47, 49, 52–3, 54, 58–60, 78, 150, 200–01, 210; divergence of 40, 42–5, 47–9, 60–1, 67, 76–80, 84, 86, 125, 156, 181, 185, 190, 193–4, 200–2, 206–7; configuration of 45, 47–8, 210n2;

polarisation of 192, 202 (*see also* policy position; ideal point)

PreLex 67–8, 72, 76, 79

presidency: impatience 125–6, 156, 190, 192, 205, 207; priorities 122, 126, 140, 142, 151, 156, 193, 195, 203–8

principal-agent theory 6, 43, 54–9, 210–1; *see also* delegation

procedural models 39

proposal introduction: by Commission 13, 66–7, 72, 105, 114, 132, 150, 162–4, 173, 180–1, 183–4, 199, 202; by a Member State 65, 69

qualified majority *see* voting, rule

recitals 80, 84, 114, 116, 119–21, 137–8, 146–9, 151–2, 177

Research Council formation 74, 83

rule *see* voting, rule

sample selection 10, 32–4, 65–70, 74, 199; *see also* case selection

scheduling power 205

Secretariat of the Council 14, 20, 24, 35, 79, 99–100, 142

Security Committee 19–20

senior committees 4, 10, 14–16, 18–19, 29, 35–6, 43n1, 48, 72, 98–9, 126, 189, 203, 205–7

senior working parties 19–20

Slovakia (SK) 145–8

Slovenia (SI) 145, 147–8

social choice theory 10, 44; *see also* game theory; spatial voting model

Social Protection Committee 18–19

Socialist party group in the EP 136, 138, 142

socialization 6, 31, 36–8, 41–3, 49–53, 59–61, 76, 79–80, 86, 192–4, 202–3, 211; *see also* internalization of norms and values

Spain (ES) 109, 111–13, 116–17, 119, 121n36, 122–3, 135–6, 143, 145, 147–9, 166–71, 174–7, 179–80, 189, 194

spatial voting model 39; *see also* social choice theory; game theory

Special Committee on Agriculture (SCA) 15, 18, 29, 95–7, 103, 106–28, 151, 189–90, 192–4, 202

224 *Index*

speed *see* decision-making, duration

status quo policy 44–5, 47, 49, 51–2, 60, 118, 121, 171, 179, 182, 204

Strategic Committee on Immigration, Frontiers and Asylum (SCIFA) 20, 29–30

sufficient condition 125, 154, 185, 200, 206–8

supranational attitudes 35, 37

supranational institutions 35–6

supranational norms 38, 41, 43, 49–50, 60, 79, 86, 202; *see also* norms

supranational role perceptions 6, 36–8, 41, 49–51

Sweden (SE) 35, 109, 112, 116–17, 119, 121, 135, 143, 145–9, 165, 167, 175–6, 178–9

Taxation Council formation 162–88, 191–2, 195, 199, 201, 204

technicality of policy issue 5, 29, 99, 106, 118, 120, 153, 175, 207

Telecommunications Council formation 15, 23, 74, 76, 83

Tourism Council formation 83–4

Trade-Related International Property Rights (TRIPS) 105

transition period 108, 110–12, 125, 144–8; *see also* transposition period

Transport Council formation 15, 23, 74, 76, 83

transposition period 147–8, 167; *see also* transition period

trilogue *see* early agreement

unanimity *see* voting, rule

United Kingdom (UK) 35, 105, 109–13, 116–17, 119–21, 136, 143, 145–9, 170–1, 174–80

urgency 123, 154; *see also* presidency, impatience, priorities

utility 53, 55–7, 59; *see also* preferences

values *see* norms

veto 7, 39, 42, 44–5, 48–9, 51, 60, 66,

71, 86, 106, 193; *see also* formal institutions; voting, rule; co-decision procedure

voting 86, 123, 126, 193, 202, 211; abstain from 113, 121, 149; against 121; behaviour 1, 5, 32, 36, 40–2; explicit 40–2, 44n3, 60; in European Parliament 135–6, 142; rule 5, 13, 16–17, 35, 38–42, 44–54, 59–61, 76, 80, 84, 86, 95, 97–8, 126–7, 131, 154, 156, 162, 183–4, 186, 190–5, 202, 206, 211–12; threshold *see* voting, rule; weights 39, 44n2

winning coalition 44, 46, 52n9

winset 52–3

withdrawal of proposal by Commission 13, 66–7, 69, 179, 183

Working Party of Chief Veterinary Officers 20

Working Party on Asylum 30

Working Party on Biodiversity 23

Working Party on Biosafety 23

Working Party on Environment 95, 130–61, 163, 192, 202

Working Party on Foodstuff Quality (Geographical Indications and Designations of Origin) 103–13, 121–9

Working Party on Frontiers 20

Working Party on International Environmental Issues 95

Working Party on Migration 20

Working Party on Persistent Organic Pollutants 23

Working Party on Tax Questions (Direct Taxation) 162–88, 193

Working Party on Tobacco 104, 113–29

Working Party on Visa 20

workload 15, 24, 26, 28, 30, 35, 79, 100, 103, 117

World Trade Organization (WTO) 105

youth 15, 74n3, 76, 138